The Political Economy
of Policy Coordination

A volume in the series

Cornell Studies in Political Economy

EDITED BY PETER J. KATZENSTEIN

A full list of titles in the series appears at the end of the book.

The Political Economy of Policy Coordination

INTERNATIONAL ADJUSTMENT SINCE 1945

MICHAEL C. WEBB

CORNELL UNIVERSITY PRESS

Ithaca and London

First published 1995 by Cornell University Press

Printed in the United States of America

⊗ The paper in this book meets the minimum requirements
of the American National Standard for Information Sciences—
Permanence of Paper for Printed Library Materials, ANSI Z39.48–1984.

Library of Congress Cataloging-in-Publication Data

Webb, Michael C.
   The political economy of policy coordination : international adjustment since 1945 /
Michael C. Webb.
       p. cm.—(Cornell studies in political economy)
   Includes bibliographical references and index.
   ISBN 0-8014-2929-3
   1. International economic relations. 2. Economic policy.
I. Title. II. Series.
HF1412.W4 1995
337—dc20   94-46155

For Jane, Gregory, and Laura

Contents

✳ ✝ ✝. 1?

	Preface	ix
1.	Coordinating Macroeconomic Adjustment Policy	1
2.	The Structure of the International System and Patterns of Policy Coordination	21
3.	Insulation and Symptom Management, 1945–55	51
4.	Symptom Management, 1956–70	92
5.	Flexible Exchange Rates and the Search for Policy Autonomy, 1971–77	149
6.	Macroeconomic Conflict and Coordination, 1978–94	187
7.	Conclusions: International Structures, Domestic Politics, and Policy Coordination	251
	Index	265

Preface

Economic policy coordination among the advanced capitalist countries tries to reconcile an interest in international economic liberalization with a need to maintain domestic economic and political stability. This book examines how the macroeconomic policy implications of this basic tension have been resolved since 1945 in response to the changing structure of the international economy. Rising international capital mobility forced governments to abandon the cooperative strategies they had used to insulate national macroeconomic policy-making from international influences in the 1950s and 1960s. Since the late 1970s it has encouraged a shift toward international coordination of monetary and fiscal policies themselves. In other words, there has been a shift away from efforts to manage the international imbalances that are symptomatic of different macroeconomic policies in different countries (although concerted intervention in foreign exchange markets is heavier today than ever) and toward direct coordination of the interest rate and budget policies that drive speculative flows of international capital. Monetary and fiscal policies are difficult to coordinate, however, because they are economically and politically the most important domestic economic policy levers available to governments.

I take issue here with hegemonic stability theorists who identify an erosion in international policy coordination over recent decades because of a decline in American power. Instead, I argue that the extent of policy coordination in the Bretton Woods years has commonly been exaggerated, whereas since the 1970s it has commonly been underestimated. The ad hoc coordination of monetary and fiscal policies in recent years intrudes far more seriously into national policy-making autonomy than did the policy coordination of the 1950s and 1960s, which focused on gradual liberalization of highly protectionist policies and on balance-of-payments lending and helped to insulate domestic economic policies from international economic pressures. Policy coordination in recent years has been less successful in stabilizing the international economy than was policy coordination in the 1950s and 1960s. This lack of success stems from changes in the structure of the international economy, not from an erosion of policy coordination. International capital mobility and the enormous volume of capital that flows through currency markets make for greater international instability.

I also show how the United States continues to dominate economic policy coordination in the 1980s and 1990s, much as it did in the 1950s and 1960s. The United States was able to persuade foreign surplus countries (especially Japan and Germany) to reflate their economies in the late 1980s and (in the case of Japan) the early 1990s, something it had been unable to achieve in the 1960s. Moreover, as in the earlier period, the United States in the late 1980s persuaded foreign governments to adjust so as to reduce international market pressures for changes in American policies.

Chapter 1 introduces the argument, particularly as it relates to theories about American hegemony and international cooperation. Chapter 2 develops the economic-structural argument that explains changing patterns of coordination and presents arguments about bargaining power that help to explain the outcomes of international negotiations about macroeconomic adjustment policies. Chapters 3 through 6 discuss historical patterns of coordination in four distinct subperiods.

Between 1945 and 1955, the period discussed in Chapter 3, international market integration was very low. Consequently, national macroeconomic adjustment strategies relied heavily on external policies: trade and capital controls and exchange-rate adjustments. International coordination of trade controls and balance-of-payments financing was more extensive than one might expect solely from the level of international market integration because of the United States's cold war interest in financing its allies' trade deficits. Despite American pressure, however, exchange-rate and macroeconomic policies were largely un-coordinated.

Trade liberalization and moves toward currency convertibility made external-payments positions more sensitive to macroeconomic policies in the late 1950s, and the development of Eurocurrency markets increased this sensitivity after the mid-1960s. Nevertheless, international capital mobility was still low compared with subsequent decades. As I discuss in Chapter 4, this situation encouraged an expansion of international policy coordination to include symptom-management policies—intervention in foreign-exchange markets and multilateral balance-of-payments lending—during the period 1956–70. For example, when relatively expansive British and French macroeconomic policies generated payments deficits and pressure on the pound and the franc, Western European countries and the United States collaborated to lend money to the deficit countries and coordinate intervention in foreign-exchange markets to support their currencies. Persistent U.S. payments deficits triggered unilateral efforts to block private capital flows and international collaboration to finance those deficits and support the dollar. This coordination was sufficient to maintain stable exchange rates even though monetary and fiscal policies generally were not aligned and governments were unable to cooperate to adjust exchange-rate parities.

By the late 1960s, short-term international capital flows through the Euromarkets had become large enough (despite capital controls) to undermine governments' ability simultaneously to maintain fixed exchange rates and macroeconomic policy-making autonomy. The volume of private speculative capital flows exceeded what governments were willing and able to expend in symptom-management efforts, and governments were still unable to coordinate exchange-rate changes. Although coordination of monetary and fiscal policies might have been appropriate in this environment, states sought instead to regain macroeconomic policy-making autonomy by permitting exchange rates to fluctuate and by borrowing and lending on private international capital markets. As Chapter 5 demonstrates, policy coordination during the period 1971–77 did not erode much below its level in the preceding period, but it also did not develop to meet the new challenges posed by increasing international market integration.

By the late 1970s, most governments realized that fluctuating exchange rates did not actually permit macroeconomic policy-making autonomy, which became even more apparent with the acceleration of international capital mobility in the 1980s and early 1990s. Consequently, policy coordination in the years since 1978 has focused on monetary and fiscal policies—the only effective approach given the current structure of the international economy. The United States periodically demanded that Japan and Germany reflate their economies with relaxed fiscal and monetary policies, which they did in 1977–78, the late 1980s, and (in the case of Japan) the early 1990s. Foreign governments also called repeatedly for adjustments in American monetary and fiscal policies, although such adjustments in response to foreign pressure were rare. In the early 1990s, deficit spending on reunification in Germany was accompanied by high interest rates to contain the resulting inflation. Criticism from the United States went largely unheeded (in part because of Washington's indifference to foreign concerns about its fiscal and monetary policies), although German monetary policy relaxed somewhat in response to the concerns of other governments within the European Community. As Chapter 6 shows, domestic political obstacles to macroeconomic policy coordination remain high, and the resulting incompatibilities among national policies continue to generate considerable domestic and international economic instability.

Chapter 7 summarizes the book's findings and draws some broader implications for the study of international political economy, focusing on the contributions that an economic-structural approach can make and on lessons for theories about American hegemony.

Many people provided valuable assistance in the preparation of this book. My greatest intellectual debt is to Stephen Krasner, whose rigorous critiques helped give shape to my research. Also at Stanford University, Judith Goldstein and Alexander L. George provided guidance and trenchant criticism. Substantial parts of the research and writing were completed while I was at the Institute of International Relations and the University of British Columbia, and I am deeply indebted to Mark Zacher (then director of the institute) for his generous intellectual and moral support. Helpful comments came at various stages of the work from David Andrews, Jeffry Frieden, Geoffrey Garrett, Michael Hawes, Keisuke Iida, Jan Thomson, and Gilbert Winham. None bears responsibility for my claims, and many probably disagree with various parts of the argument. I also thank Emma Bircham and Blair Jordan for research assistance, and Erin Richmond for assistance in typing portions of the final manuscript.

Generous financial support came from the Social Sciences and Humanities Research Council of Canada, the MacArthur Foundation (by way of the Center for International Security and Arms Control at Stanford University), and the Eisenhower World Affairs Institute. I gratefully acknowledge financial support for postdoctoral research provided by the Izaak Walton Killam Memorial Fellowships (through the University of British Columbia) and the Social Sciences and Humanities Research Council of Canada.

Earlier versions of parts of the argument were published as "International Economic Structures, Government Interests, and International Coordination of Macroeconomic Adjustment Policies," *International Organization* 45 (Summer 1991), pp. 309–42, and as "Understanding Patterns of Macroeconomic Policy Coordination in the Postwar Period," in *Political Economy and the Changing Global Order*, edited by Richard Stubbs and Geoffrey R. D. Underhill (Toronto: McClelland and Stewart, 1994).

MICHAEL C. WEBB

Victoria, B.C.

The Political Economy
of Policy Coordination

CHAPTER ONE

Coordinating Macroeconomic Adjustment Policy

Recent international economic diplomacy has been marked by highly politicized debates about macroeconomic policy. Every U.S. administration since Jimmy Carter's in the late 1970s has demanded that Japan and Germany lower interest rates and stimulate domestic demand in order to reduce American trade deficits and (on occasion) to slow capital outflows from the United States. The governments of Japan and many European countries have reciprocated by demanding that Washington reduce its budget deficit, which they see as the root cause of international trade imbalances, and alter monetary policies that they believe destabilize exchange rates. Since 1991, many European governments have criticized Germany's stimulative fiscal and restrictive monetary policies, which they believe have generated recession and exchange-rate instability throughout Europe.

Two things are especially noteworthy about these recent debates. First, the degree of politicization and intergovernmental conflict appears high, which many analysts contrast with what they consider (mistakenly, I shall argue) as more cooperative relations in the 1950s and 1960s. During those years—the so-called Bretton Woods period—international policy coordination focused on promoting trade liberalization, coordinating intervention in foreign-exchange markets, and providing balance-of-payments lending to support fixed-currency parities. Many argue that international policy coordination was more extensive in those years than it is today, and certainly the earlier period was associated with much greater stability in exchange rates and international payments balances. Second, recent international debates concern the most politically sensitive domestic economic policies of governments (monetary and fiscal policies) in contrast to the focus in earlier periods on more obviously foreign economic policies (balance-of-payments financing, trade and exchange restrictions).

How can we best understand this emergence of macroeconomic policy coordination as a central issue in international cooperation since the late 1970s and the contrasts between recent patterns of coordination and those of earlier periods? In this book I argue that such patterns have to be understood in the context of the changing structure of the international economy. Specifically, the growth of international trade and capital flows has had a dramatic impact on macroeconomic policy-making in the advanced capitalist countries and on patterns of economic policy coordination among them. These changes in the structure of the international economy—in particular, the growth of international capital mobility—have constrained governments' freedom to pursue macroeconomic policies that differ from those of other large countries. Such changes, rather than any erosion of international policy coordination, have greatly increased international economic instability. National monetary and fiscal policies now have greater international spillover effects than in previous decades, which has led to changes in patterns of economic policy coordination. Governments have moved away from strategies of policy coordination that they relied on to insulate national macroeconomic policy-making from international pressures in the 1950s and 1960s and have moved toward coordination of monetary and fiscal policies themselves. The limited results reflect the serious domestic political obstacles to international coordination of such policies, not any general erosion of cooperation among industrialized countries.

THE STRUCTURE OF THE INTERNATIONAL ECONOMY AND PATTERNS OF POLICY COORDINATION

I begin to develop these arguments about economic policy coordination by constructing an informal model of how changing international economic structures affect the options that governments have for reconciling their domestic macroeconomic objectives with constraints imposed by international market pressures and diplomacy. The issue of international macroeconomic adjustment arises because differences in macroeconomic policies among countries can lead to external payments imbalances that make it difficult for governments to sustain the policies they prefer. Countries that pursue more expansive policies than those of their trading partners experience trade deficits, capital outflows, or a combination of the two, while countries that pursue more restrictive policies experience trade surpluses, capital inflows, or both. (This argument is developed in detail in Chapter 2).

The basic issue for coordinating international macroeconomic adjustment policy is to reconcile governments' different policies with international trade and capital market pressures. Indeed, the central problem can be seen through the lens of John Gerard Ruggie's idea of *embedded liberalism*.[1] Ruggie argued that postwar international trade and monetary regimes were designed to promote a kind of international liberalization that was embedded in a prior concern for domestic economic and social stability. The Great Depression of the 1930s showed that laissez-faire policies (domestic and international) simply were not socially or politically viable in industrialized, urbanized societies. Governments everywhere had assumed "much more direct responsibility for domestic social security and economic stability."[2] The challenge facing postwar planners was essentially the same issue that underlies all the strategies of international policy coordination discussed in this book: "to devise a framework which would safeguard and even aid the quest for domestic stability without, at the same time, triggering the mutually destructive external consequences that had plagued the interwar period."[3]

A number of different policies can be used to manage or eliminate external imbalances generated by differences in macroeconomic policies among countries.[4] I label these *international macroeconomic adjustment policies*. Three categories are relevant:

1. John Gerard Ruggie, "International Regimes, Transactions, and Change: Embedded Liberalism in the Postwar Economic Order," in Stephen D. Krasner, ed., *International Regimes* (Ithaca: Cornell University Press, 1983).
2. Ibid., p. 204.
3. Ibid., p. 209.
4. The following schema borrows from Richard N. Cooper, *The Economics of Interdependence: Economic Policy in the Atlantic Community* (New York: McGraw-Hill, 1968), chap. 1, and is common in the literature.

External policies. Controls can be imposed or adjusted on trade and capital flows, and exchange rates can be adjusted. Deficit countries might restrict imports and capital outflows or devalue their currencies; surplus countries might encourage imports and restrict capital inflows or revalue their currencies.

Symptom-management policies. Governments might intervene in foreign-exchange markets and balance-of-payments borrowing might be used to manage or offset the international market flows generated by different macroeconomic policies in different countries.

Internal policies. Governments can adjust monetary and fiscal policies to eliminate imbalances between savings, investment, and consumption that generate trade imbalances and to avoid crossnational interest-rate differentials that generate speculative international capital flows.

If governments always adjusted internal policies to eliminate external imbalances (as some liberal economists prescribe), no one would be interested in international policy coordination. But the kinds of monetary and fiscal policies required to eliminate external imbalances often conflict with the domestic political pressures that cause governments to pursue internationally disequilibriating policies in the first place. It is important to remember that in the advanced capitalist countries no economic policies have more extensive and visible effects on economic conditions than macroeconomic policies. Studies of voting behavior reveal that conditions such as unemployment, inflation, and income growth are among the most important influences on electoral outcomes. Consequently, governments may be very reluctant to alter monetary and fiscal policies to eliminate external imbalances if those alterations conflict with domestic political interests. For example, a government committed to full employment may find it difficult to shift to restrictive monetary and fiscal policies to eliminate external deficits (e.g., Britain at some periods in the 1950s and 1960s) without undermining its electoral position. Similarly, domestic political calculations and machinations in the 1980s and early 1990s left Washington unable to increase taxes and reduce spending sufficiently to eliminate massive American budget and trade deficits.

Domestic political pressures mean that deficit and surplus countries alike often want to avoid or postpone internal adjustment. Attempts to do so typically raise issues of international policy coordination. Governments may want to persuade their foreign counterparts to adjust their policies to help manage or eliminate the international imbalance. Deficit countries want surplus countries to reflate their economies, revalue their currencies, expand their imports, and provide financing for payments deficits. Similarly, governments may favor international agreements to limit others' use of external strategies of adjustment. Surplus countries want deficit countries to rely on the internal strategy of deflation and to refrain from restricting imports and sharply devaluing their currencies.[5] Surplus countries may be willing to provide international financing to persuade deficit countries to limit their resort to external strategies of adjustment and ease the introduction of domestic restraint.

Which types of policies will be adjusted to eliminate imbalances and which will be subject to coordination depend critically on the structure of the international economy. The degree of integration of markets for goods, services, and especially capital is a crucial determinant of the advantages and disadvantages for governments of alternative international macroeconomic adjustment strategies. (These linkages are discussed in greater detail in Chapter 2). When international trade flows are moderate and capital mobility is low, governments can manage the imbalances generated by crossnational differences in macroeconomic policies by adjusting trade controls and exchange rates (either unilaterally or in a coordinated fashion) and by coordinating balance of payments lending. These adjustments can permit governments to manage the symptoms of crossnational policy differentials without destabilizing the international economy, thereby preserving a substantial degree of macroeconomic policy-making autonomy.

But when capital flows easily across national borders, even coordinated balance-of-payments lending and exchange-rate coordination will not be sufficient to manage the symptoms of different macroeconomic policies in different countries. Surplus or deficit governments that want to lessen their burden of adjustment to imbalances must pressure foreign governments to alter their monetary and fiscal policies. When international capital flows dominate external payments positions, only adjustments to macroeconomic policies themselves will change the interest-rate differentials and the expectations that motivate capital

---

5. Surplus countries would generally oppose drastic devaluation by deficit countries but might well favor moderate changes, especially if they were an alternative to trade restrictions. In any case, surplus countries would prefer decisions about changes in deficit countries' exchange rates to be coordinated internationally to give these countries the opportunity to protect their interests.

5

holders' decisions about where to invest their money. Governments, therefore, face powerful pressures to coordinate macroeconomic policies internationally in order to achieve domestic objectives, although the impediments to coordination are also substantial.

Implicit in this argument about how changing international economic structures influence the attractiveness of alternative adjustment strategies is a recognition that different types of macroeconomic adjustment policies are interrelated and can substitute for one another under certain circumstances. For example, either or both governments could address a current account imbalance between two countries by trade controls, exchange-rate adjustments, lending from the surplus to the deficit country, adjustments to monetary and fiscal policies, or some combination of these approaches.

This recognition has important implications for our interpretation of particular instances of policy coordination. Agreements to coordinate specific types of policies need to be understood in the context of their relationship to the basic issue of macroeconomic adjustment. For example, two historically separate commitments to maintain fixed exchange rates could represent fundamentally different cases of international policy coordination, depending on the structure of the international economy and agreements regarding other types of macroeconomic adjustment policy. Most industrialized capitalist countries made commitments to maintain fixed exchange rates in the 1960s, just as most European Community members did in the 1980s. The former commitment was undertaken, however, in a context of relatively low international market integration and was accompanied by capital controls and balance-of-payments lending to reconcile fixed exchange rates with macroeconomic policy-making autonomy. In the latter case, market integration was extensive, and states had little choice but to subordinate monetary policies to the maintenance of fixed exchange rates. It would be misleading to equate these two episodes on the grounds that both involved fixed exchange rates; other aspects of economic structure and macroeconomic adjustment policies were so different. Thus, this book assesses trends in policy coordination by examining the degree to which international coordination of all types of macroeconomic adjustment policies constrains national policy-making autonomy rather than analyses changes over time in the extent of coordination of any one type of policy. As I argue above, a focus on the shift from fixed to fluctuating exchange rates has been particularly misleading in this respect.

POWER AND COORDINATION: DECLINING AMERICAN HEGEMONY?

In focusing attention on how changes in the structure of the international economy have systematically altered patterns of policy coordination, I take issue with theories of cooperation that focus attention on a purported decline in American hegemony. Scholars working from a variety of theoretical perspectives see American power as the key variable explaining changes in patterns of international cooperation. Realist international relations theorists such as Robert Gilpin and Stephen D. Krasner argue that American hegemony was necessary to overcome obstacles to international coordination arising out of security conflicts among independent countries in an anarchic world. According to this view, the United States used its predominant power in the early postwar decades to impose an international economic system that benefited all countries, especially those outside the United States.[6] International cooperation eroded, Gilpin and Krasner argue, when the United States lost the margin of power that allowed it to underwrite international agreements that benefited others to its own relative disadvantage.[7]

Hegemonic stability theories that draw on the liberal-interdependence tradition also suggest that American hegemony was critical for stabilizing the international economy and promoting international cooperation, but for very different reasons. Charles P. Kindleberger, for example, argued that stability and liberalization are collective goods, as all countries benefit from them regardless of whether the countries contribute to their production. International collective goods tend to be underproduced because states cannot be excluded from the benefits and thus have an incentive to free ride on others' efforts. Only a hegemonic country has both the power to provide the collective good on its own (or to induce others to cooperate

---

6. Robert Gilpin, *U.S. Power and the Multinational Corporation: The Political Economy of Foreign Direct Investment* (New York: Basic Books, 1975); Stephen D. Krasner, "State Power and the Structure of International Trade," *World Politics* 28 (April 1976).

7. Robert Gilpin, *The Political Economy of International Relations* (Princeton: Princeton University Press, 1987).

in providing the collective good) and a large enough stake in the system for the benefits to exceed the costs.[8] Even theorists such as Robert Keohane who argue that obstacles to the provision of international collective goods can be overcome in the absence of hegemony suggest that hegemony uniquely facilitates cooperation and that economic cooperation was most extensive when the United States was at its peak of power in the 1950s and 60s.[9]

Finally, some radical scholars argue that the United States exercised ideological hegemony, backed by economic and political coercion, to harmonize the policies of leading capitalist states in a pro-market direction in the 1950s and 60s. The posited erosion of American ideological hegemony and international power is said to have reduced its ability to resolve competition, and harmony among the advanced capitalist countries has therefore eroded.[10]

As applied to the area of international monetary cooperation, the declining hegemony argument tends to view the abandonment of fixed exchange rates in the early 1970s as the key turning point in the postwar years. Before that time, it is argued, United States–led policy coordination to maintain fixed exchange rates was extensive and was the key factor underlying international economic stability. With the decline in American hegemony apparent (to these analysts) by the late 1960s, the United States was no longer able unilaterally to underwrite international policy coordination or to persuade other governments to share the burdens of such leadership. The resulting erosion of international policy coordination led to the breakdown of the Bretton Woods system and ushered in a continuing period of economic volatility and diplomatic conflict.

My findings do not support the declining hegemony thesis. International coordination of monetary and fiscal policies closer to the core of national autonomy has actually increased in recent decades, albeit unevenly. The overall level of international coordination of all types of

8. Charles P. Kindleberger, "Dominance and Leadership in the International Economy: Exploitation, Public Goods, and Free Rides," *International Studies Quarterly* 25 (June 1981).

9. Robert O. Keohane, *After Hegemony: Cooperation and Discord in the World Political Economy* (Princeton: Princeton University Press, 1984).

10. Robert W. Cox, *Power, Production, and World Order: Social Forces in the Making of History* (New York: Columbia University Press, 1987); Fred L. Block, *The Origins of International Economic Disorder: A Study of United States International Monetary Policy from World War II to the Present* (Berkeley: University of California Press, 1977).

macroeconomic adjustment policies was at least as high in the late 1970s and much of the 1980s as it had been in the late 1950s and the 1960s (the years in which the Bretton Woods system functioned most effectively) and higher than it had been in the late 1940s and the 1950s (the years of greatest American power).

Theories of declining American hegemony also cannot explain observed changes in the types of policies subject to international coordination: a shift in focus from coordination of trade controls and balance-of-payments finance in the late 1940s and the 1950s to exchange rates and balance-of-payments lending in the late 1950s and the 1960s to macroeconomic policies since the late 1970s. Overall, we can see a move away from coordination of policies that have limited direct consequences for domestic economic and political conditions— especially balance-of-payments financing—and toward coordination of policies that are critically important for domestic politics and economics—monetary and fiscal policies. This shift toward more extensive coordination of more important policies is not consistent with theories of declining American hegemony.

Although international economic instability was much greater in the 1980s than during the Bretton Woods years, this change was a consequence less of the posited erosion of American hegemony than of the increasing international integration of capital markets. As capital became more mobile, international economic policy coordination had to become more extensive simply to maintain the 1960s level of stability.[11] Specifically, exchange-rate stability could have been achieved after the early 1970s only by direct coordination of monetary policies, in contrast to the coordination of foreign-exchange market intervention and balance-of-payments lending that stabilized exchange rates in the 1960s. Therefore, the instability of the late 1970s and the 1980s reflected the obstacles to making international policy coordination more extensive than it had been in the 1960s; it was not a breakdown of coordination.

These criticisms of the declining hegemony thesis do not mean that international power relationships are unimportant for explaining patterns of policy coordination. They are, in fact, extremely important, as I discuss in greater detail in Chapter 2. International bargaining power

11. For an early argument about the link between increasing economic interdependence and increased pressures for cooperation, see Cooper, *Economics of Interdependence.*

shapes the distribution of the burden of policy adjustment among co-operating governments far more than does the concern about maxi-mizing welfare that motivates many theoretical discussions of international policy coordination. Not surprisingly, governments of weak countries generally adjust their policies more through interna-tional negotiations than do the governments of powerful countries, regardless of which bears most responsibility for international imbal-ances. Thus, a focus on international political structures *complements* the economic-structural argument developed earlier in this chapter. An un-derstanding of international economic structures—especially the de-gree of international capital market integration—is crucial for understanding which types of policies will be the focus of negotiated adjustments, while an understanding of the international political struc-ture—especially the distribution of power among states—is crucial for understanding why the burden of adjustment is distributed as it is among countries.[12]

But my observation of the distribution of international bargaining power contrasts sharply with the situation depicted by declinists. The United States has dominated international negotiations throughout the postwar period. In all periods, including the 1970s and 1980s, it was able to persuade foreign governments to alter their policies to a much greater degree than it altered its own policies. American bargaining power was striking even in periods in which American macroeconomic policies were the primary cause of international imbalances. In the late 1980s, the United States persuaded Japan and Germany to adjust more in the direction of macroeconomic expansion than the United States itself adjusted in the direction of restraint, even though American fiscal deficits were the most important cause of large international payments imbalances since the early 1980s. Similarly, coordinated moves to sta-bilize currencies in the 1960s in the face of large American payments deficits involved larger adjustments to foreign policies (mainly balance-of-payments and international reserve policies) than to American pol-icies. At the same time, American bargaining power (measured in terms

12. The two types of explanations are interrelated in practice. For example, an ina-bility or unwillingness of the government of a powerful country to adjust certain policies (e.g., the United States and fiscal policy in the 1980s) may encourage all countries to coordinate other types of policies (such as symptom-management policies, including foreign-exchange market intervention in the case just noted), even though that type of coordination may be relatively ineffective.

of the United States's ability to persuade foreign governments to adjust their policies) appears to have been less in the late 1940s and early 1950s than argued by some proponents of the declining hegemony thesis, as evidenced by U.S. inability to persuade aid recipients to co-ordinate their recovery programs or monetary and fiscal policies. Such persistent patterns in bargaining outcomes (American preeminence but not dominance) suggest that the American power position has changed much less than proponents of the declining hegemony theory suggest.[13]

CONCEPTUALIZING AND MEASURING POLICY COORDINATION

Recent literature on international cooperation has developed a number of useful definitions and typologies, and it is important at this point to identify how my study relates to the broader theoretical literature. Throughout the book, *international coordination* is defined as negotiated mutual adjustment that causes states to pursue different policies than they would have chosen had policy-making been unilateral.[14] This is what Helen Milner has described as the consensus definition.[15] It is important to note that according to this definition, coordination involves both negotiation and policy adjustment. The definition differs from the way economists tend to use the term, as in Henry C. Wallich's widely cited definition of coordination as "a significant modification of national policies in recognition of international economic interdependence."[16] Wallich's definition is not appropriate for this book because it does not distinguish independent policy-making that takes international factors into account from internationally negotiated adjustments to national policy.

Coordination does not necessarily reflect national interests or enhance welfare, two assumptions often made in the international coop-

13. Joseph Nye, Susan Strange, and Henry Nau, among others, have made similar arguments about continuing American power.

14. This definition closely resembles Keohane's definition of cooperation in *After Hegemony*, pp. 51–52.

15. Helen Milner, "International Theories of Cooperation among Nations: Strengths and Weaknesses," *World Politics* 44 (April 1992), pp. 467–68.

16. Henry C. Wallich, "Institutional Cooperation in the World Economy," in Jacob A. Frenkel and Michael L. Mussa, eds., *The World Economic System: Performance and Prospects* (Doyer, Mass.: Auburn House, 1984), p. 85.

eration literature (especially literature that uses game theory). The policy adjustments demanded and negotiated by states reflect each government's perception of its own interests, which may be widely at variance with how independent analysts define the national interest. For example, according to theories about political business cycles, politicians may have a self-interest in preelection stimulus, even if the national interest suffers from the resulting postelection inflation.[17] Similarly, one could argue that the American national interest in the mid-to-late-1980s would have been best served by changes in domestic policy to eliminate the fiscal deficit; instead, the Reagan and Bush administrations focused on persuading foreign governments to reflate in hopes of reducing the American trade deficit and making it easier for Washington to attract foreign financing for its budget deficit.

As these examples make clear, international policy coordination does not need to enhance welfare, national or global, and I do not assume anything about its welfare effects. In fact, as economists critical of policy coordination have argued, negotiated mutual policy adjustments may enable governments to avoid making politically difficult choices that could enhance welfare in the long run.[18] I define and measure policy coordination empirically with no a priori assumptions about its desirability. The historical record does reveal that choices not to coordinate policies in a highly integrated international economy can be destabilizing, but certain kinds of policy coordination can be equally damaging.

Another important component of the mainstream definition of cooperation is the distinction made between cooperation and harmony. According to Robert Keohane, who developed this conceptualization in its most widely used form, "harmony refers to a situation in which actors' policies (pursued in their own self-interest without regard for others) *automatically* facilitate the attainment of others' goals. . . . Where harmony reigns, cooperation is unnecessary."[19] The distinction

---

17. For such an argument, see Edward Tufte, *Political Control of the Economy* (Princeton: Princeton University Press, 1978). For a sophisticated test of the political business-cycle hypothesis in the American context, see Nathaniel Beck, "Elections and the Fed: Is There a Political Monetary Cycle?" *American Journal of Political Science* 31 (February 1987). For a classic, class-based explanation for political business cycles, see Michal Kalecki, "Political Aspects of Full Employment," *Political Quarterly* 14 (October–December 1943).

18. Martin Feldstein, "International Economic Cooperation: Introduction," in Feldstein, ed., *International Economic Cooperation* (Chicago: University of Chicago Press for the National Bureau of Economic Research, 1988).

19. Keohane, *After Hegemony*, p. 51.

between cooperation and harmony is important because the absence of negotiated mutual adjustment of certain policies has sometimes reflected unresolvable conflicts of interest among governments (what Keohane labels *discord*) and at other times a situation of harmony in which each government has unilaterally chosen to pursue policies consistent with the interests of other states.

The importance of this distinction can be seen in two cases. The first concerns the use of trade restrictions as instruments of international macroeconomic adjustment. From the mid-1940s to the early 1960s, restrictions were widely used to prevent trade deficits from undermining expansionary domestic policies. Because these restrictions were so widespread and because they interfered with the realization of foreign countries' export interests, they were a primary focus of international macroeconomic adjustment policy coordination. In contrast, there was very little explicit coordination of trade policies as instruments of international macroeconomic adjustment after the mid-1970s because each government independently abstained from proposing to introduce comprehensive trade restrictions to insulate its policies from external payments pressures (see Chapter 6; the United States Congress was a partial exception). The absence of policy coordination in this case reflected the success that earlier coordination had in changing governments' perceptions of self-interest, not any erosion of coordination.

A second potential example of harmony concerns monetary and fiscal policies. Harmony would exist if each country automatically adjusted its own macroeconomic policies to eliminate external imbalances. Thus, there would be little interest in explicit coordination of any type of international macroeconomic adjustment policy. Some analysts have suggested that harmony did exist in the late 1950s and the 1960s as a consequence of the commitment most countries made to maintain fixed exchange rates. According to this view, governments independently adjusted national monetary and fiscal policies to eliminate external imbalances that threatened fixed exchange rates, thereby obviating any need for negotiated mutual adjustment of monetary and fiscal policies. The evidence presented in Chapter 4, however, shows that governments generally did not independently adjust macroeconomic policies to eliminate payments imbalances; consequently, the absence of negotiated mutual adjustment in this period cannot be attributed to harmony.

Widespread agreement in the literature on a definition of coordination does not imply agreement on how to measure coordination empirically, as Helen Milner has pointed out.[20] To determine whether policies were coordinated, my definition directs us to look for evidence that national policies were different as a result of international agreements (formal or informal) from what they would otherwise have been. This means comparing the policies actually pursued with a counterfactual assessment of the policies likely to have been pursued in the absence of international negotiations, which is difficult to do precisely except through detailed study of particular events. For example, Robert D. Putnam and C. Randall Henning examined policy debates in three countries in considerable detail (some seventy pages of text) in order to support their contention that the Bonn Summit agreement of 1978 involved adjustments to the policies of the German, Japanese, and American governments.[21] Because I examine changes in patterns of coordination of a variety of policies over an extended period of time, I cannot compare in detail the outcomes of policy coordination with counterfactual estimations of unilateral policies. Instead, my judgments about the impact of policy coordination rely on the assessments made by contemporary participants and observers and the findings of other scholars' detailed studies of particular episodes.[22]

One important general observation can be made about the significance of government policy adjustments. As I discuss in some detail in Chapter 2, it is generally more difficult for governments unilaterally to sustain expansionary macroeconomic policies in the face of external deficits than it is for governments unilaterally to sustain relatively restrictive policies in the face of external surpluses. (The United States is a partial exception, as explained in Chapter 2.) The implication for measuring coordination is that negotiated adjustments to the policies of surplus states generally involve greater departures from unilateral policy-making than do negotiated adjustments to the policies of deficit states because deficit states are under greater market pressure to make

20. Milner, "International Theories of Cooperation," p. 468.

21. Robert D. Putnam and C. Randall Henning, "The Bonn Summit of 1978: A Case Study in Coordination," in *Can Nations Agree? Issues in International Economic Cooperation,* by Richard N. Cooper, Barry Eichengreen, C. Randall Henning, Gerald Holtham, and Robert D. Putnam (Washington, D.C.: Brookings Institution, 1989), pp. 27–98.

22. Because my purpose is to identify broad historical patterns, controversy about the impact of specific negotiations is unlikely to undermine the book's overall conclusions.

adjustments in the absence of international coordination. This is especially important in terms of monetary and fiscal policies. In the absence of policy coordination, it would be extremely difficult for deficit states to avoid some deflation, while surplus states may be able to avoid reflation. Thus, other things being equal, negotiations that generate policy adjustments by surplus states represent a higher level of coordination than do agreements involving policy adjustments only by deficit states.

INTERNATIONAL STRUCTURES AND DOMESTIC POLITICS

My explanation for international policy coordination is focused at the systemic level of analysis, although the elements of the international system that I stress are not those emphasized in much recent literature on international cooperation. In neorealist theory, the structure of the international system is generally described in terms of political anarchy (the absence of an authority to resolve disputes among sovereign states) and the distribution of power among states.[23] I point to the inadequacy of the neorealist definition of international structure.[24] The distribution of power alone cannot explain patterns of macroeconomic policy coordination, an area central to the concerns of governments; we also need to look at characteristics of the international economy that persist over time and systematically influence how governments relate to each other. As the empirical chapters of this book show, the governments of advanced capitalist countries have responded in similar (though not identical) fashion to changes in international capital mobility. According to Kenneth N. Waltz, if different states act similarly in response to similar phenomena, we are justified in thinking that there may be some kind of structural effect at work.[25]

My emphasis on how changes in the structure of the international

23. Kenneth N. Waltz, *Theory of International Politics* (Reading, Mass.: Addison-Wesley, 1979). See also Milner, "International Theories of Cooperation," which critiques this characteristic of recent literature on international cooperation.

24. For more fundamental challenges, see John Gerard Ruggie, "Continuity and Transformation in the World Polity: Toward a Neorealist Synthesis," *World Politics* 35 (January 1983); and Alexander E. Wendt, "The Agent-Structure Problem in International Relations Theory," *International Organization* 41 (Summer 1987).

25. Waltz, *Theory of International Politics*, pp. 69–73.

15

economy influence the possibilities for domestic macroeconomic policy choices should not obscure the fact that those structural changes were themselves the product of policy choices: to liberalize trade and trade-related capital flows and not to regulate international capital markets when regulation might have been feasible (e.g., the early years of the Eurocurrency markets centered in London).[26] The technology of international finance did not develop in a political vacuum, nor was the growth of private international capital flows inevitable or economically determined. Nevertheless, it is important to emphasize that the constraints that international capital mobility imposes on national policy-making autonomy were not intended and may now be practically unavoidable.

Leading states permitted the Eurodollar market to flourish in the mid-1960s because it offered them short-term advantages. Deposit taking in dollars outside the United States eased balance-of-payments pressures on the governments of surplus and deficit countries by encouraging private agents to hold on to dollars instead of converting them into stronger currencies or gold. Conversion would have increased pressure on the United States to correct its deficit by devaluing or deflating and would have increased pressure on surplus states to revalue or reflate. The British government encouraged the development of Eurocurrency markets as part of its strategy to make the City of London a leading international financial center.

The permissive attitude toward the Euromarkets adopted by most Western governments reflected their belief that the emerging international capital market would serve as a minor adjunct to national capital markets and that national markets could be effectively insulated from Euromarket influences.[27] For most of the 1960s, economists and central bank officials generally believed that Euromarket transactions would have little impact on national macroeconomic conditions and policies.[28] Not until the Euromarkets became well established did state leaders

Failure of N-S's to anticipate effects of Euromarkets.

26. Susan Strange, *Casino Capitalism* (Oxford: Basil Blackwell, 1986); Geoffrey R. D. Underhill, "Markets beyond Politics? The State and the Internationalisation of Financial Markets," *European Journal of Political Research* 19 (March/April 1991).

27. Susan Strange, *International Monetary Relations*, vol. 2 of Andrew Shonfield, ed., *International Economic Relations of the Western World, 1959–1971* (London: Oxford University Press for the Royal Institute of International Affairs, 1976), p. 190.

28. George W. McKenzie, *The Economics of the Euro-currency System* (London: Macmillan, 1976), pp. 9–10.

realize that they might have an interest in preventing the development of markets that facilitate international capital flows. Thus, "the Euro-dollar business began with the approval or at least the silent blessing of the main governments concerned, even though it may prove to have been the most important single development of the century undermining national monetary sovereignty."[29]

Once these crucial permissive decisions were taken, international capital liberalization took on a self-fulfilling character, and short-term international capital markets quickly became deeply entrenched. Governments faced incentives to liberalize capital controls in order to attract foreign and domestic investment in the financial sector or to forestall a loss of business to less controlled foreign financial centers. Deregulation and liberalization are attractive to financial industries because they lower costs and permit increased profits. Once a major state begins to liberalize its capital markets, others are forced to follow if they do not want to lose business to foreign financial centers. This process of competitive deregulation can lead to a situation in which international capital controls are signficantly less restrictive than would be preferred by any individual state.[30]

By the early 1980s, most governments were trying to make a virtue out of a necessity. Controls on speculative capital flows were no longer effective in insulating national macroeconomic policies from international market pressures. As early as 1973, the German central bank concluded that recent experience had "made it abundantly clear that even stronger administrative action against capital flows from foreign countries . . . does not suffice when speculative expectations run particularly high."[31] In 1983 the failure of the French socialist government's efforts to use capital controls to insulate its expansionary policies from international market pressures confirmed that controls were no longer

29. Susan Strange, *Sterling and British Policy: A Political Study of an International Currency in Decline* (London: Oxford University Press, 1971), p. 209.

30. John B. Goodman and Louis W. Pauly, "The Obsolescence of Capital Controls? Economic Management in an Age of Global Markets," *World Politics* 46 (October 1993); Ethan B. Kapstein, "Resolving the Regulator's Dilemma: International Coordination of Banking Regulations," *International Organization* 43 (Spring 1989); Edward J. Kane, "Competitive Financial Reregulation: An International Perspective," in Richard Portes and Alexander K. Swoboda, eds., *Threats to International Financial Stability* (Cambridge: Cambridge University Press, 1987).

31. Cited in D. C. Kruse, *Monetary Integration in Western Europe: EMU, EMS, and Beyond* (London: Butterworths, 1980), p. 130.

an effective instrument of macroeconomic adjustment policy. The declining effectiveness of capital controls and the increasing importance of financial flows for international production and trade thus encouraged most advanced capitalist countries to abandon attempts to achieve policy-making autonomy by controlling speculative capital flows. A wave of liberalization and deregulation in the early 1980s combined with recent advances in the technology of international communications and information processing to produce what has been called the globalization of international finance: rapid growth in international financial flows and the integration of national capital markets with the Eurocurrency market.[32]

In light of this history, the constraints on macroeconomic policy-making autonomy imposed by international capital mobility are best understood as an *unintended* consequence of earlier choices to liberalize trade and long-term investment. If government policies contributed (even unintentionally) to the development of international capital mobility, one might argue that governments could change the structure of the international economic system to eliminate the constraint that capital mobility imposes on macroeconomic policy-making autonomy.[33] However, given the character of the international economic interdependence that has emerged in the wake of trade and investment liberalization, it now would be extremely difficult for any government to escape these constraints. Any government, including the United States, would find it difficult and costly to reverse the process of capital market integration. As I discuss in detail in later chapters, the experience of the 1970s and 80s shows that it is not possible for governments selectively to control speculative capital flows when international capital markets become entrenched and international ties of trade and direct investment are extensive. International capital market integration could be reversed only by reintroducing comprehensive trade and exchange controls. But a return to autarky would be extremely disruptive for national economies and therefore also politically destabilizing. It would be strongly opposed by most of the large influential firms and industries in advanced capitalist countries. For these reasons, govern-

32. Bank for International Settlements (BIS), *Recent Innovations in International Banking* (Basle: BIS, 1986), pp. 149, 195. Globalization has so far been restricted mainly to the advanced capitalist countries.

33. For a theoretical discussion of the meaning of structure and its relationship to the actions of individual units, see Wendt, "The Agent-Structure Problem."

ments of these countries are unlikely to block international capital mobility, short of a severe depression (which is made less likely by the policy coordination that capital market integration has encouraged) or large-scale international conflict. Capital mobility has persisted over time and even accelerated through the worst world recession since the 1930s, and it is likely to continue to persist. We are therefore justified in considering it an element of the international economic structure and studying the effects of this structure on the policies of individual governments.

Structuralist or systemic explanations for international cooperation have been sharply criticized for their neglect of domestic politics.[34] I focus attention on constraints that the structure of the international economy imposes on national policy-making autonomy, but this in no way denigrates the importance of domestic politics. As I argued earlier, the explanatory model is based on the view that domestic political considerations are of primary importance. States want to maintain macroeconomic policy-making autonomy because monetary and fiscal policies are crucial to their domestic political fortunes; and when governments favor international policy coordination, they are often attempting to defend that autonomy by persuading other states to adjust their policies. Domestic politics also explains why states are more reluctant to coordinate monetary and fiscal policies than other types of macroeconomic adjustment policies, such as balance-of-payments financing and intervention in foreign-exchange markets. Monetary and fiscal policies are harder to coordinate because their domestic political consequences are much more serious than those that follow from coordination of symptom-management policies or external policies of adjustment.

Arguing that changing international economic structures constrain domestic policy choices does not mean that international structures determine domestic choices.[35] As we shall see, governments retain considerable freedom to adopt policies tailored to their domestic political circumstances, even though the costs of policies inconsistent with international market pressures can be high. Similarly, the outcome of any

34. Milner, "International Theories of Cooperation."
35. I also do not attempt to deduce national interests from countries' positions in the international system. Instead, I focus on the expressed interests of governments, which are usually more closely related to domestic political concerns than to abstract concepts of welfare maximization or improving the state's international power position.

particular set of negotiations is heavily influenced by domestic political debates within participating countries.[36] Thus, if one's purpose is to understand fully any particular instance of international coordination of macroeconomic adjustment policies that has important domestic implications, one would devote far more attention to chronicling domestic political debates than I have done in this book. My purpose is to help readers understand broad changes in patterns of international policy coordination over time and how changes in the structure of the international economy affect the opportunities and constraints that governments face when trying to adopt macroeconomic policies that serve their domestic political interests.

36. Robert D. Putnam's work on two-level games provides a helpful analogy; see "Diplomacy and Domestic Politics: The Logic of Two-level Games," *International Organization* 42 (Summer 1988); and Putnam and Henning, "Bonn Summit of 1978."

CHAPTER TWO

The Structure of the International System
and Patterns of Policy Coordination

How and why have patterns of international coordination of macro-economic adjustment policies changed since 1945? I focus on how changes in the structure of the international economy have encouraged states to move toward coordination of monetary and fiscal policies themselves and away from coordination of external policies of adjustment and strategies for symptom management that prevailed in the 1950s and 60s. Accordingly, this chapter starts with a model of how the structure of the international economy shapes the opportunities and constraints that governments face when setting macroeconomic policies and choosing among alternative patterns of international policy coordination.

Market integration is not the only element of the international system that consistently shapes patterns of policy coordination. International power relationships are also critically important for understanding the outcome of negotiations, especially the distribution of the burdens of adjustment to international macroeconomic disequilibria. Negotiated policy adjustments have much more to do with the bargaining power of the governments involved than with welfare maximization or each government's responsibility for international macroeconomic imbalances. Consequently, this chapter also outlines some arguments about bargaining power between deficit and surplus countries and between the United States and other countries, which help to explain patterns of policy coordination identified in subsequent chapters.

INTERNATIONAL ECONOMIC STRUCTURES AND PATTERNS OF POLICY COORDINATION

Domestic Politics and Interest in International Policy Coordination

Any understanding of international policy coordination must begin with an appreciation of the importance of macroeconomic policies in domestic politics. Interest in international coordination of any type of macroeconomic adjustment policy arises out of the domestic political interest all governments have in pursuing policies appropriate to their circumstances. Governments favor coordination that permits them to externalize some of the burdens of adjustment to international macroeconomic imbalances and that limits other governments' ability to do so at their expense, all in order to obtain some freedom to pursue macroeconomic policies that address domestic political and economic concerns. Governments seek favorable domestic economic conditions because severe economic problems hurt the reelection prospects of incumbent governments and at worst could bring a return to the political and social instability of the 1920s and 30s.

The pursuit of favorable domestic economic conditions can lead different governments to choose different macroeconomic policies, depending on domestic political circumstances. For example, conservative governments may put greater emphasis on keeping interest rates high to prevent inflation or maintain the value of capital, while left-wing governments may put a higher priority on maintaining full employment. Economic problems also vary across countries, encouraging different governments to address different problems and thereby pursue different policies. Varying institutional structures can also cause governments to adopt different monetary and fiscal policy mixes. For example, the difficulty of coordinating fiscal policy between the executive and legislative branches in the United States contrasts with the relative independence of the Federal Reserve, contributing to frequent divergence between monetary and fiscal policies. Finally, governments may be unable to make coherent choices for a variety of political and institutional reasons, as in the United States and Canada since the mid-1980s.

When different countries pursue different macroeconomic policies, external-payments imbalances and exchange-rate movements are likely to result. As I outlined in Chapter 1, there are three types of international macroeconomic adjustment policies that could be used to reconcile national macroeconomic objectives with international constraints: external policies, symptom-management policies, and internal policies. If governments always adjusted internal policies to eliminate external imbalances, there would be no interest in international policy coordination. But the kinds of monetary and fiscal policies required to eliminate external imbalances often conflict with the domestic political pressures that initially cause governments to pursue disequilibriating policies. Because of these domestic political pressures, deficit and surplus countries alike often want to avoid or postpone internal adjustment.

Governments are also reluctant to coordinate macroeconomic policies, especially fiscal policies, for historical and institutional reasons. The strong contemporary desire for fiscal-policy autonomy is in part a legacy of the battles that led to the triumph of the sovereign state over competing claims for political authority in sixteenth- and seventeenth-century Europe, where the system of sovereign states was born. Disputes over who had the right to raise taxes and spend public money were at the heart of these battles, and the victorious sovereigns have jealously protected their rights ever since. These historical struggles encouraged an inward orientation toward revenue raising and spending by state institutions forced to defend their rights against challengers inside and outside their territory.[1] Furthermore, when macroeconomic management began to be consciously practiced by leading states in the 1930s and 40s, national economies were insulated from international market pressures. This encouraged a national orientation in fiscal and monetary policy-making because the external consequences of domestic policy choices were minor. In contrast, policies regarding trade controls and exchange rates are inherently international, and governments have always expected others to express an interest in them. Only in the 1970s and 80s, I argue, did the international consequences of monetary and fiscal policy choices become so important that governments were compelled to demand changes in the macroeconomic policies of foreign governments, even at the risk of opening up their own policies to foreign criticism. As we shall see in Chapter 6, efforts to coordinate fiscal policies have been impeded by the institutional difficulty of integrating international consultations into domestic policy-making pro-

---

1. Monetary policy coordination does not face this particular institutional impediment. There is a long tradition of consultations among central bankers, although coordinated policy adjustments were rare before the 1980s.

cedures,[2] although broader political differences among states and domestic fiscal policy-making pathologies in leading countries are also important obstacles to coordination.

Thus, the domestic political importance of macroeconomic policy generates international differences in macroeconomic policies that create payments imbalances and creates powerful obstacles to international coordination of monetary and fiscal policies. Macroeconomic policies are the most powerful instruments that governments have to influence economic conditions within their countries, and governments are therefore more reluctant to coordinate these policies than any other. Monetary and fiscal policy coordination is a last resort, to be used only if other strategies fail; and even when alternative strategies are not viable, we can expect governments to be reluctant to coordinate monetary and fiscal policies. Because the domestic obstacles to international coordination are higher for monetary and fiscal policies than for other types of macroeconomic adjustment policies, we are justified in viewing that coordination as representing a more significant departure from unilateral policy-making than the coordination of external policies of adjustment or symptom-management policies.

Governments that want to avoid adjusting their own monetary and fiscal policies to eliminate international macroeconomic imbalances could do so by relying on external strategies of adjustment or by persuading foreign governments to alter their macroeconomic adjustment policies. Either course of action raises issues of international policy coordination. External strategies of adjustment raise questions of international coordination because trade restrictions and exchange-rate changes in any one country impose burdens of adjustment on foreign countries. For example, during the depression of the 1930s, many countries depreciated their currencies and restricted imports in the hope of stimulating domestic employment; but in so doing they also exported unemployment to their former trading partners. More generally, the exchange rate for any country's currency is effectively its price in terms of other currencies. Thus, a move by one government to alter its exchange rate inevitably alters the exchange rates of other countries, which have their own views about which exchange rate is

2. This lesson is emphasized by Wendy Dobson, *Economic Policy Coordination: Requiem or Prologue?* Policy Analyses in International Economics No. 30 (Washington, D.C.: Institute for International Economics, April 1991).

appropriate. Governments are interested in international coordination of external policies of adjustment mainly to discourage foreign governments from restricting imports or devaluing their currencies, although governments suffering from external macroeconomic imbalances may also call on foreign governments to alter their own external policies of adjustment. For example, deficit countries may call on surplus countries to revalue their currencies or relax their import restrictions.

Symptom-management strategies require international policy coordination virtually by definition. International payments imbalances cannot be managed unilaterally for very long because the amount of financing needed to prevent payments imbalances from forcing governments to alter macroeconomic policies or exchange rates may be quite substantial. National reserves of foreign currencies are rarely large enough to finance deficits for more than a brief period, and surplus countries cannot indefinitely add surpluses to their national reserves without inflating the domestic money supply.[3] These constraints on unilateral symptom-management policy become more serious as international market integration increases. Thus, successful attempts to finance payments imbalances and prevent market-driven currency fluctuations usually require coordinated action by a number of governments, with surplus governments in effect lending money to deficit governments to finance the payments imbalances of the latter.

Governments that want to avoid adjusting their own monetary and fiscal policies to reduce international payments imbalances can call on foreign governments to alter their monetary and fiscal policies. For reasons already discussed, foreign governments are usually reluctant to do so if such alteration conflicts with the domestic imperatives of macroeconomic policy, but diplomatic pressure and mutual adjustments of other types of policies provide a basis for coordination—even of monetary and fiscal policies.

My preceding discussion indicates that interest in international coordination of macroeconomic adjustment policies stems from government efforts to externalize burdens of adjustment to macroeconomic imbalances and to limit others' ability to externalize them. As I noted in Chapter 1, deficit countries favor international policy coordination to encourage surplus countries to reflate their economies, revalue their currencies, expand their imports, or finance deficit countries. Surplus

---

3. That is, their ability to sterilize foreign exchange market intervention is limited.

countries favor international coordination to deter deficit countries from restricting imports and sharply devaluing their currencies and to encourage them to rely on the internal strategy of deflation. Surplus countries may be willing to provide international financing to persuade deficit countries to limit external strategies of adjustment and make it easier for them to deflate by giving them time to do so gradually.

My argument assumes that these key interests motivate governments; but other motivations may also exist, as the historical record indicates. First, governments are often internally divided over which policy course to adopt and may face significant opposition to preferred policies from the public and interest groups. Those government branches that have access to international forums may seek support to help them overcome internal opposition to these policies.[4] International support could come in the form of declarations that help justify a certain course of action or in the form of alterations in foreign government policies that defuse domestic opposition to the preferred course of action. For example, leaders of a country who want to restrain macroeconomic policies to eliminate an external deficit but who fear that this could lead to recession and unemployment might seek foreign reflation to help sustain demand for their country's production.

Another motivation for international macroeconomic policy coordination could be a joint desire to avoid policies that are individually appropriate but collectively harmful. For example, a cycle of increasingly restrictive monetary policies can occur when countries individually restrain demand to strengthen their payments balances, causing others to adopt more restrictive policies to prevent payments balances from worsening and slowing growth more than anyone had intended. (This argument has been made about the recession of the early 1980s.) Alternatively, governments' simultaneous but noncoordinated pursuit of expansionary policies could generate higher inflation than intended. International coordination of macroeconomic policies could account for transmission effects to avoid making all countries worse off.

This special case exemplifies a more general argument made by some economists, who suggest that there may be global and national welfare gains from international policy coordination. Coordination could, they

4. See, for example, Robert D. Putnam and C. Randall Henning, "The Bonn Summit of 1978: A Case Study in Coordination," in *Can Nations Agree? Issues in International Economic Cooperation*, by Richard N. Cooper, Barry Eichengreen, C. Randall Henning, Gerard Holtham, and Robert D. Putnam (Washington, D.C.: Brookings Institution, 1989).

argue, move countries to higher levels of welfare than they could achieve with optimal but noncoordinated policies.[5] The problems with this argument are manifest and are discussed in detail in Chapter 6. Most important, the argument depends upon a number of unrealistic assumptions: that governments choose macroeconomic policies in order to maximize welfare, that different governments agree about the international effects of national policies, that international transmission effects are large enough to make fine tuning worthwhile, that information is good, that economic agents are rational, and so on.

I do not assume that governments are motivated by a desire to maximize national or global welfare. Macroeconomic policy-making is an intensely political process, not a technical exercise in welfare maximization. Therefore, the policies pursued may have little to do with maximizing national welfare. International coordination results from government attempts to evade constraints imposed by international market forces and is not a technical exercise in collective welfare maximization. In fact, some economists decry international macroeconomic policy coordination because they believe that coordination would make it easier for governments to pursue inflationary policies by reducing balance-of-payments constraints on economic stimulus.[6] If one interprets this point of view as an explanatory theory rather than a normative argument, it indicates that there are potential political gains from macroeconomic policy coordination, regardless of its effects on national or global welfare.

How International Market Integration Conditions Policy Choices

Interest in international coordination of macroeconomic adjustment policies can exist whenever countries are not completely autarkic. But which types of policies will be adjusted to eliminate disequilibria and which will be subject to international coordination depend critically on

5. Accessible explanations of this argument and summaries of the literature can be found in Michael Artis and Sylvia Ostry, *International Economic Policy Coordination*, Chatham House Paper No. 30 (London: Routledge and Keegan Paul, 1986); and Michael Devereux and Thomas A. Wilson, "International Coordination of Macroeconomic Policies: A Review," *Canadian Public Policy* 15, supp. (February 1989).

6. Martin Feldstein, "International Economic Cooperation: Introduction," in Feldstein, ed., *International Economic Cooperation* (Chicago: University of Chicago Press for the National Bureau of Economic Research, 1988); W. Lee Hoskins, "International Policy Coordination: Benefits and Costs," *Economic Impact* 67 (1988).

Table 1. Types of policy likely to be coordinated under different conditions of international market integration

| | | Degree of international capital mobility | |
		Lower	Higher
Level of international trade	Lower	External: Trade controls, exchange rates (late 1940s and 1950s)	Monetary and fiscal (no historical cases)
	Higher	Symptom management (late 1950s and 1960s)	Monetary and fiscal (since mid-1970s)

the structure of the international economy. Two aspects of the international economic structure are important: the degree of international integration of markets for goods and services and the degree of international capital market integration.[7] In practice, the two may be more or less closely linked, but for purposes of explication, I consider them separately. Table 1, preceding, summarizes the discussion in a highly simplified manner. It indicates which types of international macroeconomic adjustment policy are likely to be coordinated, depending upon the degree of international integration of markets for goods and services and the degree of international capital mobility, and identifies how the historical periods considered in this book correspond to the general economic-structural argument.

The level of international integration of markets for goods and services is important because differences among countries in the expansiveness of macroeconomic policy spill over into trade balances. Expansionary policies stimulate demand at home, which tends to increase imports and depress exports. (The latter effect is created when domestic firms shift production to meet strong domestic demand at the expense of production for export.) Higher imports and lower exports worsen the trade balance. The reverse process occurs in countries that pursue relatively restrictive macroeconomic policies.

For both deficit and surplus countries, trade imbalances increase as international trade increases relative to the size of the national economy.[8] Thus, as international trade becomes more important, countries

7. These are the two most important variables in the period 1945–94 among advanced capitalist countries. If one were to consider a longer time period, or a different (perhaps less homogeneous) group of countries, other variables might well become important.

8. The multiplier effect of demand stimulus on the domestic economy (and therefore the policy's efficacy) declines as international market integration increases.

face larger payments imbalances as a consequence of divergent macroeconomic policy choices; and each government's interest in international policy coordination to reduce its burden of adjustment increases. Nevertheless, if economies are linked only by trade,[9] the international payments imbalances that result when different countries pursue different policies will be relatively small and slow to emerge—relative, that is, to the imbalances generated by short-term capital flows.

When national economies are linked only by trade, governments can deal with their payments imbalances by implementing moderate adjustments to external policies or turning to symptom-management policies. When trade flows are low, few industries in either deficit or surplus countries would be hurt, so the likelihood of a protectionist response to deficits is higher. But when trade flows are moderate or high, numerous domestic industries in both surplus and deficit countries are likely to oppose deficit countries' intensification of trade restrictions,[10] encouraging governments to search for alternative ways to deal with the payments imbalance. Thus, increasing trade integration both increases the volume of payments imbalances that result when different countries pursue different macroeconomic policies and reduces the attractiveness of trade restrictions as an instrument of international adjustment.

One alternative would be to manipulate exchange rates, allowing them either to depreciate and eliminate deficits or to appreciate and eliminate surpluses. In theory, this alternative would be feasible if national capital markets were not linked internationally and governments did not intervene to accelerate or block changes driven by current account imbalances.[11] If governments preferred to maintain fixed

9. Economies may also be linked by long-term investment, but this investment is not highly sensitive to short-term macroeconomic policy differentials and therefore does not seriously constrain policy-making autonomy.

10. Some domestic industries in deficit countries will always favor protection; my argument here is that as the importance of trade increases, there will be more industries that oppose restrictions that interfere with their international operations. See, for example, Helen Milner, "Resisting the Protectionist Temptation: Industry and the Making of Trade Policy in France and the United States during the 1970s," *International Organization* 41 (Autumn 1987); and Stephen D. Krasner, "United States Commercial and Monetary Policy: Unravelling the Paradox of External Strength and Internal Weakness," in Peter J.Katzenstein, ed., *Between Power and Plenty: Foreign Economic Policies of Advanced Industrial States* (Madison: University of Wisconsin Press, 1978).

11. These conditions have not been met in any historical period. In the late 1950s and the 1960s, a period of moderate trade flows and insulated national capital markets,

exchange rates, international macroeconomic imbalances could be managed by having surplus countries lend money to deficit countries. This option would appeal to deficit countries seeking to avoid drastic deflation or trade protectionism and might appeal to surplus countries seeking to avoid reflation or the loss of access to the markets of deficit countries.

The appeal of this form of symptom management, however, is crucially dependent on the sums involved. If payments deficits are relatively small, as they are when economies are linked internationally only by trade, surplus countries may well be willing to finance them, even if deficit countries show little sign of implementing more fundamental adjustments.[12] This can give governments considerable freedom to pursue independently chosen macroeconomic policies in the face of trade deficits or surpluses.

The second element of the international economic structure that is critical for understanding coordination of macroeconomic adjustment policies is the degree of market integration for short-term capital. When short-term capital markets are highly integrated internationally, there is little autonomy in macroeconomic policy-making, even for the largest states, because differences in the policies pursued by various countries immediately trigger large flows of capital. Capital flows respond quickly to changes in investors' expectations about interest rates and exchange rates, and these flows have immediate effects on exchange rates.

The effects of monetary and fiscal policies when capital is internationally mobile are much different than the effects when it is not.[13]

---

many economists argued that freely fluctuating exchange rates would have adjusted moderately and gradually to restore payments equilibrium; see Ronald I. McKinnon, *An International Standard for Monetary Stabilization*, Policy Analyses in International Economics No. 8 (Washington, D.C.: Institute for International Economics, 1984). Most leading governments, however, supported the IMF-centered fixed exchange rate regime because they feared a repeat of the disastrous exchange-rate volatility of the 1920s and 30s.

12. Surplus countries lent money year after year to Britain and the United States in the mid-1960s. For a detailed discussion of why creditor countries and institutions did not insist on fundamental reforms to eliminate Britain's balance-of-payments weakness, see Susan Strange, *Sterling and British Policy: A Political Study of an International Currency in Decline* (London: Oxford University Press, 1971), pp. 289–95.

13. This section is based on open-economy macroeconomic theory. A good textbook source is Francisco L. Rivera-Batiz and Luis Rivera-Batiz, *International Finance and Open Economy Macroeconomics* (New York: Macmillan, 1985).

When capital is highly mobile across national borders, arbitrage between domestic and world capital markets keeps domestic interest rates from diverging very far from international interest rates.[14] This, in turn, makes fiscal policy less effective. Fiscal expansion puts upward pressure on domestic interest rates. Capital floods in as international investors take advantage of higher domestic interest rates, causing the domestic currency to appreciate. The international competitive position of domestic producers erodes, exports decline, and imports increase. Not only does the country suffer from a trade deficit, but the harm done to domestic producers can offset the stimulating effect that fiscal expansion was intended to have on output and employment.[15]

When international capital mobility is high, monetary policy is effective in theory but not in practice. Monetary expansion puts downward pressure on domestic interest rates, causing a massive exodus of capital as investors seek higher returns abroad. Capital outflows depreciate the domestic currency, which shifts demand away from foreign goods (imports) and into domestic goods (import-competing products and exports). Therefore, monetary expansion in the context of high capital mobility could stimulate the economy by both reducing interest rates (as in the case of a closed economy) and depreciating the currency and improving the trade balance.

In practice, however, governments are not willing to tolerate the drastic exchange-rate fluctuations that would accompany monetary policy choices based solely on domestic conditions. Expansionary monetary policy can trigger capital flight and a collapse in the value of the currency, both of which could damage a government's domestic standing and undermine its economic policies. Similarly, restrictive monetary policy would push the exchange rate up sharply, thereby damaging the government's standing with exporters and causing a more severe slowdown than intended. Examples of exchange-rate constraints on both expansionary and restrictive monetary policies can be found in the 1980s. France abandoned expansionary monetary policies in 1983 in the face of capital flight and severe downward pressure on the franc; the United States relaxed monetary policy in 1985 in part because tight

14. In the context of flexible exchange rates, domestic interest rates equal the international interest rate plus the expected rate of depreciation of the domestic currency.

15. Trade flows adjust more slowly to exchange-rate changes than do capital flows. Thus, there is potential for a temporary fiscal stimulus; its length depends upon how long it takes goods and services markets to adjust to the instantaneous currency appreciation.

monetary policy had (in combination with fiscal expansion) driven the dollar up to a level that severely eroded American industry's international competitiveness; and Germany relaxed monetary policy after the October 1987 stock-market crash to slow the mark's appreciation against the United States dollar (weakened by loose monetary policy) and other European currencies.

The high costs of exchange rate volatility mean that, despite economic theory, international capital mobility does *not* increase the real-world effectiveness of monetary policy. Capital mobility would increase the effectiveness of monetary policy only if governments were completely indifferent to the exchange rate; and recent experience shows that few governments can afford to be indifferent to the exchange rate for very long.

I have already argued that the trade imbalances generated by macroeconomic policy differences can be managed by intergovernmental lending from surplus to deficit countries. But international capital flows are difficult to manage in this way, for two reasons. First, international capital markets react much more quickly to macroeconomic policy changes than do international trade flows. Capital flows generate payments imbalances immediately, while trade balances are not affected until after macroeconomic policies affect domestic demand and prices.[16] Governments have less time to put symptom-management policies into effect when capital is mobile than they have when trade deficits are the main symptom of divergence.

Second, the size of capital flows makes them more difficult to manage than trade imbalances. The volume of capital that can flow internationally in response to macroeconomic policies is enormous, and governments are not able to lend to each other on a large enough scale to permit management of this symptom of crossnational policy differentials. Coordinated intervention in foreign-exchange markets, even when backed by international lending, cannot stabilize exchange rates if investors believe that the currency values sought by central banks are unrealistic. The reason is that the volume of short-term private capital flows can be so large. Prominent recent examples include the failure to defend fixed European exchange rates despite tens of billions of dollars worth of coordinated intervention in 1992–93.

16. McKinnon, *International Standard*, pp. 24–25.

The basic problem facing efforts to stabilize currencies by intervening in foreign-exchange markets is that central bank reserves now are far smaller than the volume of foreign-exchange trading. In fact, by the late 1980s the *daily* volume of trading on foreign-exchange markets typically equaled or exceeded the combined foreign reserve holdings of leading central banks. Surveys by central banks estimated the average daily volume of foreign-exchange trading at $218 billion in April 1986, $431 billion in April 1989, and $880 billion in April 1992.[17] In contrast, the combined foreign-exchange reserves of all industrialized capitalist countries totaled $259 billion in 1986, $453 billion in 1989, and $487 billion in 1992.[18] Governments of countries experiencing speculative capital inflows are unlikely to be able to lend the tens or even hundreds of billions of dollars needed to prevent other countries' exchange rates from depreciating. Even the most complacent expansionist government is likely to become concerned at foreign indebtedness measured in the hundreds of billions of dollars.

In the short run, governments can borrow funds on private international capital markets to finance macroeconomic imbalances. International capital market integration both increases the volume of external payments imbalances that result from a given degree of divergence and enhances the ability of governments to finance international macroeconomic imbalances by unilateral borrowing and lending on private international capital markets. But borrowing on private international markets to finance payments deficits usually requires a reversal of the expansionary monetary policies that generated the outflow in the first place. Deficit countries trying to borrow on international markets soon find that they must raise interest rates because private investors are not willing to lend indefinitely to governments that do not move quickly to restore balance in their domestic and international accounts.

This constraint on the ability to borrow on private international markets to insulate domestic policies from external deficits has become especially tight with the recent globalization of financial markets, a

17. Estimates for 1986 and 1989 reported in the *Globe and Mail,* 14 September 1989, pp. B1, B4; 1992 estimate from Bank for International Settlements (BIS), *Sixty-Third Annual Report* (Basle: BIS, 1993), p. 196.

18. Calculated from special drawing rights figures (SDR) in International Monetary Fund (IMF), *International Financial Statistics,* various issues.

trend that involves the erosion of barriers between national and international capital markets.[19] As recently as the late 1970s, governments could issue Eurobonds at interest rates different from rates within their own countries. Private international borrowing and lending could therefore help to finance payments imbalances without adjusting domestic interest rates. Once financial capital was able to flow freely between the national and international markets, however, such interest-rate differentials could not be sustained. Governments that wanted to encourage private capital inflows or outflows to finance current account imbalances found that they could do so only by altering domestic interest rates. Once national and international financial markets became integrated this closely, private international borrowing was no longer a separate macroeconomic adjustment strategy; it became an aspect of monetary policy, an internal strategy of adjustment.[20]

To reiterate, symptom-management policies alone cannot reconcile divergent national macroeconomic policies when capital markets are integrated internationally. Governments that face external imbalances must turn to other types of adjustment policies. Trade restrictions are not an attractive alternative because powerful domestic groups oppose controls that would interfere with transnational economic linkages. Nevertheless, the possibility remains that threatened industries in deficit countries will succeed in their demands for trade protection, as demonstrated in the United States in 1985. Controls on capital flows would have to be comprehensive to be effective, which would cut off the country's economy from all but the simplest forms of international commerce. Even if the ultimate welfare losses associated with autarky would be small (as one might argue for the United States), the transitional economic and political costs would discourage such a choice. Comprehensive controls would be vehemently opposed by powerful domestic groups and would be extremely disruptive.

Problems with external strategies of adjustment and symptom management mean that when capital is internationally mobile, governments with international macroeconomic imbalances face powerful incentives

19. This is a central theme of BIS, *Recent Innovations in International Banking* (Basle: BIS, 1986).

20. This argument is discussed in greater detail in Chapter 6, as is the somewhat exceptional position of the United States. Evidence of declining interest-rate differentials between national and international capital markets is given later in this chapter.

to press foreign countries to alter their internal policies. Deficit countries try to persuade surplus countries to reflate, and surplus countries try to persuade deficit countries to deflate.[21] Asymmetries in bargaining power generally favor countries with trade surpluses and capital inflows (as I discuss later in the chapter), but even large surplus countries can be pressured to reflate in order to stabilize the international economy and keep deficit countries from restricting imports. Merely lending money to deficit countries is not sufficient to ease imbalances when capital is internationally mobile.

More generally, the discussion of the effectiveness of fiscal and monetary policies suggests that independent macroeconomic policy-making is simply less effective when capital is internationally mobile—that is, in achieving domestic economic conditions that favor the political prospects of governments. Thus, when short-term capital flows easily across national borders, governments face powerful incentives to coordinate their macroeconomic policies *internationally* in order to achieve their *domestic* objectives. If they do not coordinate policies, they will be unable to achieve domestic and international economic objectives. Coordination is necessary to reduce differences among the policies pursued by various countries and to instill confidence in private capital holders, all to lessen the incentives for private investors to shift speculative funds in directions that prevent governments from achieving national macroeconomic objectives. The international imbalances that have prevailed since the mid-1970s, despite periodic bouts of policy coordination, have severely undermined governments' ability to achieve domestic macroeconomic conditions that win public approval, indicating that autonomous policy-making is not effective in achieving domestic objectives if it does not also consider external implications.

To summarize, I have argued in this section that different international economic structures, characterized by different degrees of international market integration, generate distinct incentives for governments to choose among alternative strategies for coordinating macroeconomic adjustment policies. As international market integration increases—and especially as financial capital becomes internation-

21. The exact demands depend on the mix of monetary and fiscal policies being pursued; for example, in the early 1980s, foreign governments called on the United States to restrain fiscal policy and relax monetary policy.

ally mobile—external strategies of adjustment become less attractive and symptom-management policies less effective, and governments face incentives to coordinate monetary and fiscal policies themselves.

The existence of incentives for macroeconomic policy coordination does not guarantee that governments will coordinate. Other political, economic, and intellectual considerations may well interfere. For example, because of political differences between Congress and the President, the United States did not join in negotiated mutual adjustments of fiscal policy in the 1980s.[22] Macroeconomic coordination may also be blocked by different national views of the desirability of specific policy adjustments, a lack of consensus within the economics profession about the international implications of monetary and fiscal policies,[23] disputes about how the burdens of adjustment should be divided among participating countries, and conflicting views about appropriate trade-offs between growth and price stability.

Despite these obstacles, governments have responded to economic-structural incentives for macroeconomic policy coordination. Immediately after World War II, private international markets were moribund and governments relied heavily on the external strategies of trade and capital controls and unilateral exchange-rate adjustments. Coordination of symptom-management policies became more prevalent as private trade markets became more integrated in the 1960s. The emergence of active international capital markets in the 1960s and their subsequent growth encouraged coordination of monetary and fiscal policies beginning in the late 1970s.

Trends in International Market Integration since 1945

In order to understand how the structure of the international economy influences patterns of policy coordination in particular periods, we need to be able to measure the degree of market integration. Ide-

22. The United States was uniquely able to force other countries to adjust their policies to compensate for destabilizing American monetary and fiscal policies. This is an example of the bargaining asymmetries discussed later in the chapter.

23. See, for example, Jeffrey A. Frankel, *Obstacles to International Macroeconomic Policy Coordination*, Princeton Studies in International Finance No. 64 (Princeton: International Finance Section, Department of Economics, December 1988). I stress, however, that governments did coordinate macroeconomic policies after 1985, despite substantial disagreement about the appropriateness of specific policies.

ally, we want measures of the sensitivity of international trade and capital flows to macroeconomic policies, but they are not available for enough countries for much of the period in question. As an approximation, the degree of international integration of national markets for goods and services can be roughly measured by the share of imports and exports relative to the size of the national economy, or gross domestic product (GDP). In general, higher levels of trade relative to domestic economic activity should be associated with larger international spillover effects and therefore with tighter international market constraints on national macroeconomic policies. Table 2 presents data on import and export shares for the seven leading advanced capitalist countries since the 1950s.

While there is considerable variation across countries concerning the importance of international trade, all but Japan have become more trade dependent since World War II.[24] Trade proportions grew especially rapidly between 1960 and 1985. For many countries, trade proportions were as high in the 1950s as in the 1960s, but this masks an important difference between the two periods: the sensitivity of trade flows to macroeconomic policies. In the early 1950s, most governments outside North America exercised comprehensive controls over large import programs designed to contribute to ambitious national reconstruction programs. By the 1960s administrative controls had been relaxed, and import demand was no longer driven by government-directed purchases. This made trade flows more sensitive to market pressures and therefore to crossnational macroeconomic policy differentials in the 1960s. Table 2 suggests, then, that the international spillover effect of national macroeconomic policies and the impact of policies on trade balances have increased sharply since the early 1950s. For many countries, the increase was especially dramatic in the 1970s and 1980s.

Measuring the international integration of capital markets is perhaps more difficult. Broadly speaking, there are two approaches: measuring the volume of international capital flows, and attempting to measure capital mobility directly. One problem common to both measures is that reliable data are not available for the late 1940s, the 1950s, and

24. In Japan's case, trade flows have become more sensitive to international market forces, as direct government control over imports was relaxed in the 1970s and 80s.

Table 2. Exports plus imports of goods and services as a proportion of GDP, major advanced capitalist countries, in percent

	1950	1955	1960	1965	1970	1975	1980	1985	1990	1992
Canada	48	39	35	38	43	47	54	54	51	54
France	32	27	27	25	31	37	45	47	46	45
Germany	25	37	36	36	40	47	53	62	58	61
Italy	25[a]	23	27	28	32	42	44	44	38	36
Japan	25[b]	24	21	19	21	26	29	25	22	19[c]
U.K.	53	48	43	39	45	54	52	57	51	48
U.S.	9	9	10	9	12	17	21	17	21	22

SOURCES: 1950 data from Organization for Economic Cooperation and Development (OECD), *National Accounts of OECD Countries: 1950–1968* (Paris: OECD, n.d.); 1955 data from OECD, *National Accounts Statistics: 1952–1981. Volume I: Main Aggregates* (Paris: OECD, 1983). 1960–75 data from OECD, *National Accounts Statistics: 1960–1988. Volume I: Main Aggregates* (Paris: OECD, 1990). 1980–92 data from OECD, *Quarterly National Accounts* 1 (1993).
[a]1951
[b]1952
[c]1991

much of the 1960s. In one sense this lack of data is itself an important indicator; data were not collected because the phenomenon was not substantively important. Short-term capital flows were very small, so governments and intergovernmental organizations did not consider measurement worthwhile. This also means, of course, that international capital flows did not play an important role in shaping incentives for coordination of macroeconomic adjustment policies before the 1960s.[25]

Using capital flows as a measure of international capital market integration is also problematic because a low volume of flows may indicate either obstacles to capital mobility or lack of private market interest in international lending and depositing.[26] Despite these prob-

25. Speculation against currencies before international capital markets began to develop in the early 1960s mainly took the form of lags and leads in current account payments. For example, a private trading company would delay converting its national currency into a foreign currency to make a payment for imports if it believed that the foreign currency was about to be devalued. Alternatively, a private company would convert a payment into a foreign currency as soon as possible if it believed that its national currency was about to be devalued. Speculation was therefore possible but was limited in volume to some portion of current account flows.

26. For helpful discussions of the problem of measuring capital market integration, see David M. Andrews, "The Structural Roots of European Monetary Convergence: Exploring the Capital Mobility Hypothesis" (Paper prepared for delivery at the 1992 Annual Meeting of the American Political Science Association, Chicago, 3–6 September 1992),

lems, it is worthwhile examining the available measures of short-term capital flows. Since the mid-1960s, the Bank for International Settlements (BIS) has gathered data on international bank lending and bond financing in a consistent form. Table 3 presents the BIS's calculations of short-term international lending before adjustments for double counting.[27] The volume of lending is compared to the combined volume of foreign-reserve holdings of advanced capitalist countries to give some indication of the adequacy of central bank reserves for offsetting international market flows. This comparison is important because governments must be able to offset international market flows if they are to manage the symptoms of crossnational macroeconomic policy divergences without adjusting monetary and fiscal policies. If international market flows are very large relative to national reserves, symptom-management policies alone are not viable, and governments may pressure each other to coordinate monetary and fiscal policies themselves.

It is clear from Table 3 that short-term international capital flows have increased dramatically, if unevenly, over the past three decades. Increases were particularly notable in the late 1960s and in the second half of the 1980s, followed by declines generally attributed to recession. The volume of international lending has become very large in relation to the international reserve holdings of the advanced capitalist states.

Other data confirm that the volume of international capital flows has grown enormously. During the late 1940s and early 1950s, private foreign-exchange markets outside New York were largely inoperative, closed by comprehensive exchange controls outside North America. Private trading in foreign exchange began again in earnest in the late 1950s after the adoption of currency convertibility by most Western European states. Governments that wanted to maintain fixed exchange rates now had to intervene in foreign-exchange markets to offset fluctuations in private demand and supply that threatened to depreciate or appreciate the currency. The volume of private foreign-exchange trading grew rapidly in the 1960s, but reliable estimates of trading volumes are not available before the 1980s. As I noted earlier, studies by

---

pp. 7–9; and Jeffrey A. Frankel, "Measuring International Capital Mobility: A Review," *American Economic Review: Papers and Proceedings* 82 (May 1992).

27. Estimates of net lending are available for more recent years, but are not reported here because I am interested in trends over a longer period of time. Data are converted to SDRs to compensate for fluctuations in the value of the United States dollar, in which such flows are commonly reported.

Table 3. Short-term international capital flows and international reserves

	1964	1965	1966	1967	1968	1969	1970	1971	1972	1973	1974	1975	1976	1977	1978	1979	1980	1981	1982	1983	1984	1985	1986	1987	1988	1989	1990	1991	1992
Total international lending, billion SDR	5	6	8	11	23	31	25	30	44	82	70	84	121	124	174	190	215	262	231	168	226	393	629	575	504	728	618	208	407
Total international reserves, billion SDR[a]	57	58	58	59	66	59	73	102	132	159	211	188	194	239	297	460	549	454	511	492	472	462	502	587	594	626	630	597	585
Lending/reserves, percent	9	10	14	19	35	53	34	29	33	52	33	45	62	52	59	41	39	58	45	34	48	85	125	98	85	116	98	35	70

SOURCES: International reserves data from International Monetary Fund (IMF), *International Financial Statistics Yearbook,* 1987 and 1992; all other data from BIS, *Annual Report,* various issues.

NOTE: SDR = special drawing rights

[a]International reserves of industrial countries, with gold reserves calculated at contemporary market prices after 1967.

central banks estimated the total daily volume of foreign-exchange trading at $880 billion by 1992, many times the value of international trade
in goods and services.

Directly comparable data for earlier periods are not available, but
the magnitude of the contrast between the situation in the 1980s and
that in the 1960s is suggested by isolated pieces of information. For
example, foreign-exchange trading was considered exceptionally heavy
in one period (April–May 1969) when the German central bank had
to purchase $4.4 billion over a week and a half of trading in a successful
effort to prevent the mark from appreciating.[28] In contrast, approximately $100 billion was spent by European central banks in September
1992 in unsuccessful efforts to prevent the British, Italian, and other
European currencies from depreciating against the German mark.[29] It
is estimated that more than $20 billion was spent by the German cen-
tral bank in only one day.[30] The scale of foreign-exchange trading in
the 1990s is many times larger that it was in the 1960s, even if inflation
is taken into account.

The degree of international integration of national capital markets
can also be assessed by measuring capital mobility directly. The best
way is to measure differences in interest rates for similar instruments
in different national and international markets.[31] For example, one can
measure the divergence between national interest rates and Euromarket interest rates for lending in specific currencies (e.g., interest rates
in Japan compared with Euroyen interest rates). The underlying assumption is that interest rates in the loosely regulated Euromarkets
reflect investors' beliefs about the true value of loans and deposits in
different currencies (taking into account inflation and exchange-rate
expectations), while national interest rates can be distorted by controls
on capital inflows or outflows. The lower the interest-rate differential,
the higher the degree of capital mobility between the national market
and the international market and the higher the degree of international market integration.

28. Susan Strange, *International Monetary Relations*, vol. 2 of Andrew Shonfield, ed.,
International Economic Relations of the Western World, 1959–1971 (London: Oxford University
Press for the Royal Institute of International Affairs, 1976), p. 327.

29. Estimates of the volume of intervention are presented in BIS, *Sixty-Third Annual
Report*, p. 188.

30. *Globe and Mail*, 2 August 1993, p. B2; *Economist*, 10 October 1992, p. 71.

31. Andrews, "Structural Roots of European Monetary Convergence."

In the 1960s and 70s, national interest rates often diverged sharply from Euromarket interest rates because of national capital controls and the relatively undeveloped state of international capital market linkages. Evidence from these periods is spotty but suggestive. During 1969, Eurodollar deposit rates rose to 11.5 percent while U.S. treasury bills paid only 7.7 percent and certificates of deposit issued by domestic U.S. banks paid only 6 percent. In the early 1970s, interest rates in Germany were as much as 11 percentage points higher than Euromark interest rates.[32]

In contrast, differences between Euromarket and national interest rates for most leading currencies have been minimal since the 1980s. Data for the period 1979–84 indicate that differentials for Japan, Britain, Germany, and Switzerland all averaged well under 0.5 percentage points. "By that criterion, Japan, the United Kingdom, Germany, Switzerland, Canada, and the United States all currently have open capital markets."[33] Interest-rate differentials were quite large for France in the early 1980s because it was one of the last leading countries to liberalize international capital flows. After France liberalized controls in 1987–88, however, the differential between interest rates in France and Eurofranc interest rates dropped to negligible levels.[34]

Another way to measure capital mobility is to compare interest rates on identical investments in different national markets, adjusted for exchange-rate risk (what economists call *covered interest parity*, with the difference between spot and forward exchange rates used as the measure of exchange rate risk). According to this measure, interest-rate differentials on short-term investments in different currencies virtually disappeared by the late 1980s, indicating considerable international mobility for short-term finance capital.[35] Other forms of capital are not nearly as mobile, providing governments with some limited ability to choose real interest-rate levels different from those in other countries.[36] Nevertheless, the mobility of short-term financial capital imposes seri-

32. Richard C. Marston, "Exchange Rate Policy Reconsidered," in Feldstein, ed., *International Economic Cooperation*, pp. 111–12.

33. Jeffrey A. Frankel, *The Yen/Dollar Agreement: Liberalizing Japanese Capital Markets* (Washington, D.C.: Institute for International Economics, 1984), p. 24.

34. *Economist*, 18 March 1989, p. 85.

35. Frankel, "Measuring International Capital Mobility."

36. Andrews, "Structural Roots of European Monetary Convergence," pp. 8–9; Jeffry A. Frieden, "Invested Interests: The Politics of National Economic Policies in a World of Global Finance," *International Organization* 45 (Autumn 1991).

ous constraints on governments' ability to sustain domestic interest rates that differ from international levels.

The data just presented provide a basis for characterizing trends in international capital market integration in specific periods. It is difficult to be precise about the starting and end points of these periods or about thresholds between one type of international capital market structure and another, primarily because we lack precise data on capital mobility before the 1980s. Nevertheless, the following characterization is consistent with available data.

International capital market integration was extremely limited in the late 1940s and for most of the 1950s and therefore did not seriously constrain national macroeconomic policy-making autonomy for most countries. The introduction of convertibility for most Western European currencies and the Japanese yen in the late 1950s and early 60s increased international capital mobility somewhat, but it was not until the Eurodollar market became well established in the late 1960s that most governments began to experience significant international capital market constraints on macroeconomic policy autonomy. Capital mobility grew substantially during the 1970s as private market linkages developed and as controls on capital flows became less effective and widespread. International mobility for short-term financial capital became nearly complete by the mid-1980s, and the late 80s and early 90s witnessed rapid growth in short-term speculative movements through foreign-exchange markets. By the late 1970s macroeconomic policy-making autonomy was seriously constrained for most countries by international capital market pressures; subsequent developments have made those constraints unavoidable for all governments.

It is also important to note that the timing of national capital market integration into international markets varied among the major industrialized countries, at least until the past few years. Differences in the degree of openness to international financial flows meant that different countries experienced different international market constraints on national macroeconomic policies during certain periods. Among the Group of Seven countries, the United States and Canada have the longest history (in the post-1945 period) of openness to international capital movements. In the case of Canada, the ease of capital mobility between national markets and the American market imposed serious

43

constraints on policy-making autonomy as early as the late 1940s, encouraging the Canadian government to abandon fixed exchange rates twenty years earlier than other industrialized countries (1950 versus the early 1970s). United States openness to international capital flows did not seriously impinge upon American macroeconomic policy-making autonomy until well into the 1960s because international capital flows were small relative to the huge domestic economy and the United States was able to use its bargaining power to persuade other countries to adjust their policies. These characteristics continue to permit the United States to evade international capital market constraints on its macroeconomic policies, as I discuss later in the chapter.

Britain and Germany were the next industrialized countries to experience significant international capital market linkages. Both governments were more committed to international liberalization than were their counterparts in most of Europe and Japan. In Britain's case, this commitment took the form of encouraging international markets to develop in London as early as the late 1950s. Until 1979 British governments attempted to separate the national capital market from the international markets based in London, but these attempts were never fully successful and became less effective over time. This openness to international capital flows (despite government controls) helped to make British macroeconomic policies sensitive to the country's international capital accounts in the late 1950s and early 1960s; and as we shall see in Chapter 4, Britain was the only country whose policies were subject to internationally negotiated adjustments during these years.

Among the large continental European countries, Germany had the most liberal economic policies and experienced substantial international capital inflows in the mid-1960s. Nevertheless, these inflows did not constrain German macroeconomic policies until the late 1960s: it is easier for governments to avoid adjusting policies in the face of capital inflows than outflows, and the German government was willing to intervene with selective controls on undesirable capital inflows—at least until the mid-1970s, by which time these controls were becoming ineffective.

Capital markets in France and Italy did not become highly integrated with international markets until the mid-1980s because of their governments' traditional desire to manage national capital markets to serve national (or governmental) interests. French and Italian efforts to control international capital flows were not very effective after the late

1960s and early 1970s, and by the mid-1970s the governments of both countries found their macroeconomic policies seriously constrained by international capital flows.

Japan was the last of the large industrialized countries to experience significant linkages between national capital markets and international capital markets, due to traditionally strong government control over the domestic financial industry and international capital flows. Consequently, Japanese monetary policies were insulated from international capital market pressures until well into the 1970s, which meant, for example, that during the 1960s the government was able to provide subsidized credit to selected industries in order to stimulate very rapid economic growth without being constrained by capital outflows seeking higher returns abroad. This insulation eroded significantly by the early 1970s, and by the 1980s Japan's prominence as an international financial center made it a leading player in international policy coordination and the main target of American pressure for changes in foreign macroeconomic policies.

As this brief review suggests, international capital mobility developed at a different pace in different countries in the 1950s, 60s, and 70s. With the exception of Canada, macroeconomic policy-making was not seriously constrained by international capital mobility in any of the industrialized countries before the late 1960s. Most were affected by the early 1970s, although to varying degrees. By the early 1980s, all were experiencing similar levels of capital mobility; however, the degree to which it constrained policy-making autonomy varied according to a country's status as source or destination for international capital movements and its bargaining power.

International Power and Bargaining Outcomes

According to realist theory, the distribution of power among states is the most important international structural variable for explaining international political outcomes, including patterns of policy coordination. As I discussed earlier, I do not accept the widespread view that declining American power led to an erosion of economic policy coordination, but I do argue that the international distribution of power is a crucial influence on patterns of policy coordination. The outcomes of international negotiations are more closely related to the bargaining power of the governments involved than they are to abstract calculations of welfare-maximizing policy adjustments or to each government's responsibility for imbalances. Governments of weak countries generally make more substantial policy adjustments than do governments of more powerful countries. Thus, a focus on international political structures *complements* the economic-structural argument developed earlier in this chapter. An understanding of international economic structures, especially the degree of capital market integration, is crucial for understanding which types of policies will be the focus of negotiated adjustments, while an understanding of the international political structure, especially the distribution of power among states, is crucial for understanding the distribution of the burden of adjustment among countries.[37]

The game theory literature on international cooperation tends to neglect bargaining power as a central explanatory variable.[38] Such neglect clearly is not possible in this case. Models of international cooperation based on the logic of collective goods and, more specifically, the prisoners' dilemma game identify the central problem as moving from a noncooperative situation in which welfare is not maximized to a cooperative one in which welfare is improved for all (or at least none suffer while some gain)—that is, from a Nash equilibrium to a Pareto equilibrium. The key obstacle to cooperation is the risk that myopically self-interested players will cheat. All countries are treated as having equal power, which is revealed by the identical payoffs and preference orderings in the standard prisoners' dilemma game.[39]

The record of international macroeconomic adjustment policy coordination that I have reviewed suggests that the key issue in interna-

37. The two types of explanations are interrelated in practice. For example, the inability or unwillingness of the government of a powerful country to adjust certain policies (e.g., the United States and fiscal policy in the 1980s) may encourage all countries to coordinate other types of policies (such as symptom-management policies, including foreign exchange market intervention in the case just noted), even though that coordination may be relatively ineffective.

38. Stephen D. Krasner, "Global Communications and National Power: Life on the Pareto Frontier," *World Politics* 43 (April 1991). The following paragraph draws from this article.

39. The only widely considered exception is a situation of hegemony in which one player is powerful enough to implement the cooperative solution unilaterally.

tional negotiations has been determining how burdens of adjustment to international macroeconomic disequilibria will be distributed among countries, not overcoming obstacles to cooperation posed by the fear of cheating in an anarchic world.[40] Historically, there have rarely been cooperative solutions to the game of adjustment policy coordination that serve the interests of all governments equally; the payoffs vary according to how much adjustment to national policies is required. Governments may often prefer no coordination to coordination involving policy adjustments that improve global welfare at the expense of a politically undesirable change in national policies. This is especially true when capital is mobile because effective policy coordination under such conditions must involve macroeconomic rather than symptom-management policies—another example in which coordination is more difficult when capital is mobile.

Certain structural asymmetries in the degree of interest in international coordination of macroeconomic adjustment policies affect the bargaining power of different countries[41] and can influence the interstate distribution of the burdens of adjustment to international disequilibria. First, it is generally more difficult for governments to prevent trade deficits and capital outflows from having a deflationary impact than it is to insulate domestic economies from the potential inflationary consequences of trade surpluses and capital inflows. Governments of countries experiencing trade and capital-account deficits will eventually run out of national reserves of foreign currencies that can be sold to finance their deficits, while surplus countries are freer to conduct sterilized intervention in foreign-exchange markets to stabilize currency values without inflating the domestic money supply. Sterilized intervention involves making sales of government securities (or purchases, in

40. Similarly, based on their analysis of the 1978 Bonn Summit, Putnam and Henning argue that the issue of voluntary cheating on international agreements has received far too much attention in the theoretical literature on international cooperation, in contrast to its relative insignificance in international negotiations; see their "Bonn Summit of 1978," pp. 98–104.

41. These arguments about international economic asymmetries as sources of bargaining power are inspired by Albert O. Hirschman, *National Power and the Structure of Foreign Trade* (Berkeley: University of California Press, 1945 and 1980); and Robert O. Keohane and Joseph S. Nye, *Power and Interdependence: World Politics in Transition* (Boston: Little, Brown, 1977).

the case of deficit countries) in the domestic market to offset the impact of changes in central bank holdings of foreign reserves on the total supply of monetary reserves.

Germany's position as a consistently low-inflation surplus country is the basis for its preponderant power in European Community (EC) efforts to coordinate international macroeconomic adjustment policies. Coordination within the EC has involved substantial adjustments to non-German macroeconomic policies, while negotiated adjustments to German monetary and fiscal policies have been less substantial. Nevertheless, even the power of a surplus country such as Germany is not unlimited. The ability to set macroeconomic policies in response to domestic conditions while simultaneously maintaining a fixed exchange rate (i.e., in the case of Germany, preventing currency appreciation) relies on the effectiveness of sterilized foreign exchange market intervention. This is eroded when capital mobility increases, as recent German experience demonstrates. If capital inflows are very large, foreign exchange market intervention can lead to huge additions of foreign currency to national reserves; and the central bank may not have enough salable government securities to offset that addition to monetary reserves. In this case (as Germany has recently shown), the high interest rates that the central bank is relying on to dampen domestic monetary growth may in fact exacerbate inflationary pressures by stimulating inflows of foreign capital that swell the money supply. In the German example, growth in the money supply due to foreign capital inflows that cannot be sterilized have encouraged the central bank to keep interest rates high, thereby perpetuating the problem.[42] Thus, when capital is highly mobile, even surplus countries cannot maintain monetary policy autonomy and a fixed exchange rate at the same time.

The economic pressure on governments of countries with trade deficits and capital outflows is generally stronger than that facing governments of surplus countries. Deficit countries also face severe domestic political problems when investors lose confidence in national policy, the currency depreciates rapidly, or capital flees to safer havens abroad. These asymmetries between deficit and surplus countries mean that deficit countries typically have a stronger interest in international coordination to spread the burden of adjustment to others, matched with a lesser ability to bargain for changes in foreign government policies.

42. On the recent German experience, see *Globe and Mail*, 2 August 1993, p. B2.

But surplus countries can also have a strong interest in international coordination, especially if their agreement to share some of the burden of adjustment is necessary to persuade deficit countries not to restrict imports.

Second, the size of a country affects its power and interest in international coordination. Larger countries are better able to sustain payments disequilibria of a given volume than are smaller countries and thus are under less pressure to adjust, which puts the larger country in a stronger position in international bargaining. Larger countries also have (virtually by definition) larger domestic markets, and the threat of restricting access to that market can be a powerful lever in international bargaining.

Third, countries have different degrees of trade dependence. Less trade-dependent countries experience smaller external imbalances (relative to the size of the national economy) than do more trade-dependent countries, taking into account a given divergence between the expansiveness of national macroeconomic policy and the policies of major trading partners. This means that less trade-dependent countries are under less pressure to adjust policies to eliminate imbalances, which can enhance their bargaining position in international negotiations.

Fourth, bargaining power is affected by the international status of the national currency. Governments of countries whose currencies serve as international reserve and transactions currencies are able to borrow from abroad at less cost than other countries, since foreigners will be willing to hold at least some of the excess currency because of its usefulness in international trade and finance. Conversely, countries whose currencies do not serve as international currencies must often pay higher interest rates on their foreign borrowings because lenders demand a premium to account for the likelihood that the currency will depreciate in the face of persistent deficits.[43]

As we shall see, while the United States was a deficit country in the 1960s and 1980s, it had a dramatic advantage over the other three dimensions of power. U.S. payments deficits were small relative to the domestic economy but occasionally very large relative to the interna-

---

43. The United States has become less different from other countries in this respect since 1987 as foreign lenders have increasingly demanded interest-rate premiums that reflect the likelihood that the U.S. dollar will depreciate (see Chapter 6).

tional economy. The United States has also been much less trade dependent than most other industrialized countries, which helped to minimize the domestic political consequences of international imbalances—at least until the mid-1980s. Because the dollar has provided the world's primary reserve and transactions currency throughout the postwar era, foreigners have been willing to hold dollars without demanding a high interest rate premium. Therefore, the United States is the only country that has been able to borrow substantial sums from foreigners in its own currency without paying a high premium.[44]

The pattern of international policy coordination has reflected this preponderant American power throughout the period that I examine. The distribution of negotiated policy adjustments has generally favored the U.S. in the sense that the country has made fewer departures from the likely course of unilateral policy-making than have others. The main exception was during the late 1940s and the 1950s when American approaches to international policy coordination were dominated by the desire to help Western Europe and Japan resist domestic and foreign communism.

44. Susan Strange, "The Persistent Myth of Lost Hegemony," *International Organization* 41 (Autumn 1987), pp. 568–69.

CHAPTER THREE

Insulation and Symptom Management, 1945–55

The late 1940s and the first half of the 1950s were formative years for postwar international relations. World War II had ended with two superpowers poised on opposite sides of a devastated Europe. If the description of the United States as hegemonic was ever truly valid, it was during the years before the Soviet Union developed nuclear weapons and Western Europe began to recover. The United States took the lead in trying to negotiate agreements that touched on all aspects of international macroeconomic adjustment policy.

This chapter examines the coordination of macroeconomic adjustment policy in the period 1945–55, focusing on how the relatively insular structure of the international economy encouraged governments to coordinate certain types of policies and not others, and how the international distribution of power (U.S. predominance in a context of bipolarity) shaped the distribution of policy adjustments. The key problem in the late 1940s and early 1950s was the tremendous trade and payments imbalance between the United States on the one hand and Western Europe and Japan on the other. These imbalances resulted from the impact that World War II had on different regions of the world. The war had stimulated the American economy: wartime demand had finally pulled the economy out of depression, and American productive capacity had grown very rapidly. U.S. economic planning was driven in part by fears of a postwar recession similar to the one at the end of World War I. Leaders hoped that export demand would help to maintain production and employment in this postwar transition. The focus on export-led prosperity also reflected domestic opposition to Keynesian demand-management policies, which were seen to involve too much government intervention in the private economy.

In contrast, the economies of Western Europe and Japan had been devastated by the war, and the central problems for economic policy were much different than those of the United States. These governments faced the daunting task of reconstruction, combined in many cases with intense domestic pressures to prevent the return of the economic insecurities and unemployment of the 1920s and 30s. Consequently, most Western European governments pursued expansionary economic policies. Demand stimulus combined with depressed productive capacities (a legacy of the war) and relatively restrained macroeconomic policies in the United States to produce substantial trade deficits. American analysts have tended to view anti-inflationary macroeconomic policies in the late 1940s and the 1950s as a source of international economic stability.[1] From the perspective of governments bent on domestic expansion, however, macroeconomic restraint in the United States was a major source of international instability.

In theory, this imbalance—American surpluses and foreign deficits—could have been resolved with coordinated changes in any of the macroeconomic adjustment policies identified in Chapter 2. Surplus and deficit countries could have adjusted internal policies to eliminate external imbalances, and foreign demands for monetary and fiscal policy adjustments were often heard in international meetings. Nevertheless, this option was generally not attractive because of intense domestic opposition to the adjustments required to eliminate external imbalances and because alternatives existed. The United States could have reduced its export surplus by stimulating domestic demand, but mainstream conservative opinion would have been vehemently opposed—as the debates over the Employment Act of 1946 revealed. Western European governments could have scaled back reconstruction and full employment plans, but this action would have exposed them to severe domestic unrest. Furthermore, all governments rejected international coordination as an infringement on their sovereign right to pursue whatever domestic policies they saw fit.

1. Henry R. Nau, *The Myth of America's Decline: Leading the World Economy into the 1990s* (New York: Oxford University Press, 1990), especially chaps. 1 and 3.

Resistance to adjustments, unilateral or coordinated, caused governments to turn to external strategies and symptom-management policies. Controls on trade and capital flows were pervasive as deficit governments sought to direct all foreign exchange to the purchase of essential imports and protectionist forces retained the upper hand even in surplus countries such as the United States. Many countries unilaterally depreciated their exchange rates to improve their international competitive positions and reduce their trade deficits. Comprehensive exchange controls, private investors' fears of international political risk, and the virtual absence of markets for trading in foreign exchange meant that little capital flowed internationally in response to macroeconomic policy differentials. Given the strength of domestic demand in most countries outside North America, interest in expanding exports was limited; so there was little immediate pressure to open foreign markets. Overall, trade imbalances could have been managed simply by extreme protectionism and unilateral exchange-rate adjustments. There was little immediate need, in terms of the argument developed in Chapter 2, even for coordination of symptom-management policies.

Nevertheless, in the first half of the 1950s there was international coordination to maintain fixed exchange rates and to liberalize trade and exchange controls. The widespread fear of a return to the competitive devaluations of the 1930s encouraged most governments to maintain fixed exchange rates after 1949, as did the International Monetary Fund (IMF). Trade liberalization was made possible by extensive coordination of symptom-management policies in the form of large-scale American balance-of-payments assistance to foreign countries. Marshall Plan foreign aid and heavy American military spending overseas strengthened the balance-of-payments positions of foreign countries and permitted their governments gradually to liberalize trade and exchange controls without sacrificing domestic expansion.

American willingness to provide balance-of-payments assistance reflected two related concerns. First, the United States wanted to strengthen non-Communist governments and increase their ability to resist the challenges posed by the Soviet military threat and Communist parties in Western Europe. Anticommunism and the cold war were necessary conditions for the Marshall Plan and for American military spending in Europe and Japan that lasted well beyond the Marshall Plan period. Second, American leaders wanted to create an open international economy in which American industry was expected to thrive, and they recognized that foreign governments could not liberalize their economies without assistance. The American ability to provide assistance was a function of its hegemonic status in the international system; only a country as large, rich, and insulated as the United States could have provided enough funds to establish conditions favorable for the future liberalization of the international economy. In contrast to many versions of hegemonic stability theory, however, it is important to recognize that the United States probably would not have provided such large-scale assistance without the Soviet threat. In other words, hegemony and bipolarity are both necessary parts of the explanation.

The United States offered balance-of-payments assistance to persuade foreign governments to coordinate international macroeconomic adjustment policy, but its success was limited. American bargaining power proved to be less than its structural position in the international system might indicate. The country was in a advantageous position regarding all of the structural determinants of bargaining power noted in Chapter 2: it had a large trade surplus throughout the period, its economy was large and insular, and its currency was unquestionably the most desirable and widely used. Conversely, the much smaller economies of Western Europe and Japan were all experiencing trade deficits, were more dependent on international trade, and were undergoing severe problems of reconstruction. West Germany and Japan were even subject to the authority of occupying American forces (as well as British and French forces in the case of Germany) for part of this period. Because of the broader cold war context, however, these structural weaknesses actually strengthened their bargaining power with the United States. Governments were able to resist American demands for economic policy adjustments by pointing to the threat of domestic Communist political forces and (after 1950) the pressures imposed by American-led rearmament efforts. As we shall see, American bargaining power was also undermined by divisions within the United States government.

Consequently, American aid contributed to policy changes in foreign countries only when it enabled governments to pursue policies they already favored but had been unable to adopt beforehand. For example, the United States was almost completely unsuccessful in its attempts to get foreign governments to alter their monetary, fiscal, and exchange-rate policies. It was more successful in persuading governments to liberalize trade and exchange controls and in encouraging European economic integration, although the form pursued by European governments was different from what Washington preferred. For their part, governments of deficit countries were completely unsuccessful in their efforts to persuade the United States to reflate or liberalize import controls on goods and services they could export competitively. In other words, deficit countries succeeded in persuading the United States to provide a large amount of financial assistance but not to alter its own internal or external adjustment policies.

This pattern of policy coordination is consistent with the model developed in Chapter 2: governments agreed to coordinate only external and symptom-management policies because international market flows were still small enough to allow external payments imbalances to be managed without coordinating monetary and fiscal policies. Governments of deficit countries did have to restrain macroeconomic policies when faced with trade deficits larger than American aid and military spending could finance; but this was in response to market pressure, not negotiated mutual policy adjustment. Coordination of balance-of-payments financing was relatively easy because it had few adverse effects on domestic politics (compared with monetary and fiscal adjustments), although it was possible to mobilize U.S. domestic support for spending in Europe and Japan only because of the cold war Communist threat. Coordinated trade liberalization was possible only because it was limited, and governments retained considerable freedom to reintroduce controls in the face of imports that posed a threat to macroeconomic expansion or particular industries.

This chapter examines the historical record of international coordination of each category of macroeconomic adjustment policies from 1945 to 1955. It looks at external, symptom-management, and internal policies in order to establish the argument I have outlined in this introduction. A concluding section summarizes the findings and shows how the arguments about international economic and political structures developed in Chapter 2 help to explain the pattern of international coordination.

THE POLITICAL ECONOMY OF POLICY COORDINATION

INTERNATIONAL COORDINATION OF EXTERNAL POLICIES OF ADJUSTMENT

The international economic institutions created in the mid-1940s were intended to control states' use of external strategies of adjustment—to prevent a repeat of the beggar-thy-neighbor policies of the 1930s. The IMF, the abortive International Trade Organization (ITO), and the General Agreement on Tariffs and Trade (GATT) all incorporated rules to discourage states from restricting trade and devaluing currencies to export the costs of adjustment to foreign countries. The rules did provide exemptions for countries experiencing serious difficulties in the postwar transition period; and in fact, virtually all states relied heavily on external strategies of adjustment to insulate national economies from international market pressures. Nevertheless, there was international coordination underwritten by the United States to liberalize trade and exchange within Europe. As I examined the impact of international coordination on states' use of external strategies of adjustment, I found that there was substantial negotiated mutual adjustment of trade restrictions and of exchange controls on current account transactions but little negotiated mutual adjustment of capital controls or exchange rates.

Trade Controls and Controls on Current Account Payments

From 1945 to 1955 states outside North America relied heavily on controls on trade and payments to insulate national macroeconomic conditions from international market pressures. In the aftermath of a devastating world war, states in Western Europe and Japan were determined to pursue ambitious reconstruction programs and, in many cases, expansive full employment policies intended to prevent a return of the unemployment and sociopolitical strife that had accompanied the Great Depression in the 1930s. Comprehensive trade and exchange controls were used to minimize international market presures for restrictive macroeconomic policies and to direct scarce foreign earnings toward the purchase of those foreign goods that would make the greatest contribution to the achievement of state objectives. Most Western European states agreed that higher levels of trade were desirable but only if they did not threaten reconstruction programs and full employment policies. As an Organization for European Economic Cooperation (OEEC) report argued in 1950, trade liberalization depended upon the success of full employment policies.[2]

In contrast, American officials tended to believe that trade liberalization was more important than the achievement of full employment (at least in Western Europe; American import policies continued to be protectionist)[3] and that it was a prerequisite for full employment. Consequently, the United States rapidly sought to dismantle foreign trade and exchange controls and to wean foreigners from their reliance on controls as instruments of international macroeconomic adjustment.

GATT tariff negotiating rounds in 1947, 1949, and 1951 had little impact on effective levels of tariff protection.[4] The GATT included a general prohibition against the use of quantitative restrictions on trade, but it was qualified by provisions that permitted members to impose quantitative restrictions (even in ways that discriminated against hard-currency countries such as the United States) to strengthen their balance-of-payments and international reserve positions.[5] Governments in Western Europe relied on these provisions to ensure that scarce foreign currencies were used for state objectives and successfully resisted pressure for liberalization from the United States, Canada, and the GATT secretariat.[6]

High trade barriers were paralleled in the 1940s and most of the 1950s by restrictive state controls on payments for international transactions. These controls prevented individuals and businesses from gaining and using foreign exchange for purposes not specifically approved by the state and were acceptable until 1952 under the transitional pro-

---

2. Cited in William Diebold, Jr., *Trade and Payments in Western Europe: A Study in Economic Cooperation 1947–51* (New York: Harper and Brothers for the Council on Foreign Relations, 1952), p. 204.

3. Stephen D. Krasner, "United States Commercial and Monetary Policy: Unravelling the Paradox of External Strength and Internal Weakness," in Peter J. Katzenstein, ed., *Between Power and Plenty: Foreign Economic Policies of Advanced Industrial States* (Madison: University of Wisconsin Press, 1978), p. 77.

4. Jock A. Finlayson and Mark W. Zacher, "The GATT and the Regulation of Trade Barriers: Regime Dynamics and Functions," in Stephen D. Krasner, ed., *International Regimes* (Ithaca: Cornell University Press, 1983) p. 283.

5. Kenneth W. Dam, *The GATT: Law and International Economic Organization* (Chicago: University of Chicago Press, 1970), pp. 150–51; John H. Jackson, *World Trade and the Law of GATT* (Indianapolis: Bobbs-Merrill, 1969), pp. 691–92.

6. Jackson, *World Trade*, pp. 158–59, 682, 695–701, 707–8; Gardner Patterson, *Discrimination in International Trade: The Policy Issues, 1945–1965* (Princeton: Princeton University Press, 1966), pp. 37, 53–54, 63.

visions of the IMF. Most governments took advantage of these provisions to impose whatever controls on trade and payments they independently determined were appropriate. After 1952 the IMF had the right to demand that members withdraw restrictions it deemed inconsistent with the articles of agreement. Most governments, however, simply ignored IMF advice—strongly supported by the United States and Canada—that they relax exchange restrictions and eliminate payments deficits by pursuing less expansionary macroeconomic policies.[7] The IMF was supposed to gain leverage over national policies by controlling access to balance-of-payments financing, but this was irrelevant in the late 1940s and early 1950s because Marshall Plan aid recipients were declared ineligible for IMF loans.

In contrast to the ineffectiveness of the GATT and the IMF, international policy coordination underwritten by the United States did encourage liberalization of trade and payments within Western Europe, although it had little immediate impact on relations between Western Europe and North America. The United States viewed trade liberalization within Western Europe as a prerequisite for liberalization of transatlantic trade as well as a way to encourage political integration and improve Western Europe's ability to contribute to joint defense against the Soviet Union.[8] Consequently, one of the primary conditions attached to the offer of Marshall Plan aid was that European states cooperate to promote the expansion of foreign trade by liberalizing controls on trade and payments.[9]

Most Western European governments agreed with the United States that increased trade within Europe was a desirable objective but felt that it should be pursued only as long as it did not interfere with other national economic objectives. They agreed to negotiate a series of codes of liberalization of import quotas in the OEEC only after the United States insisted that it would not provide financing for the European

7. IMF, *The International Monetary Fund, 1945–1965: Twenty Years of International Monetary Cooperation.* Volume 2: *Analysis,* by Margaret Garritsen de Vries and J. Keith Horsefield (Washington, D.C.: IMF, 1969), pp. 245–46; W. M. Scammell, *International Monetary Policy,* 2d ed. (London: Macmillan, 1961), pp. 179–81.

8. Alan S. Milward, *The Reconstruction of Western Europe, 1945–51* (Berkeley: University of California Press, 1984), chap. 6; Imanuel Wexler, *The Marshall Plan Revisited: The European Recovery Program in Economic Perspective* (Westport, Conn.: Greenwood Press, 1983), pp. 201, 224.

9. Wexler, *Marshall Plan Revisited,* pp. 5, 18–19, 22.

Payments Union until they had done so. The OEEC codes eliminated discrimination among European suppliers and required that governments remove quotas on a large proportion of private imports.[10] These agreements had a modest impact. Quotas were relaxed, although the effect was moderated by high tariffs, state trading, and safeguard provisions that allowed members temporarily to restore quantitative restrictions when their payments positions came under strain.[11]

European governments rejected the broad American effort to stimulate European economic and political integration through trade liberalization and instead adopted a regulatory approach. European integration on the market-driven American model was viewed by most governments not just as a potential constraint on their macroeconomic policy-making autonomy,[12] but also as a "comprehensive threat to their national economic and political existence."[13] France led European efforts to organize economic integration along lines radically different from those proposed by the United States. In place of market rationality and the removal of governmental barriers to private trade flows, France proposed extensive European regulation of specific sectors. This approach was manifested most clearly by the European Coal and Steel Community (ECSC), an organization designed to capture certain benefits from international integration of a key industrial sector (and to determine in advance how the benefits would be distributed among member countries) while minimizing the pressures that international trade would put on national economic policies. The United States strongly objected to the elements of cartelization and regulation inherent in the ECSC but had to support the French initiative (the Schuman Plan) if it wanted to promote European integration; this was the only model acceptable to the important European governments.[14]

---

10. Ibid., p. 173; Diebold, *Trade and Payments in Western Europe*, pp. 162–81.

11. Diebold, *Trade and Payments in Western Europe*, pp. 172–85; I. Kravis, *Domestic Interests and International Obligations: Safeguards in International Trade Organizations* (Philadelphia: University of Pennsylvania Press, 1963), pp. 24, 148, 153, 160; Patterson, *Discrimination in International Trade*, pp. 110–11.

12. It *was* a constraint. Wexler, *Marshall Plan Revisited*, p. 236.

13. Milward, *Reconstruction of Western Europe*, p. 123.

14. See especially Milward, *Reconstruction of Western Europe*, pp. 388–89, 398–99, 474–77, 497–98; and Wexler, *Marshall Plan Revisited*, pp. 239–40. Michael J. Hogan emphasizes American support for the ECSC and its congruence with certain elements in American postwar planning in *The Marshall Plan: America, Britain, and the Reconstruction of Western Europe, 1947–1952* (Cambridge: Cambridge University Press, 1987), p. 378, but the ele-

American efforts to persuade European governments to liberalize exchange controls within Europe were more successful. Foreign aid and diplomatic pressure underwrote the creation of the European Payments Union (EPU) in 1950. The obstacles to payments liberalization in the late 1940s were very high. Liberalization would directly challenge the ability of European governments to insulate their reconstruction programs and full employment policies from deflationary international market pressures. Pervasive economic and political uncertainty made governments extremely reluctant to constrain their future options. The British convertibility fiasco in 1947 (discussed later in the chapter) had an important cautionary impact on all European governments.[15] The British government was also concerned that a European arrangement would threaten the integrity of the sterling area and reduce sterling's role as an international reserve currency.[16]

European governments looked to the United States to provide external financing to ease payments liberalization within Europe. At first, Washington was reluctant because of fears that this response would create a discriminatory soft-currency area in Europe.[17] By 1949–50, however, many American leaders realized that efforts to pressure European states into establishing full currency convertibility and ending trade discrimination against the United States were not working. A European payments system, supported financially by the United States, came to be viewed as an interim step toward multilateral liberalization, one that would strengthen Western Europe's competitive position, accelerate the date at which states were willing to accept IMF and GATT obligations, and hasten European integration.[18] In order to encourage

---

ment of European market regulation inherent in the ECSC far exceeded American preferences.

15. Robert Triffin, *Europe and the Money Muddle: From Bilateralism to Near Convertibility, 1947–1956* (New Haven, Conn.: Yale University Press, 1957), p. 141; Milward, *Reconstruction of Western Europe*, pp. 258, 262.

16. Milward, *Reconstruction of Western Europe*, pp. 259–60, 265–66, 278. See Susan Strange, *Sterling and British Policy: A Political Study of an International Currency in Decline* (London: Oxford University Press, 1971), for a discussion of the reasons for the British government's desire to maintain the special status of sterling.

17. Milward, *Reconstruction of Western Europe*, p. 77; Wexler, *Marshall Plan Revisited*, pp. 124–28.

18. On internal debates in the U.S. about the desirability of a Europe-only payments scheme, see Wexler, *Marshall Plan Revisited*, pp. 155–56, 161–65; Fred L. Block, *The Origins of International Economic Disorder: A Study of United States International Monetary Policy from World War II to the Present* (Berkeley: University of California Press, 1977), pp. 101–2;

agreement, the United States made the disbursement of some Marshall Plan funds conditional on European acceptance of multilateral payments liberalization.[19]

The EPU established a multilateral clearing system backed by American credits. Each national monetary authority would report its monthly balances with central banks in the other participating countries to the Bank for International Settlements (BIS, the agent for the EPU), which would then calculate a net surplus or deficit position for each country in terms of the EPU as a whole. This procedure used countries' claims against certain EPU members to offset their liabilities with others. Settlements of individual national balances against the EPU would be made partly in gold or dollars and partly in credits. A managing board was created that had some power to pressure countries to adopt policies consistent with the objectives of the agreement.

The central issue in the EPU negotiations was the degree of hardness in the terms of settlement. The United States wanted the terms to be very hard—that is, to require countries in net deficit to settle their debts quickly by paying gold or dollars to the EPU. This would force countries to restore equilibrium in their balance of payments by adopting deflationary policies, even at the expense of full employment—something Washington had been unable to persuade European countries to do.[20] The United States position was supported by those European countries that expected to be net creditors to the EPU. Predictably, governments that expected to be in deficit rejected the demand for hard terms of settlement because of the constraint imposed on their expansionary macroeconomic policies. France, Britain,[21] and other governments made it clear that they were willing to consider less liberal alternatives. Excessively hard terms of settlement could also have slowed the process of trade liberalization.[22]

The terms of the EPU provided for settlements of net deficit positions in a mixture of credits and gold, with the proportion of gold to

---

Milward, *Reconstruction of Western Europe*, pp. 321–24; and Hadley Arkes, *Bureaucracy, the Marshall Plan, and the National Interest* (Princeton: Princeton University Press, 1972), pp. 196–97.

19. Wexler, *Marshall Plan Revisited*, p. 169; Diebold, *Trade and Payments in Western Europe*, pp. 147–48.

20. Wexler, *Marshall Plan Revisited*, p. 169.

21. Britain expected to be in surplus within Europe but feared that its position at the center of the sterling area could lead to a drain of its reserves through the EPU.

22. Milward, *Reconstruction of Western Europe*, pp. 306–21.

increase as the size of the deficit increased relative to the member's quota. This system provided some financing for intra-European balance-of-payments deficits, but it also encouraged countries to correct their deficits by requiring them to pay larger proportions of gold or dollars for larger deficits. This compromise, plus other minor concessions and intense diplomatic pressure from the United States, finally persuaded Britain and others to relent.[23]

The second key issue in the negotiations concerned the powers of the EPU managing board. I will discuss this issue in greater detail later in the chapter. Briefly, however, the United States wanted to give the managing board the power to harmonize European monetary and fiscal policies to minimize payments imbalances and facilitate liberalization, but European resistance forced the United States to drop its demand.

The EPU agreement represented a significant degree of adjustment policy coordination. American efforts to promote European coordination were more successful in liberalizing international payments than in any other policy area.[24] The EPU eased the pressures on European countries' payments positions, thereby permitting them to liberalize controls on payments and trade without seriously undermining the expansionary policies that many were determined to pursue.[25] In the long run, the EPU agreement and related developments represent a crucial turning point in European policy, encouraging a shift away from statist and autarkic tendencies, especially in Britain.[26] Despite its overwhelming structural power, the United States did have to make significant concessions in the EPU negotiations, in part because other governments might have followed policies even more damaging to the American vision. Once on the path toward liberalization, however, and with the continuing support of American military aid and spending, European governments would have had difficulty turning back toward autarky.

The EPU had no immediate impact on the exchange controls that European countries imposed on transactions with the United States

23. Diebold, *Trade and Payments in Western Europe*, pp. 91–107; Triffin, *Europe and the Money Muddle*, pp. 164–68, 172; Milward, *Reconstruction of Western Europe*, pp. 327–30.

24. Harry B. Price, *The Marshall Plan and Its Meaning* (Ithaca: Cornell University Press, 1955), pp. 315, 318; Wexler, *Marshall Plan Revisited*, p. 121.

25. The trade liberalizing effects of the EPU are discussed in Triffin, *Europe and the Money Muddle*, pp. 168–69, 250–51.

26. Hogan, *Marshall Plan*, chap. 7.

and other hard-currency countries. Before 1952, convertibility between European currencies and North American currencies was blocked by huge European current account deficits and an unwillingness to deflate to reduce them. Deficits shrank after 1952 as European production and trade revived and American aid and military spending strengthened international reserves. Some governments unilaterally relaxed exchange controls in the mid-1950s, but all continued to resist American pressure to make their currencies formally convertible. The British government took an especially cautious approach because of its fear that a premature move would lead to a repeat of the 1947 convertibility fiasco. Continental European countries were unwilling to precede Britain, so no concerted move was possible before the late 1950s.[27] Even as conditions improved, many European governments still feared that U.S. deflationary policies or trade protectionism could lead to payments deficits that would threaten domestic prosperity unless they retained the freedom to impose trade and exchange controls to insulate their economies from external deflationary pressures.[28]

Controls on Capital Account Transactions

Speculative international capital flows proved extremely disruptive in the 1930s, and states decided at Bretton Woods that such flows should be strictly controlled while capital flows for current account purposes (such as trade financing) were liberalized.[29] In practice, however, states did not follow this path. As European governments gradually introduced elements of transferability between their currencies and hard currencies, they often applied it to capital account as well as current account transactions. The readiness to relax capital controls unilaterally reflected an independent interest in attracting and retaining inflows of investment capital. In fact, capital controls were often more effective in discouraging capital inflows than they were in preventing outflows.[30] Consequently, although the IMF called for strict capital controls as an

---

27. IMF, *The International Monetary Fund, 1945–1965: Twenty Years of International Monetary Cooperation.* Volume 1: *Chronicle*, by J. Keith Horsefield (Washington, D.C.: IMF, 1969), pp. 353–55; vol. 2, pp. 257–58, 266–69; Triffin, *Europe and the Money Muddle*, pp. 90–93, 209–16; Strange, *Sterling and British Policy*, pp. 64–65.

28. Triffin, *Europe and the Money Muddle*, pp. 86, 274.

29. IMF, *International Monetary Fund, 1945–1965*, vol. 1, pp. 503–4.

30. Triffin, *Europe and the Money Muddle*, pp. 214–16, 236.

instrument of international adjustment policy coordination, states determined unilaterally how to reconcile their interest in attracting capital inflows with preventing international flows that would constrain national policy-making autonomy.

Exchange-rate Adjustments

In the Bretton Woods negotiations, states did agree to maintain fixed exchange rates and to seek IMF approval for exchange-rate adjustments, but during the postwar decade this did not seriously constrain national policy-making autonomy. Most states were independently determined to maintain fixed exchange rates regardless of the IMF agreement and were determined to use an extensive battery of recent trade and payments controls for that purpose.[31] Private foreign-exchange markets were not permitted to become active until after 1956, thereby freeing states from the need to intervene to maintain fixed currency values.[32]

Despite the general preference for fixed exchange rates and IMF commitments, many states demonstrated that they were not willing to sacrifice domestic macroeconomic objectives to maintain fixed exchange rates. The most glaring departure from the IMF's rules was Canada's adoption of a fluctuating exchange rate in 1950. The government had decided to let the dollar float to prevent speculative capital inflows from fueling inflation.[33] The IMF staff strongly disapproved of the Canadian decision and feared that the "use of floating rates by a major developed country could undermine the credibility of the Bretton Woods system and lead to widespread disregard for its rules."[34] Nevertheless, the IMF did not impose sanctions, and Canada continued

31. Ibid., p. 291.

32. Susan Strange, *International Monetary Relations*, vol. 2 of Andrew Shonfield, ed., *International Economic Relations of the Western World, 1959–1971* (London: Oxford University Press for the Royal Institute of International Affairs, 1976), p. 59.

33. Paul Wonnacott, *The Canadian Dollar, 1948–1958* (Toronto: University of Toronto Press, 1960); A. F. W. Plumptre, *Three Decades of Decision: Canada and the World Monetary System, 1944–75* (Toronto: McClelland and Stewart, 1977), pp. 142–48; IMF, *International Monetary Fund, 1945–1965*, vol. 2, pp. 159–62. Controls on capital flows between Canada and the United States were much less restrictive than European controls at this time.

34. Kenneth W. Dam, *The Rules of the Game: Reform and Evolution in the International Monetary System* (Chicago: University of Chicago Press, 1982), pp. 128–29 (quotation); IMF, *International Monetary Fund, 1945–1965*, vol. 1, p. 273.

to permit its dollar to fluctuate until 1962. France and Italy also refused to name official par values until 1958 and 1960, respectively. Both governments maintained fixed exchange rates for most of the period, but neither wanted to lose the freedom to adjust exchange rates unilaterally to reconcile domestic objectives with balance-of-payments pressures. In 1948 the IMF declared France ineligible to use the fund's resources, but this was not an effective sanction because Marshall Plan aid and American military spending provided more assistance for France's balance of payments than would have been available from the IMF.[35]

Even states that did not violate IMF exchange-rate rules were able to maintain fixed exchange rates without serious constraints on adjustment policy-making because there was very little international coordination of initial exchange-rate levels or adjustments. Member countries unilaterally established official par values for their exchange rates, and the IMF accepted all of these even when IMF staff believed they were inappropriate.[36]

The IMF articles of agreement did ask members to coordinate exchange-rate adjustments in cases of "fundamental disequilibrium," and the fund had the right to refuse to lend money to members that devalued or revalued by more than ten percent without IMF approval. American proposals to give the fund a veto over any exchange rate proposed by a member and the right to propose and demand changes in exchange rates were rejected at Bretton Woods; the British government in particular wanted the freedom to devalue if necessary to protect full employment policies from external deficits.[37]

The most significant exchange-rate adjustments during the period 1945–55 were the 1949 devaluations of European currencies, establishing an exchange-rate structure that persisted with few changes for two decades. The devaluations therefore represent key cases for international coordination. Some analysts have interpreted the 1949 devaluations as a case of U.S.-directed international coordination,[38] but

35. IMF, *International Monetary Fund, 1945–1965*, vol. 2, pp. 55–56, 129–30; vol. 1, pp. 200–202.

36. Ibid., vol. 1, pp. 153–56; vol. 2, pp. 52–54; Triffin, *Europe and the Money Muddle*, pp. 116–17.

37. Dam, *Rules of the Game*, pp. 88–91.

38. Krasner, "United States Commercial and Monetary Policy," pp. 76, 82; Sidney E. Rolfe and James Burtle, *The Great Wheel: The World Monetary System. A Reinterpretation* (New York: Quadrangle/New York Times Book Company, 1973), pp. 67–69.

evidence suggests that negotiated mutual adjustment was less important than market pressure and independent national decision making.

By 1948, many European currencies were overvalued, an obstacle to international adjustment. The United States took the lead in encouraging Western European states to devalue, believing it would reduce European deficits and demands for American aid and improve the prospects for trade and payments liberalization.[39] Most continental European governments wanted to devalue their currencies against the dollar to improve their international competitive positions; in fact, several had already done so unilaterally. The main obstacle to a general European devaluation was Britain's determination to maintain sterling at the prewar level, an important attitude because of the country's leading role in European trade and payments. Its reluctance to devalue apparently was linked to tradition and a desire to maintain sterling's status as an international reserve currency and preserve the overseas sterling area.[40]

Thus, the main focus for international coordination of exchange rates in 1948–49 was American pressure on Britain to devalue. Several European countries tried to persuade Britain to discuss exchange-rate adjustments multilaterally, but it rejected all initiatives.[41] Decision makers initially were unswayed by diplomatic pressure from the United States, the IMF, and other governments. Britain's attitude changed, however, in the face of an accelerating loss of international reserves.[42] Its current account was undermined by a loss of exports due to recession in the United States and by speculation that sterling was about to be devalued.[43] Speculation had been fueled by American officials calling publicly for devaluation and by American-instigated investigations in the IMF.[44] Most members of the British cabinet were reluctant to

39. Milward, *Reconstruction of Western Europe*, p. 287; Block, *Origins of International Economic Disorder*, pp. 93–97.

40. Alec Cairncross, *Years of Recovery: British Economic Policy, 1945–51* (London: Methuen, 1985), pp. 166–73; Milward, *Reconstruction of Western Europe*, p. 288; Strange, *Sterling and British Policy*.

41. Milward, *Reconstruction of Western Europe*, pp. 287–89.

42. Ibid., pp. 288, 291; Cairncross, *Years of Recovery*, p. 197.

43. Speculation took the form of uncontrollable capital account flows as well as lags and leads in current account payments intended to delay purchases of sterling until after the expected devaluation and to complete purchases of dollars before devaluation; Cairncross, *Years of Recovery*, pp. 205–6.

44. On discussions in the IMF, see IMF, *International Monetary Fund, 1945–1965*, vol. 1, pp. 234–37.

devalue sterling and did so because the only alternative seemed to be "cuts in public expenditure and deflation, . . . exactly what [the Labour government] had been elected to avoid."[45]

American pressure undoubtedly had an impact on the decision, especially because private markets were responsive to U.S. attitudes. The British government offered its decision to devalue in efforts to get concessions from the United States, including improved access for British and sterling-area exports and more generous American financial assistance. The American government did make some concessions in September 1949 after the British government decided to devalue (although before that decision was announced).[46]

To assess the degree of negotiated mutual policy adjustment involved in these decisions, we must compare what happened to a plausible counterfactual. Some commentators have suggested that Britain was forced to devalue because the United States would not provide additional credits,[47] but this view is paradoxical at best. It suggests that if the United States had been more willing to adjust its policies, Britain would have been under less pressure. Although this may be true, the comparison should concern what would have happened without negotiated mutual policy adjustment. In such a case, Britain's growing trade deficit and accelerating loss of reserves would almost certainly have forced it to devalue even in the absence of American diplomatic pressure, and possibly to adopt deflationary macroeconomic policies. As the American government feared, the Labour government could have reacted to the payments crisis by retreating into a more insular sterling bloc, complete with tighter trade and exchange restrictions against the dollar and more extensive internal government intervention. Thus, American-led policy coordination had its greatest impact on Britain's trade and exchange policies. Neither devaluation nor deflation was made significantly more likely through international diplomacy, but American actions were crucial in persuading the Labour government to abandon the option of a strengthened sterling bloc insulated from the dollar area.[48]

Britain unilaterally determined the size of the British devaluation, which was considerably larger (at 30.5 percent) than most American

45. Milward, *Reconstruction of Western Europe*, p. 288.
46. Hogan, *Marshall Plan*, pp. 261–65.
47. This was the view of many in the British Cabinet. Hogan, *Marshall Plan*, p. 249.
48. Ibid., chap. 6.

officials felt was appropriate.[49] This issue has important theoretical implications. Some hegemonic stability theorists claim that the United States deliberately encouraged European countries to adopt undervalued exchange rates as a way to stimulate their economies without paying much attention to the long-term costs to American competitiveness. The analysis here, however, suggests that the United States preferred more realistic (i.e., less undervalued) European exchange rates but was unable to persuade Britain to adopt an exchange rate that met this criteria.

The IMF executive board quickly approved Britain's proposed devaluation, despite the country's failure to seek prior IMF approval (as called for in the articles of agreement) and the fact that the size of the devaluation was "deemed unquestionably excessive by most Fund members."[50] Britain's devaluation was immediately followed by most sterling area and Western European countries. The amounts of their devaluations were determined unilaterally,[51] and the IMF approved all of them.[52]

The lack of international coordination undoubtedly made it easier for states to meet their IMF exchange-rate commitments without actually constraining national policy-making autonomy or their ability to use exchange-rate changes as an instrument of international macroeconomic adjustment. Of course, the United States did not have to modify its policies in any way to support the exchange rate for the dollar (either into gold or other currencies). But the establishment of the IMF with its rules on fixed exchange rates did create a structure that constrained national adjustment policy from 1956 to 1970. It was easy for states to agree to adhere to the IMF's rules when they did not

49. Cairncross, *Years of Recovery*, pp. 186–88, provides a detailed account of the choice of the new exchange rate. For the American view that a devaluation of more than 25 percent would have drastic and unpredictable effects on Britain and the international economy, see the Economic Cooperation Administration internal document cited in Milward, *Reconstruction of Western Europe*, pp. 291–92.

50. Triffin, *Europe and the Money Muddle*, pp. 119–20 (quotation); Block, *Origins of International Monetary Disorder*, p. 98; IMF, *International Monetary Fund, 1945–1965*, vol. 1, p. 239.

51. The new Federal Republic of Germany was an exception. It agreed to devalue the mark by only 20 percent rather than the initially proposed 22.5 percent in response to pressure from France and the American and British occupying authorities. Milward, *Reconstruction of Western Europe*, pp. 386–87.

52. Triffin, *Europe and the Money Muddle*, p. 120; IMF, *International Monetary Fund, 1945–1965*, vol. 1, pp. 239–40.

constrain national policy-making; in this sense, widespread trade and exchange controls and a loose interpretation of IMF rules made it possible to establish a system that did have a constraining impact after controls were relaxed. It would have been much more difficult to persuade states to agree to the IMF's rules on exchange rates in the 1960s, when such agreement would have immediately imposed constraints on policy-making autonomy.

INTERNATIONAL COORDINATION OF SYMPTOM-MANAGEMENT POLICIES

Governments can try to manage the international payments imbalances caused by their different macroeconomic policies by lending from surplus to deficit countries. The IMF originally was intended to be the major source of international financing for payments imbalances, attaching conditions to financial assistance that would result in international coordination of other adjustment policies. The IMF was to insist upon the maintenance of fixed par values for exchange rates and the minimization of controls on current account transactions. Its financial assistance was supposed to permit countries to restore equilibrium in their international payments without border controls, exchange-rate adjustments, or drastic policy shifts.

In April 1948, the executive directors of the IMF decided that countries receiving Marshall Plan aid would not be permitted to draw United States dollars from the fund.[53] IMF dollar resources were clearly inadequate for financing the balance-of-payments deficits generated by ambitious European reconstruction programs and would soon have been exhausted.[54] Western European countries did not draw significantly from the fund from 1950 to 1955. Among the developed countries, only Japan (which drew $124 million in 1953) relied on the IMF as a source of international finance for payments imbalances, and no substantive conditions were attached to its borrowings.

Consequently, international financing of payments imbalances was provided during the immediate postwar years mainly through bilateral agreements—most important, the Anglo-American loan agreement of 1946. The United States agreed to lend Britain $3.75 billion (an

53. IMF, *International Monetary Fund, 1945–1965*, vol. 1, pp. 217–20.
54. Scammell, *International Monetary Policy*, pp. 205–6.

amount far greater than the American contribution of $2.1 billion to the IMF)[55] with the condition that Britain liberalize its trade and exchange policies. Specifically, Britain was required to restore sterling convertibility within one year.[56] Congressional reluctance to lend such a large sum to the interventionist Labour government was eventually overcome only because the loan came to be seen "as an investment in the political and economic strength of the non-Soviet world."[57] American economic interests as a hegemonic industrial power were not sufficient to persuade Congress to finance Britain's payments deficit, but its security interests in the emerging bipolar world were sufficient and decisive.

The gradual introduction of convertibility in 1946–47 led to Britain's enormous loss of dollar reserves, much of which was directly financed by the American loan. Convertibility was therefore suspended on 20 August 1947. The loss of reserves could be traced in part to the expansionary macroeconomic policy of the Labour government, which worsened Britain's current account position and undermined confidence in sterling. The loan agreement said nothing about macroeconomic policies. The American government apparently hoped that the convertibility commitment would encourage Britain to restrain domestic expansion, but the Labour government spoke and behaved as if it were free to continue the stimulative full employment policies it had already adopted.[58]

The 1947 failure to make sterling convertible made Britain and other European governments more cautious about American proposals for liberalizing trade and payments and delayed the introduction of general European convertibility until the late 1950s.[59] The episode also revealed some limits to American bargaining power. Determined bargaining might produce policy concessions on the part of debtor governments; but if those concessions were inconsistent with debtors' political and economic conditions they could not be fulfilled. Further-

55. Triffin, *Europe and the Money Muddle*, p. 139.

56. Richard N. Gardner, *Sterling-Dollar Diplomacy in Current Perspective: The Origins and the Prospects of Our International Economic Order*, expanded ed. with rev. intro. (New York: Columbia University Press, 1980), pp. 199–206; Block, *Origins of International Economic Disorder*, pp. 55–58.

57. Gardner, *Sterling-Dollar Diplomacy*, pp. 249 (quotation), 248–53.

58. Ibid., pp. 234, 309–16.

59. Triffin, *Europe and the Money Muddle*, p. 141; Gardner, *Sterling-Dollar Diplomacy*, pp. 339–42.

more, meeting stringent policy conditions could undermine domestic stability in the borrowing country, possibly leading to increased support for leftists. Thus, American bargaining power was limited by the very weakness of its allies.

The Marshall Plan was by far the most important source of international finance for payments deficits during the late 1940s and early 1950s. Through it the United States provided approximately $12 billion in assistance (mainly grants) to seventeen European countries between April 1948 and June 1951.[60] From the perspective of this study, the essence of the Marshall Plan was its offer of American financing for European-U.S. payments deficits in exchange for a range of European policy adjustments. Most payments deficits were generated by ambitious reconstruction programs and stimulative full employment policies. U.S. protectionism and restrained macroeconomic policies also contributed to the imbalance. As I have discussed, there were major political obstacles blocking policy adjustments that could have reduced this imbalance. European countries naturally sought American aid because the United States was the largest and richest country in the world and leader of the anti-Communist alliance.

Scholars have exhaustively examined American motives for providing aid to Western Europe. Here I identify two central objectives. First, aid was linked to the American desire to create an open world economy; and second, aid was an essential component of the national security strategy of containment.

Regarding the first motive, financial assistance was intended to encourage recipients to liberalize controls on trade and payments. American leaders feared that if the United States did not provide assistance and persuade European governments to open their economies, payments deficits could force these governments to intensify international and domestic economic controls, thereby heading Western Europe toward socialism or national capitalism, either of which would have closed the continent to American exports and investment.[61] This is the argument of hegemonic stability theory: the United States, as the richest, most advanced, and largest economy in the world, had both the interest

60. W. A. Brown, Jr., and Redvers Opie, *American Foreign Assistance* (Washington, D.C.: Brookings Institution, 1953), pp. 246–47.
61. Block, *Origins of International Economic Disorder.*

71

and the ability to make necessary short-term sacrifices to create a liberal international economy. Nevertheless, the explanation is incomplete. There was strong opposition to a large-scale European aid effort within the United States in the late 1940s. Hardline multilateralists in the Treasury Department blamed Europe's external deficits on interventionist and socialist policies and felt it should be pressured to immediately accept Bretton Woods obligations to liberalize trade and payments. Opposition also came from isolationists (including many in Congress) who did not want the United States to become more deeply involved in Europe or to send good money after bad when government spending austerity was in vogue in the United States.

Internal American opposition to the Marshall Plan was overcome only because aid to Europe was considered essential to national security. Thus, the second central motive that explains why the United States provided aid to Western Europe and Japan was the desire to contain the perceived threat from the Soviet Union.[62] American military power alone was deemed insufficient to prevent the Soviet Union from dominating Western Europe, despite the American monopoly of nuclear weapons. U.S. ground forces had been withdrawn from Europe in response to strong domestic pressure and discontent at overseas military bases. Economic assistance appeared to be the only way to strengthen Western Europe against the perceived threat of Soviet military domination.[63]

By all accounts, anticommunism was critical to congressional approval of the Economic Recovery Program (ERP) in 1948. The Truman administration consciously used anticommunism and fear of Soviet domination in Europe to win public and congressional support for the Marshall Plan. The security motive underlying American financial support for Western Europe's payments deficits became more explicit after 1950. In the wake of the Korean War, the Truman administration began a massive rearmament program and pressed European allies to undertake similar programs to contain the threat of Soviet expansion. The emphasis on rearmament interfered with achievement of the Marshall Plan's economic objectives by diverting resources from the civilian economy to defense and encouraging European governments to spend

62. John Lewis Gaddis, *Strategies of Containment: A Critical Appraisal of Postwar American National Security Policy* (Oxford: Oxford University Press, 1982); Hogan, *Marshall Plan.*

63. Robert A. Pollard, *Economic Security and the Origins of the Cold War, 1945–1950* (New York: Columbia University Press, 1985).

Table 4. Selected United States balance-of-payments accounts with Western Europe, in millions of dollars

	1946	1947	1948	1949	1950	1951	1952	1953	1954	1955
Trade balance	3472	4892	3500	3246	1684	2042	1450	714	1462	1915
FDI income	62	81	93	94	110	119	127	143	186	255
FDI outflow	−22	−43	−62	−22	−117	−61	8	−51	−50	−139
Total private	3512	4930	3531	3318	1677	2100	1585	806	1598	2031
Military aid	0	−43	−254	−170	−463	−1112	−2151	−3435	−2313	−1706
Military expenditures	−16	−164	−298	−305	−168	−313	−739	−1171	−1455	−1647
Other aid	−2668	−4325	−3958	−4347	−2782	−2176	−1567	−973	−788	−628
Total government	−2684	−4532	−4510	−4822	−3413	−3601	−4453	−5579	−4556	−3981

SOURCES: U.S. Department of Commerce, *Survey of Current Business: Balance of Payments Statistical Supplement* (Washington, D.C.: Department of Commerce, 1958), pp. 20–26.

NOTES:

Trade balance: Merchandise exports minus imports, excluding military exports under aid programs and military expenditures abroad.

FDI income: Income on foreign direct investment (gross).

FDI outflow: Net foreign direct investment outflow.

Total private: Trade balance plus FDI income minus FDI outflow.

Military aid: Military transfers under aid programs.

Military expenditures: Military expenditures abroad for goods and services.

Other aid: Nonmilitary foreign aid grants plus government long-term capital outflows (net of repayments).

Total government: Military aid plus military expenditures plus other aid.

heavily on defense even at the cost of renewed inflation, continued payments deficits, and trade and exchange controls.[64] In this way, national security concerns encouraged the United States to pursue policies that conflicted with its presumed hegemonic interest in creating an open international economic system. The change of emphasis was symbolized by a 1951 change in the official name of the aid program, from the Economic Recovery Program to the Mutual Security Program (MSP).

American financial assistance to Western Europe continued at a high level even after the Marshall Plan ended in 1951. The U.S. provided assistance in the form of military aid and expenditures, again revealing the importance of security rather than hegemonic economic interests. Table 4 shows that the United States had large surpluses in its trade and foreign direct investment (FDI) accounts with Western Europe

64. Hogan, *Marshall Plan*, chap. 9.

throughout this period. In all years after 1947, American government spending in Europe on economic and military aid and military expenditures far exceeded Europe's combined trade and FDI deficits with the United States. Military aid and expenditures became especially significant after 1951. This inflow of American dollars was crucial in permitting Western European governments to rebuild their foreign-exchange reserves and liberalize trade and exchange controls without exposing expansionary domestic policies to deflationary international market pressures. The importance of this effect can hardly be exaggerated. European trade and payments liberalization in the 1950s was financed by American military spending in Europe—spending that would not have occurred without the Soviet military threat, a factor outside the purview of conventional hegemonic stability theory.

The United States attempted to attach wide-ranging economic and political conditions to the offer of Marshall Plan aid. Had this attempt been successful, there would have been negotiated mutual adjustment of all types of international adjustment policy, not just symptom-management policy. There were four major conditions.[65] First, aid was to be used to finance a high rate of capital investment in order to build Europe's productive capacity and its ability to be economically self-sustaining in the future. This was consistent with the wishes of European states and therefore involved no serious departure from national priorities. Marshall Plan aid permitted recipient countries to maintain a high rate of investment without depressing consumption to politically unacceptable levels.

Second, recipients were to coordinate their reconstruction programs through a European organization with supervisory powers over national reconstruction and macroeconomic policies. This condition was intended to encourage economic and political integration. European governments resisted American demands for coordination tenaciously and successfully; there was virtually no coordination among Marshall Plan aid recipients in these areas. After the first two years, the United States gave up even trying to get the Europeans to coordinate and determined national aid allocations in bilateral negotiations with individual countries.

65. These conditions are detailed in Wexler, *Marshall Plan Revisited*, and Price, *Marshall Plan and Its Meaning*.

Third, the United States called on recipient governments to pursue internal fiscal and monetary stability and to cooperate to stabilize exchange rates at appropriate levels. International coordination of monetary and fiscal policies was minimal, as I discuss later in the chapter; and governments rejected the American demand that they coordinate exchange rates as a condition for aid.[66]

Fourth, the United States wanted European countries to work together to liberalize trade and payments within Europe. As I have shown, American diplomacy and financial assistance did encourage this liberalization, helping to set the stage for trade liberalization and currency convertibility in the late 1950s and the 1960s.

The United States's mixed success in altering European macroeconomic adjustment policies reveals the limits of American power, even in the period when its international hegemony was most pronounced. American efforts were successful when its objectives coincided with those of European governments—stimulating capital investment and liberalizing payments within Europe.[67] European governments were able to resist American pressure for policy changes that conflicted with their objectives, as in trade liberalization, the creation of a powerful European organization to coordinate reconstruction and macroeconomic policies, and the stance of macroeconomic policy.

Washington's leverage over aid recipients' policies was limited because the recipients were both weak and crucial to the achievement of American security interests. American leaders feared that if they withheld financial assistance or demanded unpopular policy adjustments, Soviet sympathizers in aid-receiving countries would gain strength, thereby undermining American efforts to create a strongly anti-Communist Europe. Thus, the economic problems of European countries proved to be a source of strength in bargaining with the United States. Similarly, the U.S. could not terminate the military aid and expenditures that strengthened 1950s European payments positions without undermining its own strategy for containing the Soviet security threat.

66. Milward, *Reconstruction of Western Europe*, pp. 116–18.
67. For a similar assessment, see Hogan, *Marshall Plan*, p. 436.

International Coordination of Internal Policies of Adjustment

The widespread use of trade and exchange controls and unilateral adjustments in exchange rates, combined with American financing of Western European payments deficits, insulated national macroeconomic conditions from international market pressures in the late 1940s and the first half of the 1950s. Consequently, there was relatively little need for states to coordinate macroeconomic policies to achieve international stability. States wanted to maintain policy-making autonomy because of intense domestic political pressures, as I discussed earlier in this chapter. The United States government could not overcome severe domestic opposition to the stimulative policies that many foreign governments urged it to adopt in order to expand imports and reduce its trade surplus; conversely, most European governments would have faced severe domestic instability if they had pursued orthodox macroeconomic policies rather than rapid reconstruction and, in many countries, full employment.

Given the magnitude of international payments imbalances, governments often did call on foreign governments to alter their macroeconomic policies and bear a greater burden of adjustment to disequilibria. They made many attempts to persuade foreign governments to adjust monetary and fiscal policies during the period 1945–55. These attempts can be grouped into three categories: direct multilateral coordination through the IMF and other United Nations agencies; direct and implicit coordination in United States relations with ERP countries; and indirect coordination as a consequence of coordinating other types of adjustment policy.

Multilateral Organizations

Various states attempted to incorporate provisions into international agreements that would have constrained the macroeconomic policies of foreign states. All these attempts were rejected by the states whose policy-making autonomy would have been affected by the proposed measures. Even the United States, with its undisputed hegemony, was unable to force foreign states to accept international diplomatic constraints on national policy choices.

Policy guidelines were a major issue in the IMF negotiations at Bretton Woods. The original American plans for the IMF were designed to ensure that states with payments deficits would restrict monetary and fiscal expansion in order to eliminate deficits without restricting trade. British plans were designed to ensure that states with payments surpluses caused by deflationary macroeconomic policies had to stimulate their economies, thereby allowing states with payments deficits to avoid deflation. The United States and Britain (with Britain backed by many other states) rejected each other's efforts to impose policy constraints, and many states viewed giving the IMF power over macroeconomic policy as an infringement on national sovereignty. Consequently, the fund's articles of agreement contained no positive guidelines for international adjustment of macroeconomic policies and included many restrictions on its power over national policy-making autonomy.[68] This was part of the compromise of embedded liberalism: while the IMF could encourage international liberalization, it could not force states to adopt policies that their governments believed would threaten domestic stability.[69]

Once the IMF was established, the United States continued to use it to pressure deficit states to pursue less expansionary policies. In annual consultations held with countries whose currencies were not officially convertible, IMF staff urged them to pursue orthodox macroeconomic policies and eliminate exchange controls, but these arguments had little impact. The fund had no leverage over the major developed countries because Marshall Plan aid recipients were not eligible to borrow from it and American aid alleviated payments constraints on many European expansionary policies. This meant that the fund's conditionality policies (then being developed at American insistence) had no impact on advanced capitalist states until the 1960s.[70]

68. Gardner, *Sterling-Dollar Diplomacy*, pp. xxxix–xl, chaps. 5 and 7. Various drafts of American and British plans for the IMF are reprinted in IMF, *The International Monetary Fund, 1945–1965: Twenty Years of International Monetary Cooperation*. Volume 3: *Documents*, ed. J. Keith Horsefield (Washington, D.C.: IMF, 1969).

69. John Gerard Ruggie, "International Regimes, Transactions, and Change: Embedded Liberalism in the Postwar Economic Order," in Stephen D. Krasner, ed., *International Regimes* (Ithaca: Cornell University Press, 1983), pp. 209–212.

70. American efforts to use the IMF to promote orthodox policies were matched by equally unsuccessful efforts by Britain and others to turn it into the ready source of international credit originally envisaged by Keynes. On these debates, see Block, *Origins of International Economic Disorder*, pp. 112–13; IMF, *International Monetary Fund, 1945–1965*, vol. 1, pp. 287–88, 332–35; and Scammell, *International Monetary Policy*, pp. 385–92.

Debates about macroeconomic policies also played a central role in the negotiations for the abortive International Trade Organization (ITO). The United States wanted to avoid any reference to employment in the ITO charter, arguing that the Economic and Social Commission (ECOSOC) of the United Nations was the proper forum.[71] In contrast, Britain called for the adoption of a convention on international employment and trade policy that would, in effect, commit signatories to the pursuit of full employment policies. According to this plan, surplus countries would bear much of the responsibility for correcting payments imbalances that threatened full employment in deficit countries.[72]

The United States did succeed in diverting discussion of the most controversial British proposals out of the ITO and into ECOSOC, where they subsequently died.[73] But many countries (including Britain) would not commit themselves to trade liberalization unless it included some reference to international measures to promote full employment. The United States delegation therefore had to accept provisions in the draft ITO charter which allowed governments to impose discriminatory trade restrictions in order to maintain full employment and which put the onus on surplus countries to reduce international imbalances that threatened employment in deficit countries.[74] Otherwise, many countries would not accept the commercial policy obligations sought by the American government. Again, despite its overwhelming structural power, the United States was not able to persuade foreign governments to accept agreements that would undermine their macroeconomic policy-making autonomy.

The employment provisions of the draft ITO charter were one of the main reasons why the United States did not ratify the charter. Critics believed the charter suggested that surplus countries such as the United States would bear the main burden of correcting international payments imbalances. At the same time, it appeared to leave foreign coun-

71. Gardner, *Sterling-Dollar Diplomacy*, pp. 146–47; W. A. Brown, *The United States and the Restoration of World Trade* (Washington, D.C.: Brookings Institution, 1950), p. 58.

72. Gardner, *Sterling-Dollar Diplomacy*, p. 271.

73. For debates in ECOSOC, see ibid., pp. 278–79; Block, *Origins of International Economic Disorder*, p. 112; IMF, *International Monetary Fund, 1945–1965*, vol. 1, pp. 288, 333.

74. Brown, *United States and the Restoration of World Trade*, pp. 91–93, 96–97, 285; Gardner, *Sterling-Dollar Diplomacy*, pp. 275–78.

tries free to pursue inflationary policies and impose discriminatory trade restrictions on U.S. imports.[75]

The collapse of the ITO did not result from the American president's inability to persuade Congress to support an institution that promoted national interests.[76] Rather, American negotiators were unable to persuade foreign states to accept proposals that promoted American interests. The ITO collapsed because the United States was not sufficiently powerful, even at the height of its hegemonic power, to force foreign states to abandon their commitment to central macroeconomic policy objectives. At the same time, the failure revealed that other states could not force the United States to accept even the appearance of constraints on its own freedom to make macroeconomic policy.

The Marshall Plan and Macroeconomic Policy

As I have already discussed, the United States provided an enormous amount of balance-of-payments assistance in the late 1940s and early 1950s. In theory this might have given it some leverage over the macroeconomic policies of recipient countries. In fact, the United States did try very hard to persuade Western European countries to alter their policies in exchange for Marshall Plan aid, but its efforts had little success. Governments were required to pursue internal monetary and exchange-rate stability as a condition for American aid. This did not involve much of a concession, however, for most European governments agreed in the abstract that inflation and currency volatility were bad things.

Nevertheless, Western European states resisted all American efforts to extract specific policy commitments. The United States wanted aid recipients to pursue restrained macroeconomic policies coordinated within Europe. In this way, the U.S. attempted to create supranational monetary and fiscal policy-making institutions through bilateral nego-

75. William Diebold, Jr., *The End of the ITO*, Essays in International Finance No. 16 (Princeton: Department of Economics and Social Institutions, Princeton University, 1952), pp. 14–17; Gardner, *Sterling-Dollar Diplomacy*, pp. 375–76; Brown, *United States and the Restoration of World Trade*, p. 364.

76. This argument is made by Krasner, "United States Commercial and Monetary Policy," especially p. 74.

tiations. American hopes initially focused on the Organization for European Economic Cooperation (OEEC)—which, it argued, should have the power to harmonize national monetary and fiscal policies. This idea was rejected by most European countries, who were led by Britain and France. Divisions within the United States government also undermined Marshall Plan efforts to establish strong European institutions. Washington's "general preoccupation with defense and security considerations . . . led the State Department and the ECA to recognize the principle of British exceptionalism," which made it difficult to overcome the critical European focus of opposition to a stronger OEEC. The Treasury Department also opposed some plans for stronger central European institutions, fearing that regionalism would impede multilateral economic liberalization.[77] Consequently, "in formulating and pursuing their national production goals and in implementing domestic stabilization measures, the ERP nations acted pretty much independently of each other."[78]

After their OEEC failure, Marshall Plan organizers tried to use the EPU as a spearhead for fiscal and monetary policy coordination. Their initial proposal provided for the establishment of a managing board with wide-ranging powers to harmonize European fiscal and monetary policies.[79] But European opposition led by Britain forced the United States to abandon this proposal, and the managing board was given no coordinating power.[80] It had limited authorization to encourage policy adjustments in states that accumulated very large net deficit or surplus positions.[81] Large imbalances persisting throughout the EPU's life span had to be settled by ad hoc negotiations concerning long-term bilateral credits between deficit and creditor countries.

American efforts in bilateral negotiations to change European macroeconomic policies were hardly more successful than their attempts in multilateral negotiations. American advisors constantly urged European governments (except Italy, as I will discuss) to pursue less inflationary policies. The Truman administration and Congress expected

77. Hogan, *Marshall Plan*, p. 335.

78. Wexler, *Marshall Plan Revisited*, p. 121.

79. Arkes, *Bureaucracy*, p. 195; Price, *Marshall Plan and Its Meaning*, p. 126.

80. Milward, *Reconstruction of Western Europe*, pp. 332–33.

81. Triffin, *Europe and the Money Muddle*, pp. 168, 177–78, 250; Diebold, *Trade and Payments in Western Europe*, pp. 97–99. See Wexler, *Marshall Plan Revisited*, p. 200, on the weakness of the EPU's adjustment mechanism.

that the power to withhold aid and approve the release of counterpart funds would give American aid officials a great deal of leverage over European policies.[82] Keynesians in the ECA hoped to use consultations about counterpart releases to educate governments about American macroeconomic management techniques.[83] Most observers, however,—including the official historian of the ERP—agreed that actual leverage was minimal.[84] Counterpart funds were generally used to finance investment or retire government debt. In either case, they eased the financial burden on the recipient government, thus possibly discouraging deflation (if the alternative was a lower level of investment) or inflation (if the alternative was to print more money to make up the difference). If the ECA refused to release counterpart funds, European governments could always find other sources of money. One was the printing press; the government could simply print more money, thereby creating exactly the outcome (inflation) the United States sought to avoid.

More generally, American efforts to compel European governments to pursue restrictive macroeconomic policies were constrained by political considerations. Stabilizing prices in Europe might entail higher unemployment and lower standards of living, which could increase the appeal of radical political forces.[85] Washington's desire to contain socialism and Soviet influence made it willing to continue aid to countries that rejected U.S. policy advice when the recipient government argued that rapid expansion was necessary for political reasons. The United States was even more willing to sacrifice European price stability to strategic concerns after the Korean War began in 1950. National contributions to the rearmament effort (which tended to be inflationary) then became an important criterion for aid disbursement, and less attention was paid to anti-inflationary efforts.

82. When an ERP country received goods paid for by the ERP, the actual purchaser had to pay for them in the local currency equivalent of U.S. dollars. These payments created counterpart funds, which could be used by the European government for purposes approved by the ECA.

83. Hogan, *Marshall Plan*, pp. 152–53.

84. Price, *Marshall Plan and Its Meaning*, pp. 315–16; Wexler, *Marshall Plan Revisited*, pp. 112, 117; Hogan, *Marshall Plan*, p. 152. The country-specific chapters in Peter A. Hall, ed., *The Political Power of Economic Ideas: Keynesianism across Nations* (Princeton: Princeton University Press, 1989), also suggest that the influence of American Keynesian advice was minimal.

85. Hogan, *Marshall Plan*, pp. 152–55.

ECA policy advice to European governments was no more effective than its attempts to use counterpart releases and aid distribution to pressure governments toward less inflationary policies. Larger governments ignored American exhortations and resented attempts to interfere in internal policies.[86] A brief review of American attempts to influence policy reveals that even sustained pressure had little influence, except in the special case of occupied Germany.

The United States did have a great deal of influence over occupied Germany and during the first years of the new West German state. The crucial 1948 monetary reform in the Bizone was largely designed and implemented by American and British occupation authorities, although local German authorities also participated. A new currency was introduced in a manner that favored particular groups and destroyed part of the wealth of others; this was not a reform that could have been implemented by a democratic government.[87] West Germany also agreed to restrain fiscal and monetary expansion in 1950–51 in return for special EPU credits to finance a large deficit, although it is not clear that the German government would have behaved differently in the EPU's absence.[88] Such international coordination was obviously exceptional because Germany was not a sovereign country (especially at the time of monetary reform) and had recently been defeated in war.

The most determined ECA effort to use counterpart funds to influence macroeconomic policies occurred in France and peaked in 1948.[89] The ECA initially refused to release funds because they would permit the French government to sustain inflationary policies. It demanded that the government increase tax revenues and introduce monetary reforms to reduce inflation and threatened that a refusal might mean a congressional aid cut. In the end, the ECA did agree to release counterpart funds to cover the French budget deficit in exchange for a commitment to lower the ceiling on government bor-

86. Price, *Marshall Plan and Its Meaning*, pp. 314, 326.

87. Henry C. Wallich, *Mainsprings of the German Revival* (New Haven, Conn.: Yale University Press, 1955), pp. 68–73.

88. Germany had already introduced monetary and fiscal restraint before seeking credits from the EPU, and the restraint measures agreed to with the EPU had actually been proposed by German officials. Diebold, *Trade and Payments in Western Europe*, pp. 114–29.

89. A good account of this episode can be found in Wexler, *Marshall Plan Revisited*, pp. 101–7.

rowing from the central bank, just one of the demands made earlier.[90] The United States backed down from its initial demands to avoid a worse outcome—an inflationary increase in central bank lending to finance the government's deficit.[91] The United States was also sympathetic to the French government's claim that austerity would strengthen radical political forces.[92]

The ECA felt that its pressure had made an important contribution to bringing about French monetary and fiscal stability.[93] Yet France continued to pursue expansionary policies through the early 1950s, and the resulting balance-of-payments deficits continued to be financed in large part by American aid and military spending. For example, when France experienced large deficits in 1950–51, strict import controls were reintroduced, and American aid prevented the remaining deficits from seriously constraining macroeconomic policy.[94] American diplomatic pressure for less expansionary policies had a marginal effect because the ECA was willing to finance France's budget and payments deficits for political reasons and American military spending financed a substantial portion of France's external deficit.

In the case of Italy, American officials called for stimulative fiscal policies to increase investment and living standards and reduce Italy's payments surpluses with other European countries.[95] The conservative Italian government resisted intense diplomatic pressure, eventually accepting more ERP investment funds than it had initially requested, although still not as much as the ECA wished to give.[96] Italy continued

90. Wexler, citing internal ECA documents, states that this was "the only condition" attached to ECA approval of the release of counterpart: ibid., pp. 107, 279. Others suggest that the French government made other concessions but do not provide direct evidence; Price, *Marshall Plan and Its Meaning*, p. 105; Hogan, *Marshall Plan*, p. 155.

91. Wexler, *Marshall Plan Revisited*, p. 107.

92. Price, *Marshall Plan and Its Meaning*, p. 105; Hogan, *Marshall Plan*, pp. 154–55.

93. Price, *Marshall Plan and Its Meaning*, p. 105; Lincoln Gordon, former ECA official, cited in Stanley Hoffmann and Charles Maier, eds., *The Marshall Plan: A Retrospective* (Boulder, Colo.: Westview Press, 1984), p. 55. This view is shared by some historians; e.g., Hogan, *Marshall Plan*, pp. 206–7.

94. Triffin, *Europe and the Money Muddle*, p. 187; Milward, *Reconstruction of Western Europe*, p. 170.

95. ECA officials also urged more expansive policies on other governments at certain times, including Germany and France in late 1950 and early 1951; Hogan, *Marshall Plan*, pp. 410–11.

96. Price, *Marshall Plan and Its Meaning*, pp. 275–77; Charles Kindleberger and Lincoln Gordon, cited in Hoffmann and Maier, *Marshall Plan*, pp. 11, 67.

to pursue restrictive policies, and its European export surpluses pro-
voked complaints about its deflationary policy.[97]

The ECA also tried to influence Britain's policies but to no avail. The
Labour government was committed to maintaining full employment
and spending heavily on social services, and the impact was highly expansionary. The ECA frequently criticized the government's inflationary policies but was unable to use counterpart leverage to persuade it
to cut spending.[98] In 1949–50, the ECA cut back its aid to Britain (aid
was eliminated in 1950) in reaction to generous spending on social
services. The United States wanted Britain to devote a greater share of
national income to investment. Cuts in American aid did limit the government's spending on consumption because it preferred to maintain
a high rate of investment.[99] Nevertheless, American actions had no effect over British spending other than what was directly financed by
American aid. In other words, if the United States had provided more
aid, British policy would have been more expansionary.

Even though American diplomatic initiatives had little impact on
European macroeconomic policies, American financial assistance did
permit governments to pursue more stimulative policies than would
otherwise have been possible.[100] In fact, financial support had a far
greater stimulative effect on European policies than did diplomatic efforts to persuade governments to restrain inflationary tendencies.[101]

The United States agreed to finance expansionary Western European
policies because it feared the economic, political, and strategic consequences of failing to do so. In the absence of American aid, states would
have been forced to pursue more autarkic policies; and cuts in European government spending required to eliminate budget and trade
deficits might strengthen radical and Communist elements. Many European governments had not planned alternate strategies if American
aid was not forthcoming; they saw no politically viable alternative to
rapid economic expansion. As a senior State Department official later
stated, the need for American aid resulted from "the shape and struc-

97. Milward, *Reconstruction of Western Europe*, pp. 170, 197–98.
98. Wexler, *Marshall Plan Revisited*, pp. 111–12. Lincoln Gordon, a former ECA official, recollected that the United States made "no serious effort" to control the British
government's use of counterpart funds; in Hoffmann and Maier, *Marshall Plan*, p. 55.
99. Arkes, *Bureaucracy*, pp. 310–11.
100. This is a central theme of Milward, *Reconstruction of Western Europe*.
101. Ibid., pp. 98–99.

ture and objectives of domestic policy. And these were regarded, by all concerned, as fixed factors, as necessary conditions, as commitments that had to be supported by the program, and specifically, of course, by very large external aid."[102] This was evident from the manner in which aid was distributed. National allocations were based almost exclusively on projected payments deficits, which varied according to the degree of expansion imparted independently by national governments to national economies. This variety in national policies was simply accepted except in the most extreme cases (e.g., Italy and France). The ERP was intended to permit European governments to invest heavily for future growth and prosperity without reducing current consumption. Thus, the European political imperative of expansionary macroeconomic policies was made economically possible by the U.S. imperative of containing communism.[103]

Indirect Macroeconomic Policy Coordination

Theoretically, macroeconomic policies could be coordinated indirectly by coordinating alternative international adjustment policies. Agreements to fix exchange rates, limit the use of trade controls, and promote payment liberalization in Europe could force governments to adjust macroeconomic policies in order to meet their commitments.

IMF members agreed to maintain fixed parities, which theoretically reduced their freedom to devalue in order to eliminate payments imbalances. The United States hoped this commitment would impose the external discipline of international market pressures on foreign governments' macroeconomic policies. Some analysts assert that the fixed exchange rate commitment did discourage governments from pursuing inflationary policies that would put downward pressure on the exchange rate.[104] But in practice, fixed exchange rates posed a minimal constraint on macroeconomic policies. States unilaterally determined and adjusted exchange rates to preserve policy-making autonomy. In particular, European states devalued their currencies in the late 1940s to avoid pressure to deflate to eliminate differences between inflated European price levels and more stable American ones.[105] The United

---

102. Harold van B. Cleveland, cited in Hoffmann and Maier, *Marshall Plan*, pp. 62–3.
103. Milward, *Reconstruction of Western Europe*, pp. 53–54.
104. Ibid., p. 195.
105. Triffin, *Europe and the Money Muddle*, p. 72.

States and Canada were completely unconstrained by exchange-rate commitments. The U.S. did not have to adjust any policies to maintain the value of the dollar. Its trade surpluses did not lead to domestic inflation because the surpluses were small relative to the size of the American economy and because it gave away much of the surplus through the ERP and overseas military expenditures. Canada permitted its exchange rate to fluctuate in order to free national policy-making from the fixed exchange rate constraint.

The commitments that European states made in the EPU probably did have an indirect impact on members' macroeconomic policies. EPU members agreed to eliminate controls on payments within Europe, make settlements of net positions in a mixture of gold (or dollars) and credit, and limit their use of quantitative trade restrictions for balance-of-payments purposes. If these commitments were upheld, countries running deficits in intra-European trade would have no option but to deflate to eliminate the deficit. The consensus among students of the EPU is that it did discourage governments from pursuing highly expansionary policies. "The tendency was to push policies into a middle range of choice, mildly inflationary and expansionist" that still left countries with a considerable range for variation in policy.[106] Many governments did restrain monetary (but not fiscal) policy in response to payments deficits during these years.[107] At the same time, however, they frequently reintroduced import restrictions when faced with large deficits in order to avoid absorbing the entire burden of adjustment through deflation. American aid and military spending also allowed European states to pursue expansionary policies without generating payments crises. Thus, despite the EPU commitments, the overall effect of international coordination of all forms of macroeconomic adjustment policy was to reduce international market constraints on national policy choices.

106. Milward, *Reconstruction of Western Europe*, p. 331 (quotation); see also Triffin, *Europe and the Money Muddle*, p. 201, and Hogan, *Marshall Plan*, pp. 437–38.

107. Michael Michaely, *The Responsiveness of Demand Policies to Balance of Payments: Postwar Patterns* (New York: National Bureau of Economic Research, 1971), pp. 30–33, 42–46.

CONCLUSIONS

International coordination of macroeconomic adjustment policies in the period 1945–55 can be briefly summarized as follows. Coordination of external strategies of adjustment was minimal, with the significant exception of the EPU. States relied heavily on trade controls, capital controls, and exchange-rate adjustments to insulate national macroeconomic conditions from international market influences. Agreements made in the GATT and the IMF to liberalize trade and exchange controls had virtually no impact; states took advantage of the transitional provisions of those accords to maintain whatever controls they individually determined were necessary. Even the United States continued to rely on import restrictions to insulate its economy from international competitive pressures. Par values for exchange rates were chosen and adjusted unilaterally.

Nevertheless, American financial assistance and military spending strengthened the payments balances of European countries and permitted them to liberalize payments among themselves in the EPU as well as certain import and exchange controls. In the long run, American efforts did develop institutions that encouraged future liberalization (the GATT and the IMF), just as its financial assistance encouraged governments to turn away from alternative autarkic policies. Thus, while international coordination of external policies of adjustment had little immediate impact, it did affect the future. Trade-policy coordination was clearly liberalizing, even if policies in most countries continued to be protectionist.

Coordination of symptom-management policies was significant, primarily in the form of American financing for European payments deficits and American military spending overseas. The IMF was largely irrelevant during these years, and coordination of balance-of-payments financing occurred primarily in bilateral negotiations between the United States and individual foreign governments. Inflows of American dollars permitted Western Europe and Japan to pursue expansive reconstruction and full employment policies and sustained U.S. exports. Still, the United States was not able to persuade foreign governments to alter external or internal policies of adjustment as a condition for balance-of-payments assistance. There was no coordinated intervention in foreign-exchange markets because private foreign-exchange markets were not active. Negotiated mutual adjustment of monetary and fiscal policies was also negligible, despite occasionally intense U.S. pressure. For its part, the United States ignored foreign pleas for expansionary policies that might directly stimulate imports from Europe.

The heavy reliance on unilateral, external strategies of adjustment is consistent with the economic-structural argument developed in Chapter 2. Governments in Western Europe were determined not to coordinate monetary and fiscal policies (i.e., internal policies of adjustment). Most faced severe domestic political threats and wanted the freedom to pursue stimulative reconstruction programs and full employment policies (or restrictive anti-inflationary policies, as in Italy). The United States, of course, also rejected the idea that it should adjust its macroeconomic policies to ease payments pressures on others.

Governments were able to use external policies of adjustment to insulate macroeconomic policies from international pressures. Market integration was very low, and governments faced few incentives or domestic political pressures to avoid external strategies of adjustment. Few industries in any country were strongly interested in increasing export opportunities because domestic demand was stimulated by reconstruction programs and full employment policies. Without much industry pressure for lower trade barriers abroad, trade and exchange controls reinforced themselves.

There was also little immediate need for international coordination of symptom-management policies. Governments could unilaterally maintain fixed exchange rates by controlling international trade and capital flows and by adjusting those exchange rates when necessary. Large-scale American financing for foreign trade deficits cannot be explained by the economic-structural argument alone. International market integration was too low to generate imbalances that required such financing. In fact, the trade imbalances of the late 1940s and early 1950s were generated by the availability of American financing and inflows of dollars generated by military spending overseas.

From the perspective of the economic-structural argument alone, such extensive international coordination of balance-of-payments financing is puzzling. The United States provided large-scale financing for its allies' trade and payments deficits, and in return the allies accepted American initiatives for liberalization that had a significant future impact. It is important to explain why the United States provided foreign aid and tolerated a huge deficit generated by overseas military expenditures. According to hegemonic stability theory, by financing European payments deficits the United States was unilaterally providing the collective good of international liberalization. The United States did so because, as a hegemon, the benefits it received (in terms of enhanced trade and investment opportunities) exceeded the cost of balance-of-payments financing it provided; thus, the direct cause of American financing was the expected benefits from international economic liberalization.

Hegemonic stability theory is only a partial explanation of American policy. Hardline multilateralists in the executive branch and isolationists in Congress would have blocked American aid to Europe and Japan had the promotion of multilateralism been the only motive. It also cannot explain why the United States spent so heavily to maintain military forces in Europe and Japan, which made an enormous contribution to their balance-of-payments positions long after Marshall Plan aid had ended (see table 4).

American national security interests in the cold war help explain aid and overseas military spending during this period, as students of political-security relations (in contrast to conventional hegemonic stability theories) have always emphasized. By the late 1940s, American policymakers had come to see the world in bipolar terms, and foreign policy in all areas was driven by the desire to contain the Soviet Union and communism. The cold war made the Marshall Plan possible and motivated heavy American military spending throughout the 1950s. Indeed, aid and military spending would probably have occurred even in the absence of an American economic interest in promoting liberalization. Hegemony is a necessary part of the explanation in the sense that the funding required to permit foreign countries to move toward economic liberalization was very large and could only be provided by a large, wealthy state. But hegemony alone cannot explain such spending.

It also cannot explain other elements of the pattern of policy coordination. According to the theory, coordination should have been high among all types of adjustment policies because all were important to U.S. economic interests at a time when the country had many ways to induce cooperation from other states. As we have seen, however, American diplomacy was rarely effective in persuading European states to adjust exchange rates or macroeconomic policies or to coordinate those policies among themselves. The United States induced international cooperation only when American financial aid permitted foreign states to pursue policy courses that they independently preferred but had been unable to pursue because of external financial constraints.

We can see limits on the utility of models of bargaining power that focus on a country's structural position in the international system. The United States had a tremendous advantage in all of the sources of power I discussed in Chapter 2: its economy accounted for well over half the total industrial output of the advanced capitalist countries and was relatively insular, it ran a large trade surplus, and the dollar's status as the leading world currency was unchallenged. Centrist and conservative governments in Western Europe also looked to the United States to defend their countries against Soviet threats. Consistent with this position, the United States took the lead in all the negotiations I have reviewed in this chapter, even those in which it was not a party (e.g., the ECSC). Proposals for policy adjustments made by other governments were not even seriously discussed, as in the case of European proposals that the United States liberalize trade barriers or pursue more expansionary macroeconomic policies.

Nevertheless, American officials often were not able to persuade foreign governments to alter macroeconomic adjustment policies, particularly monetary and fiscal ones, in part because policy coordination was not essential when international market integration was so low. More generally, European structural weaknesses during the cold war actually enhanced their bargaining power. American leaders believed that if they pushed too hard (or were seen to be pushing too hard), they might strengthen Communist political forces in Western Europe and encourage governments to pursue autarkic economic strategies. Therefore, Washington tolerated expansionary European policies; and after the Korean War began, American leaders accepted European inflation as a side effect of rearmament. American bargaining power was also occasionally undermined by divisions among various agencies, which precluded a strong American position. For example, the ECA's efforts to promote policy coordination among European governments were undermined by opposition, from the Treasury Department and elsewhere, to creating a European regional bloc insulated from the dollar area.

Even though coordination of national macroeconomic adjustment policies was not very extensive in the period 1945–55, decisions taken then set the stage for more extensive coordination in the 1960s. American bargaining had a greater impact on the long-run evolution of the international economic system than it did on the policies that foreign governments actually pursued in the late 1940s and early 1950s. The IMF fixed exchange rate system was established in the late 1940s and early 1950s when pervasive controls meant that commitments to maintaining fixed exchange rates imposed minimal constraints on national policy-making autonomy. This system, however, became entrenched by the late 1950s, constraining national policy-making in the 1960s when international market flows became more substantial. Similarly, American aid and military spending in Western Europe in the late 1940s and the 1950s allowed states to relax controls on payments and trade without severely constraining policy-making autonomy. The structure of private international commerce that developed in response subsequently generated large international market flows in the 1960s and encouraged states to coordinate exchange rates and balance-of-payments financing in order to retain a narrower degree of autonomy.

CHAPTER FOUR

Symptom Management, 1956–70

The late 1950s and the 1960s are often viewed as golden years of international economic cooperation. The economies of most advanced capitalist countries grew rapidly, trade policies became much more open, and private international financial markets began to emerge. Most leading countries maintained fixed exchange rates, and this practice is thought to have contributed to the era's prosperity and economic stability. While international cooperation centered on the IMF helped to maintain these rates, many analysts have argued that governments also coordinated macroeconomic policies in order to maintain them.[1]

This chapter reviews the record of adjustment policy coordination in the late 1950s and the 1960s and finds that coordination of monetary and fiscal policies was negligible. Governments used capital controls, occasional trade controls, and extensive coordination of international financing for payments imbalances to reconcile fixed exchange rates with macroeconomic policy-making autonomy. Financing of payments deficits and surpluses enabled governments to manage the symptoms of crossnational policy differences for extended periods. All governments, surplus and deficit alike, resisted foreign pressures to adjust monetary and fiscal policies to reduce their external payments imbalances.

Symptom management by means of international borrowing and

1. Group of Thirty, *International Macroeconomic Policy Coordination* (New York and London: Group of Thirty, 1988), pp. 8–10.

lending was possible only because market integration was still relatively limited. Trade flows were hardly larger than they had been in the previous period (relative to gross domestic product), although the relaxation of trade barriers meant that import and export volumes were now more sensitive to private market trends and policy differentials. Capital flows remained minor through the mid-1960s due to government controls and the relative underdevelopment of private international capital markets. The Eurodollar market that emerged in the early 1960s initially helped governments avoid balance-of-payments pressure to alter macroeconomic policies. By the late 1960s, however, capital flows were adding to private market imbalances that had to be offset by international borrowing and lending and by coordinated foreign exchange market intervention.

In the late 1940s and the 1950s, governments maintained fixed exchange rates in the face of divergent national policies primarily by imposing extensive controls on trade and exchange and by seeking aid from the United States. By the early 1960s, with the adoption of currency convertibility and the removal of most quantitative restrictions on nonagricultural trade, governments could no longer rely heavily on external policies to insulate their economies from international market pressures. Those that wanted to maintain fixed exchange rates now had to intervene in foreign-exchange markets to offset payments deficits or surpluses resulting from the actions of private economic agents. National reserves of foreign currencies generally were not sufficient to offset private market flows, so governments turned to coordinated intervention to stabilize currencies. This action, backed by international lending and borrowing, enabled them to manage the symptoms of crossnational macroeconomic policy divergence for extended periods, thereby reducing the need to alter policies to eliminate external surpluses or deficits.

By the late 1960s, unanticipated growth in international capital mobility through the Euromarkets was making it difficult for governments to maintain policy-making autonomy and fixed exchange rates. The volume of payments imbalances that needed to be financed to stabilize exchange rates was becoming larger than governments were willing or able to provide. Consequently, after 1970 all leading governments abandoned fixed exchange rates, preferring to retain the freedom to pursue independent macroeconomic policies.

International coordination continued to be shaped by the structure of power and security that had emerged at the end of World War II. Coordination was restricted to a small group of large advanced capitalist countries, all of which were military allies (the NATO countries and Japan). The common Soviet threat had a major impact both on their payments problems and subsequent policy coordination. American and British military spending in Europe and other regions accounted for a large share of both countries' persistent international payments deficits. At the same time, U.S. military security provided to Western Europe and Japan made these governments willing to accede to many American demands for balance-of-payments support.

Extensive exchange-rate and balance-of-payments coordination in the late 1950s and the 1960s is often considered a consequence of American hegemony. The United States clearly was the acknowledged leader of the Western bloc and had a predominant influence on international coordination. But American hegemony is not the sole explanation for extensive coordination. U. S. preeminence had declined by this period, yet policy coordination actually became more extensive. I argue that the crucial difference between the two periods (1945–55 and 1956–70) was not the extent of American power but rather the degree of international market integration. Integration was higher in the later period, meaning (according to my argument in Chapter 2) that international payments imbalances were also larger for the same degree of policy divergence. Thus, coordination of symptom-management policies needed to be more extensive if governments were determined to pursue independent policies.

International market integration, especially for short-term financial capital, continued to increase in the 1960s, and by the end of the decade international capital flows and trade imbalances were putting severe pressure on the existing pattern of coordination. As I argue in Chapter 5, fixed exchange rates were abandoned in 1972–73 when the United States and other governments became unwilling to commit the sums needed to stabilize exchange rates in the face of growing speculative capital flows and trade imbalances. These changes in the structure of the international economy were more important to the change in international policy coordination than any decline in American power or change in divergence among policies.

In Chapter 1 I discussed the reasons for the growth of international capital mobility in the 1960s. It is important to recall how government policies, especially international adjustment policies, contributed to the growth of the Euromarkets. Financial institutions located outside the United States (mainly in London) increased their deposit taking and lending in U.S. dollars in part because of economic incentives. Improved information and communication technology, the growth of international trade, and the spread of American transnational corporations all stimulated the growth of international deposit taking and lending. Freedom from government regulation and the ability to avoid withholding taxes on investment proceeds gave borrowers and lenders incentives to use the Eurodollar market rather than national capital markets.[2]

But the Euromarkets could not have grown without supportive government policies, and it is important to consider why governments tolerated and encouraged this activity despite its subsequent adverse impact on national policy-making autonomy. Most Western states believed that the Euromarkets would serve as minor adjuncts to national capital markets, which could be effectively insulated from Euromarket influences.[3] For most of the 1960s, economists and central bank officials believed that Euromarket transactions would have little impact on national macroeconomic conditions and policies.[4] It was not until the markets became well established that state leaders realized they might have wanted to prevent the development of markets that facilitated international capital flows.

Individual states had narrower reasons for permitting the Euromarkets to develop. Britain encouraged their development in London in the late 1950s and the early 1960s at a time when most European monetary authorities discouraged foreign-currency banking.[5] The United States and continental European states took a permissive atti-

2. M. S. Mendelsohn, *Money on the Move: The Modern International Capital Market* (New York: McGraw-Hill, 1980), pp. 29–31, 148–49; Benjamin J. Cohen, *In Whose Interest? International Banking and American Foreign Policy* (New Haven, Conn.: Yale University Press/ Council on Foreign Relations, 1986), pp. 22–24.

3. Susan Strange, *International Monetary Relations*, vol. 2 of Andrew Shonfield, ed., *International Economic Relations of the Western World, 1959–1971* (London: Oxford University Press for the Royal Institute of International Affairs, 1976), p. 190. The intention to separate national from international capital markets was clearest in Britain, which encouraged the development of Euromarkets while seeking to prevent Britons from investing in them and foreigners from borrowing on the domestic capital market.

4. George W. McKenzie, *The Economics of the Euro-currency System* (London: Macmillan, 1976), pp. 9–10.

5. Ibid., p. 99; Susan Strange, *Sterling and British Policy: A Political Study of an International Currency in Decline* (London: Oxford University Press, 1971), pp. 213–14.

tude toward Euromarket growth primarily because the markets enabled states to achieve balance-of-payments objectives without undesirable changes in national policies. In effect, they helped governments manage the symptoms of incompatible policies—at least for a few years. For an American government struggling with the consequences of large balance-of-payments deficits, the Euromarkets provided attractive investment opportunities for dollar holders who might otherwise present their holdings to the United States Treasury for conversion into gold.[6]

United States capital controls, introduced to reduce the country's balance-of-payments deficits, stimulated Eurodollar lending and the Eurobond market. Controls were intended to slow the drain of capital caused by foreign borrowing on efficient American capital markets and by American-owned transnational corporations (TNCs) investing abroad. The Interest Equalization Tax, introduced in 1963, boosted the fledgling Eurobond market. Borrowers who could no longer tap into the American bond market developed the practice of floating Eurobond issues, which were generally denominated in dollars and intended to be bought by foreigners holding dollars outside the United States. Controls imposed on American TNCs in 1965 and later years encouraged them to raise investment funds on the Euromarkets and foreign capital markets.[7]

States in continental Western Europe and Japan also relied on the Euromarkets to achieve balance-of-payments objectives. In the early 1960s, a number of central banks directly encouraged commercial banks to participate in the Eurodollar market in order to achieve these objectives. Commercial banks were sometimes encouraged to deposit funds in the Eurodollar market to reduce a country's balance-of-payments surplus, at other times to borrow funds to finance a balance-of-payments deficit.[8] European central banks also deposited a portion of their dollar holdings into the Eurodollar market.[9] Central banks in surplus countries initially did not realize that investors would simply

6. Strange, *Sterling and British Policy*, p. 209.

7. For a general description of American capital controls and the domestic debates surrounding them, see James P. Hawley, "Interests, State Foreign Policy, and the World-System: The Case of the U.S. Capital Control Programs, 1961–1974," in Pat McGowan and Charles W. Kegley, Jr., eds., *Foreign Policy and the Modern World-System*, Sage International Yearbook of Foreign Policy Studies, vol. 8 (Beverly Hills, Calif.: Sage, 1983).

8. Mendelsohn, *Money on the Move*, p. 25.

9. McKenzie, *Economics of the Euro-currency System*, pp. 89–90.

convert these dollars back into surplus country currencies, thereby adding directly to the domestic money supply and inflation.[10] High interest rates made Eurodollar deposits especially attractive to central banks seeking to export dollars to avoid currency appreciation or inflation.

Thus, the emergence of large international capital flows in the form of Euromarket transactions can be traced directly to state decisions, which created incentives for private economic actors to increase their international financial transactions. American capital controls forced economic agents to go abroad in search of investment and borrowing opportunities, many central banks encouraged private banks to deposit and borrow dollars, and the British government encouraged the growth of dollar-based international finance in London.

Once abroad, economic agents discovered advantages to operating in the relatively unregulated and untaxed Euromarket environment, and it quickly became entrenched.[11] With each U. S. move to control capital outflows and each move by European central banks to take advantage of high Eurodollar deposit interest rates, "further impetus was given to the system and, as operators became more familiar with its potential, further growth occurred."[12]

Governments adopted policies that encouraged the growth of short-term international financial flows without fully realizing how seriously such transactions would undermine national monetary-policy autonomy.[13] Euromarkets proved to be highly sensitive to differences among countries in interest rates and other macroeconomic policies.[14]

The emergence of Euromarkets in the 1960s meant that private international short-term capital flows were vastly larger than they were in the preceding period (although still considerably smaller than they became in the 1970s and 1980s). Table 5 presents data on the absolute size of the Eurocurrency and Eurobond markets in the 1960s. The sensitivity of these growing private flows to interest-rate differentials and exchange-rate expectations (and therefore to crossnational differences in macroeconomic policies) meant that if states wanted to maintain fixed exchange rates, continue to liberalize international trade,

10. Mendelsohn, *Money on the Move*, p. 26.
11. Ibid., p. 34.
12. McKenzie, *Economics of the Euro-currency System*, p. 88.
13. Strange, *Sterling and British Policy*, p. 209.
14. Mendelsohn, *Money on the Move*, p. 29; McKenzie, *Economics of the Euro-currency System*, pp. 13, 15, 129–30.

Table 5. Estimated net size of Eurocurrency market and gross Eurobond and foreign bond issues, in billions of U.S. dollars

	1957	1960	1963	1964	1965	1966	1967	1968	1969	1970
Eurocurrency market	0	2[a]	7	9[a]	12[a]	15[a]	21	30	44	57
Eurobond & foreign bond	N/A	0.8	1.9	2.2	2.9	3.1	4.2	6.4	5.3	5.3

SOURCES: BIS, *Annual Report* (Basle: BIS), various issues; 1960 estimate of Eurodollar market size from George W. McKenzie, *The Economics of the Euro-currency System* (London: Macmillan, 1976), p. 89.

NOTE: The Eurocurrency market includes the total stock of Eurocurrency loans, net of interbank lending and redepositing.

[a]Lending in dollars only.

and maintain autonomy in national policy-making, they needed to intervene in foreign-exchange markets on a very large scale in order to offset private international capital flows.

The emergence of the Euromarkets helps to explain international coordination of adjustment policies in the 1960s. Coordination of financing for payments imbalances and intervention in foreign-exchange markets became increasingly necessary to offset capital flows as well as current and government account imbalances. By 1970–71, international capital market flows had grown so large that they overwhelmed coordinated market intervention, except at a cost deemed too high by most major states.

During the late 1950s and most of the 1960s, international market integration was weak enough to allow international payments imbalances to be managed by intergovernmental lending and coordinated intervention in foreign-exchange markets. It is useful to examine the sources of international payments imbalances during this period. The United States had a substantial balance-of-payments deficit almost continuously, a situation that was viewed favorably until the early 1960s because American deficits enabled foreign countries to achieve surpluses and rebuild their reserves of gold and foreign exchange, a prerequisite for their agreement to liberalize trade. Persistent deficits began to undermine confidence in the dollar in the early 1960s, however, and debates about the problem were prominent in international economic diplomacy for most of the decade. Many of the American policies described in this chapter were designed to deal with the payments deficit and the resulting outflow of gold without devaluing the dollar.

Differences between policies in the United States and abroad were only part of the reason for payments imbalances. Macroeconomic policy under the Eisenhower administration was relatively restrictive, which helped to produce large export surpluses. Policy became more expansive during the Kennedy administration, although not to an excessive degree in light of low inflation and relatively high unemployment levels.[15] Policies became more inflationary during the Johnson and (with brief periods of restriction) Nixon administrations, under the influence of expanding social welfare programs and the Vietnam War.

But the most persistent causes of payments deficits were not expansionary macroeconomic policies. As in the earlier period, military spending overseas and foreign aid imposed a drain on American balance of payments that exceeded the large U.S. surpluses on both trade and foreign direct investment (FDI) accounts for most of the period (see table 6). The United States would have had to impose severely deflationary policies in order to generate export surpluses large enough to pay for its government spending overseas—especially because foreign trade played a relatively small role in total U.S. economic activity. Severe deflation would likely have generated foreign retaliation, which would have prevented the United States from achieving its objectives. Thus, American balance-of-payments problems before the mid-1960s could not be corrected with the policy changes usually prescribed for a state experiencing an external deficit.

Nevertheless, most who were concerned treated the American payments deficit as a macroeconomic policy problem. Rather than cut American military spending in Europe and Japan, the United States and its allies called on each other to alter adjustment policies in ways that would generate a private trade and investment surplus large enough to offset the drain caused by American foreign-policy commitments.[16]

Britain also experienced persistent balance-of-payments deficits and recurrent crises in the late 1950s and the 1960s. These deficits were treated primarily as a macroeconomic policy problem, but other factors

15. Richard N. Cooper, *The Economics of Interdependence: Economic Policy in the Atlantic Community* (New York: McGraw-Hill, 1968), p. 217.

16. Many European governments were critical of escalating American military spending in the Vietnam War.

Table 6. Selected United States balance-of-payments accounts with Western Europe and Japan, in millions of dollars

	1956	1957	1958	1959	1960	1961	1962	1963	1964	1965	1966	1967	1968	1969	1970
Western Europe															
Trade balance	2397	2847	1374	200	2545	2781	2603	2897	3395	2708	1938	1581	335	1436	2893
FDI income	277	311	325	415	519	645	742	779	965	1149	1182	1323	1535	1748	2160
FDI outflow	-456	-254	-173	-476	-962	-724	-867	-924	-1388	-1479	-1805	-1480	-1001	-1209	-1904
Total private	2218	2904	1526	139	2102	2702	2478	2752	2972	2378	1315	1424	869	1975	3149
Military aid	-1886	-1542	-1514	-1236	-913	-611	-626	-753	-550	-538	-285	-412	-360	-295	-231
Military expenditures	-1676	-1796	-1852	-1674	-1638	-1516	-1620	-1511	-1484	-1458	-1520	-1616	-1537	-1629	-1777
Total government	-3562	-3338	-3366	-2910	-2551	-2127	-2246	-2264	-2034	-1996	-1805	-2028	-1897	-1924	-2008
Japan															
Trade balance						713	182	323	205	-376	-625	-345	-1110	-1390	-1246
Military expenditures						-385	-378	-362	-326	-346	-476	-538	-580	-651	-670

SOURCE: U.S. Department of Commerce, *Survey of Current Business*, various issues.
NOTES:
This table is comparable to table 4 except that "other aid" is not included here because the volume of nonmilitary aid to Western Europe was negligible after the late 1950s.

Data for Japan before 1961 are not available in the sources consulted. FDI and military aid are not reported for Japan because the amounts were negligible.

were at least as important. British policies during this period have been characterized as stop-and-go. Periods of monetary and fiscal expansion to generate full employment alternated with periods of restriction designed to correct payments deficits. Like the United States, much of Britain's payments problem was immune to macroeconomic policy shifts. Sterling faced periodic crises of confidence because of large balances still held abroad by sterling area countries, and British spending on foreign aid and military forces overseas imposed a constant drain on the balance of payments.[17]

Japanese policies were expansionary for most of the period, but this situation did not create international adjustment problems because of tight government control over domestic and international economic activity. Interest rates were kept very low and credit directed to government-selected industries. Fiscal policy was not used for demand management purposes before the mid-1960s; the government maintained a balanced budget, which was not difficult in a period of rapid growth and rising revenues. Budget deficits did occur in the mid-1960s, helping to stimulate the economy; but they did not produce trade deficits because of import restrictions, an undervalued currency, and the rapidly improving international competitive position of Japanese manufacturing industries. In fact, by the late 1960s Japan had a surplus in its trade with the United States (see table 6) and was urged by the United States to reflate.

Most continental European countries experienced trade and payments surpluses during the late 1950s and the 1960s. In general, West Germany, the Netherlands, and Belgium consistently pursued restrictive macroeconomic policies. The fact that these policies did not lead to unacceptably high unemployment had a great deal to do with export-led growth: undervalued currencies and American payments deficits permitted high levels of employment in export industries and reduced the need for stimulative domestic policies. Thus, it was relatively easy to achieve both price stability and full employment; "if confronted with the direct choice at home, there is little doubt that most governments would move quickly to reduce unemployment."[18] Italy also pursued restrained macroeconomic policies, with a brief inflationary interlude accompanied by a balance-of-payments crisis in 1963–64. France pur-

17. Strange, *Sterling and British Policy.*
18. Cooper, *Economics of Interdependence,* p. 202.

sued growth-oriented policies but experienced balance-of-payments problems only in 1958 and 1968–69. The franc was devalued in 1958 to an extremely competitive level, which later helped prevent expansionary policies from generating trade deficits.

International discussions of macroeconomic adjustment issues were conducted throughout the late 1950s and the 1960s in a wide variety of forums, the most important of which involved the Group of Ten (G10) states. This chapter deals with debates and policy coordination as they relate to each type of international adjustment policy identified in Chapter 2.

INTERNATIONAL COORDINATION OF EXTERNAL POLICIES OF ADJUSTMENT

Trade and Exchange Controls

International policy coordination in the late 1950s and the 1960s encouraged states to rely much less on controls on trade and current account payments as instruments of international adjustment than they had in earlier postwar years. Improved economic conditions in Europe and Japan allowed governments to liberalize trade without threatening domestic economic stability. International policy coordination helped reduce the use of trade and exchange controls to achieve equilibrium in two ways. First, general moves to liberalize trade and make currencies convertible made it harder, administratively and politically, for states to impose trade restrictions when faced with balance-of-payments deficits. Second, when states did impose trade restrictions, diplomatic pressures tended to limit their severity and prevent retaliation that could have threatened the system as a whole.

By far the most important move to liberalize the international economy was Western Europe and Japan's acceptance of currency convertibility between 1958 and 1961. Convertibility meant that nonresident holders of these currencies could present holdings to the countries' central banks to exchange for dollars or other convertible currencies.[19] It quickly became an unquestioned part of economic relations among

19. IMF, *The International Monetary Fund, 1945–1965: Twenty Years of International Monetary Cooperation.* Volume 1: *Chronicle,* by J. Keith Horsefield (Washington, D.C.: IMF, 1969), p. 466; Strange, *International Monetary Relations,* pp. 36–37.

advanced capitalist countries. Extensive trade and capital controls remained through the 1960s, but there were no moves to suspend currency convertibility, even by countries facing very large payments deficits.[20]

Western Europe's move to currency convertibility represented the achievement of an important U.S. economic objective, which American policies had made possible. Western Europe and Japan had been able to achieve payments surpluses and rebuild their gold reserves because the United States had large payments deficits and was willing to allow foreign countries to exchange some of their dollar holdings for gold. The pattern of U.S.–European financial flow described in table 4 continued into the 1960s (see table 6). As the table reveals, the United States experienced a surplus in merchandise trade and FDI accounts for most of this period as well as a substantial government account deficit generated by overseas military spending and foreign aid. Thus, American balance-of-payments deficits continued to reflect American security interests in the Cold War as much as American hegemonic interests in international liberalization.

West European currency convertibility opened up opportunities for international financial transactions at a time when rapid growth in national economies and international trade was fueling greater private interest in international finance. Private foreign exchange trading and short-term capital flows grew very rapidly in the wake of convertibility. Capital flows became responsive to crossnational differences in interest rates, increasing the volume of payments imbalances that had to be financed if exchange-rate parities were to be maintained.[21] Thus, convertibility encouraged the development of mechanisms for symptom management.

Currency convertibility was soon followed by moves to eliminate discriminatory trade and exchange controls targeted at North America. By the early 1960s, under intense diplomatic pressure from the United States, Canada, the IMF, and the GATT, most Western European countries (and, by 1964, Japan) abandoned their reliance on the IMF transitional provisions and the GATT balance-of-payments safeguards that

20. As I discuss later, the United States did suspend dollar convertibility into gold by the late 1960s and formalized the suspension in 1971, but this move did not affect the convertibility of the dollar into other currencies through foreign-exchange markets.

21. Strange, *International Monetary Relations*, pp. 57–58; Leland B. Yeager, *International Monetary Relations: Theory, History, and Policy* (New York: Harper and Row, 1966), p. 376.

had permitted them to impose discriminatory quantitative restrictions on imports.[22] Strong payments positions reduced the risks of liberalization, and rapid economic growth facilitated adjustment to international competition in previously protected industrial sectors.

Currency convertibility was the most important factor increasing the sensitivity of trade balances to macroeconomic conditions after the late 1950s, but trade liberalizing agreements also had some impact. The Kennedy Round of GATT negotiations in 1963–67 led to substantial tariff cuts by most advanced capitalist countries, but these cuts were not phased in until 1968–71 and had little impact on trade-market integration in the 1960s. Trade liberalization within the European Economic Community (EEC) and the European Free Trade Association (EFTA) substantially reduced trade barriers among the participating countries.

Nevertheless, the volume of international trade relative to the size of national economies was not much greater than it had been in the preceding period and was significantly lower than in subsequent periods. Table 2 reveals that among the Group of Seven countries only Italy experienced a substantial increase in the volume of trade (imports plus exports) relative to gross domestic product (GDP) between 1955 and 1970. What the table does not reveal, however, is that trade flows had become much more sensitive to changes in macroeconomic conditions because most governments had relaxed their earlier direct control over imports and exports.

International agreements also limited the freedom that states had to reintroduce controls for macroeconomic adjustment. For example, as long as states remained under the transitional provisions of the IMF, they were able to introduce and modify exchange controls, largely without fund interference. But once the full obligations of membership were accepted, any new restrictions had to be approved by the IMF, regardless of how bad the member's payments situation had become.[23]

22. On this process, see IMF, *International Monetary Fund, 1945–1965,* vol. 1; *The International Monetary Fund, 1945–1965: Twenty Years of International Monetary Cooperation.* Volume 2: *Analysis,* by Margaret Garritsen de Vries and J. Keith Horsefield (Washington, D.C.: IMF, 1969); Gerard Curzon, *Multilateral Commercial Diplomacy: The General Agreement on Tariffs and Trade and Its Impact on National Commercial Policies and Techniques* (London: Joseph, 1965); and Gardner Patterson, *Discrimination in International Trade: The Policy Issues, 1945–1965* (Princeton: Princeton University Press, 1966).

23. IMF, *International Monetary Fund, 1945–1965,* vol. 2, p. 284.

Coordinated measures to relax trade and exchange controls also eroded national administrative structures used to implement trade and exchange restrictions, making it significantly more difficult for states to reintroduce such controls when payments imbalances emerged.

Determined states did continue to impose trade controls unilaterally when faced with serious balance-of-payments crises in the 1960s, but such instances were rare compared with the late 1940s and the 1950s. Among the Group of Seven countries, there were only four cases in which trade restrictions were imposed in reaction to actual or anticipated balance-of-payments deficits: France in 1956–59 and 1968–69, Canada in 1962, and Britain in 1964–66. In each case, restrictions were imposed unilaterally and generated considerable international controversy, but negotiations helped to ensure that the restrictions were limited in scope and duration and that other states did not retaliate.[24] These cases indicate that leading states still did rely on trade restrictions to reduce payments deficits that threatened the maintenance of preferred macroeconomic policies and exchange-rate parities. Thus, the fact that negotiation was making the trading system more liberal should not blind us to the use of trade controls as instruments of international adjustment. Since the mid-1970s, trade restrictions have not been used to insulate national policies from international market pressures despite the magnitude of trade deficits and the slowdown in the process of negotiating liberalization.

Controls on Capital Flows

Unilateral controls on short-term capital flows were widely used in the late 1950s and the 1960s to insulate national macroeconomic policies from international influences. Currency convertibility in the late 1950s was accompanied by some easing of the comprehensive controls that had been common in most countries since World War II. When market incentives for short-term international capital flows began to

24. For more detailed discussion of these cases, see I. Kravis, *Domestic Interests and International Obligations: Safeguards in International Trade Organizations* (Philadelphia: University of Pennsylvania Press, 1963), pp. 149, 156–57; John H. Jackson, *World Trade and the Law of GATT* (Indianapolis: Bobbs-Merrill, 1969), pp. 307, 314, 711–13; Gerard Curzon and Victoria Curzon, "The Management of Trade Relations in the GATT," in Andrew Shonfield, ed., *International Economic Relations of the Western World, 1959–1971.* Volume 1: *Politics and Trade* (Oxford: Oxford University Press, 1976), pp. 216–22.

rise in the late 1950s and the early 1960s, however, many states responded by introducing new controls intended to reduce payments imbalances that threatened fixed exchange rates and to insulate national capital markets from conditions in the emerging Eurocurrency markets. Controls on capital movements were still widely thought to be valuable because they interfered with "hot money" movements that threatened exchange rates and the freedom of current account transactions.[25]

The controls imposed generally depended on whether the country had payments surpluses or deficits. The United States, which had persistent deficits, began to impose restrictions on capital outflows in 1963. The Interest Equalization Tax (IET) was introduced in 1963 to limit foreign issues of securities in the United States and to persuade international borrowers to issue bonds for sale in Western Europe, which Washington believed should be playing a larger role as a source of international investment capital.[26] Measures to encourage American TNCs and international banks to rely more on foreign financing for their overseas operations were introduced in 1965 and tightened in 1968.[27] As I noted earlier, an unintended consequence of these controls was to stimulate the growth of the Euromarkets, thereby undermining the national policy-making independence that the controls had been created to protect.

Another way in which the United States restricted capital account flows was by suspending dollar-gold convertibility in 1968.[28] Private dollar holders were still free to convert their dollars into other currencies through private markets, but the U.S. action put pressure on foreign central banks to stabilize exchange rates—if necessary, by altering macroeconomic policies. According to the two-tier arrangement worked out between foreign central banks and the United States Federal Reserve, the dollar price of gold would be permitted to fluctuate freely on the private international market while the official price would be maintained for transactions among central banks. Although the United States nominally stood ready to convert central bank dollar holdings

25. Cooper, *Economics of Interdependence*, pp. 242–48.

26. Hawley, "Interests, State Foreign Policy, and the World-System"; Robert V. Roosa, *The Dollar and World Liquidity* (New York: Random House, 1967), pp. 51, 140, 144.

27. Mendelsohn, *Money on the Move*, p. 33.

28. On the background and consequences of this decision, see Strange, *International Monetary Relations*, pp. 278–93.

into gold, in practice it put intense pressure on its allies not to present dollars for conversion. European central banks refused to agree formally to the U.S. request; but in March 1967 West Germany informally agreed,[29] and actual conversions by other American allies were minor.[30]

The suspension of dollar-gold convertibility by 1968 relieved pressure on the United States to adjust its policies to correct its deficit and imposed corresponding pressures on foreign central banks. Central banks that could no longer exchange their dollar holdings for American gold would have to absorb all of the surplus dollars in the system if they wanted to prevent their currencies from appreciating.

> [This] meant that there was little pressure on the United States when speculation against the dollar mounted. When confidence in the dollar weakened, the United States could just sit on the sidelines and watch as foreign central banks were forced to absorb huge quantities of dollars. The elimination of direct pressure on the United States of private gold purchases laid the basis for the policy of "benign neglect."[31]

Britain also experienced ongoing payments deficits during the 1960s and relied heavily on capital controls to maintain some autonomy in national macroeconomic policy-making. While London actively solicited Euromarket business, it also sought to insulate the national capital market from Euromarket influences. For example, British residents were permitted to invest in foreign securities only with so-called investment sterling, which sold at a 10–50 percent premium over sterling-dollar parity.[32]

In contrast to the practice of these two deficit countries, surplus countries such as Germany and Switzerland wanted to prevent capital inflows that could generate inflationary pressures or trigger currency revaluation. One common form of control was to prohibit interest pay-

29. David P. Calleo and Benjamin M. Rowland, *America and the World Political Economy: Atlantic Dreams and National Realities* (Bloomington: Indiana University Press, 1973), p. 284; Paul Volcker and Toyoo Gyohten, *Changing Fortunes: The World's Money and the Threat to American Leadership* (New York: Times Books, 1992), p. 43; Strange, *International Monetary Relations*, p. 283.

30. Charles A. Coombs, *The Arena of International Finance* (New York: John Wiley and Sons, 1976), pp. 171–72.

31. Fred L. Block, *The Origins of International Economic Disorder: A Study of United States International Monetary Policy from World War II to the Present* (Berkeley: University of California Press, 1977), p. 194.

32. Strange, *Sterling and British Policy*, pp. 66–67, 147, 154–57, 204.

ments on foreign deposits in domestic banks. At other times, authorities in surplus countries required national banks to recycle short-term capital inflows immediately back into foreign currencies.[33]

There was very little international coordination of capital controls in the 1960s. At the same time, there was relatively little international conflict, "since countries discouraging capital inflow have generally been in surplus, while those discouraging capital outflow have been in deficit."[34]

Exchange-rate Adjustment

One of the central goals of the international monetary regime designed at Bretton Woods had been to maintain fixed exchange rates, thereby preventing countries from manipulating currency values to achieve narrow national interests at the expense of international openness and stability. Nevertheless, the IMF articles of agreement provided for exchange-rate adjustments to eliminate *fundamental disequilibrium*—in other words, exchange rates that were so over- or undervalued that the fixed exchange rate itself became an obstacle to openness and stability. In order to ensure that countries did not take advantage of this exception to the fixed exchange rate rules, IMF members were supposed to coordinate exchange-rate adjustments through the fund.

In Chapter 3 I showed that many countries unilaterally fixed and adjusted their exchange rates in the late 1940s and the 1950s contrary to IMF rules. In the late 1950s and the 1960s, exchange-rate adjustments were rare; indeed, countries proved to be extremely unwilling to adjust rates even in the face of persistent fundamental disequilibrium. This unwillingness reflected the continuing fear of unleashing competitive devaluations and beggar-thy-neighbor trade policies and the belief that stable exchange rates were necessary to promote international trade, investment, and prosperity. These official beliefs were maintained almost without question until the late 1960s, despite much academic debate.[35]

---

33. Cooper, *Economics of Interdependence*, pp. 144–45.
34. Ibid., p. 248.
35. See John S. Odell, *U.S. International Monetary Policy: Markets, Power, and Ideas as Sources of Change* (Princeton: Princeton University Press, 1982), on the strength of official opinion in favor of stable exchange rates until the late 1960s and the gradual infiltration into the United States government of academic arguments for fluctuating exchange rates.

General objections to exchange-rate flexibility were reinforced by narrower political considerations. In surplus countries, export industries could see that a currency revaluation would undermine their international competitiveness and therefore lobbied against it. On the other hand, deficit states typically sought to avoid devaluation because it would be perceived as an admission that government policies had failed. Thus, exchange-rate adjustments that might be desirable from the perspective of external equilibrium were opposed by potential domestic losers, including governments themselves.

International coordination of exchange-rate adjustments was minimal. Governments resisted foreign pressure to alter their rates; and when adjustments did occur, they were introduced unilaterally. A major obstacle to international coordination was the fact that exchange-rate issues were so important to economic conditions and government popularity. Therefore, the IMF had not been given the right to request that members change their par values; it could only approve or disapprove changes proposed by members.

> The passive role in exchange rate changes assigned to the Fund, and the continued sensitivities of several members, had the result that, in the midst of the crucial concerns of the middle 1960's—the balance of payments deficits of major nations and the problem of international liquidity—the Board had not, by the end of 1965, discussed the general role of exchange rates in balance of payments adjustment.[36]

International coordination was a significant factor in only one adjustment of a major currency's exchange rate—the November 1967 devaluation of sterling. American diplomatic pressure helped to persuade Britain to avoid devaluing earlier in the decade, despite strong market pressure and recurring balance-of-payments crises. American leaders feared that if sterling succumbed to speculative attacks, then heavy pressure for dollar devaluation would soon follow (as indeed happened).[37] By 1967, continental European countries were equally determined that sterling must be devalued, and they refused to provide any further credits to finance British deficits until it was. The size of

36. IMF, *International Monetary Fund, 1945–1965*, vol. 2, pp. 115–16.
37. Strange, *Sterling and British Policy*, pp. 74, 344.

the devaluation (15 percent) was influenced by creditors' insistence that it be substantial, yet not so large as to give Britain an unfair advantage in international trade.[38]

In contrast, France and Germany proved unable to coordinate exchange-rate adjustments in 1968–69, even in the face of clear misalignment and strong market pressure. Neither government wanted to give in to foreign pressure on such a central economic policy issue, and the United States also refused to devalue to dollar as part of a package deal involving revaluation of the mark and devaluation of the franc.[39] Market pressure against the franc and the mark remained intense, leading to the surprise French decision to devalue by 11 percent in August 1969, "while the rest of Europe was away at the beaches."[40] Although other states were displeased by the manner of the devaluation, the amount was consistent with what had been discussed in late 1968. In October 1969 the German government let the mark float, eventually settling on a revaluation of 9 percent. Neither France nor Germany had consulted with their EEC partners before these exchange-rate changes, let alone the IMF.[41]

With the single exception of the 1967 devaluation of sterling, international coordination of adjustment policies did not extend to exchange-rate changes. Coordination among central banks to intervene in foreign-exchange markets to stabilize exchange rates was extensive and very successful, but top political leaders in each country still made unilateral decisions to adjust exchange rates.[42]

---

38. Strange, *International Monetary Relations*, pp. 138–40.

39. Central bank governors agreed on a realignment of the franc and mark in 1968, but this decision was rejected by their political superiors. Coombs, *Arena of International Finance*, pp. 181–86. On debates in 1968–69, see also Loukas Tsoukalis, *The Politics and Economics of European Monetary Integration* (London: Allen and Unwin, 1977), pp. 70–75; Robert W. Russell, "Transgovernmental Interaction in the International Monetary System, 1960–1972," *International Organization* 27 (Autumn 1973), p. 463; Edward A. Kolodziej, *French International Policy under De Gaulle and Pompidou: The Politics of Grandeur* (Ithaca: Cornell University Press, 1974), pp. 208–9; and Strange, *International Monetary Relations*, pp. 325–26.

40. Strange, *International Monetary Relations*, p. 328.

41. Tsoukalis, *Politics and Economics*, pp. 76–77.

42. Otmar Emminger, "International Cooperation—A Personal View," in *Economic Cooperation from the Inside*, by Marjorie Deanne and Robert Pringle (New York: Group of Thirty, 1984), pp. 43–44. Emminger was a central figure in the West German central bank and the BIS. Russell, "Transgovernmental Interaction," pp. 462–63.

INTERNATIONAL COORDINATION OF SYMPTOM-MANAGEMENT POLICIES

Extensive coordination of symptom management was the characteristic feature of international adjustment policies and diplomacy in the late 1950s and the 1960s. Governments relied much less on external policies of adjustment, such as trade controls and exchange-rate adjustments, than they had in earlier postwar years. Controls on capital account flows were extensive, but by the late 1960s they were undermined by the growth of the Euromarkets.

At the same time, most governments continued to formulate policies in response to domestic priorities and resist international diplomatic pressures to adjust monetary and fiscal policies. With markets more sensitive to policy differentials than they had been in the preceding decade, governments were faced with reconciling their preference for autonomy with their desire to fix exchange rates and liberalize trade. This reconciliation was achieved primarily through symptom-management policies. International financing of payments imbalances and coordinated intervention in foreign-exchange markets allowed most governments to avoid altering domestic macroeconomic policies, severely restricting international trade, or abandoning fixed exchange rates.

I discuss three types of symptom-management strategies involving intergovernmental balance-of-payments lending: coordinated intervention in foreign-exchange markets backed by short-term lending through the Bank for International Settlements (BIS), longer-term financing provided by the IMF, and special arrangements to finance ongoing U.S. payments deficits. Much of this lending, especially the IMF's, was accompanied by conditions intended to encourage deficit states to liberalize trade policies, maintain fixed exchange rates, and pursue restrained monetary and fiscal policies. As we have seen, the first two conditions were largely met; however, as I will discuss later, they had little impact on monetary and fiscal policies.

Short-term Lending and Exchange-rate Stabilization

International coordination was critical to the maintenance of fixed exchange rates in the late 1950s and the 1960s. States with currency par values threatened by private market pressures intervened using individual reserves of gold and currencies. Foreign exchange market intervention is more effective if central banks from deficit and surplus states coordinate their actions, and central banks worked closely to ensure that individual interventions were mutually supportive. Even when they believed that exchange-rate adjustments were necessary, central bankers worked together to prevent markets from forcing adjustments.[43]

Nevertheless, if a payments deficit (equivalent to an excess of supply in private foreign exchange markets) became very large, an individual state's international reserves could quickly be exhausted in an attempt to support demand for the currency at the existing par value. States facing serious payments deficits in the 1960s could draw on extensive short-term credits to supplement their limited supplies of international reserves. The largest source of short-term credit was the network of bilateral swap arrangements among the United States Federal Reserve, the central banks of eleven other advanced capitalist states, and the BIS.[44] Negotiated by U.S. initiative, the swap arrangements provided credits primarily to the United States and Britain, although Belgium, Canada, France, Italy, and Japan also borrowed money. These arrangements were bilateral agreements between central banks, each agreeing to provide standby credits that another country could drawn on without giving much notice. The borrowing central bank (i.e., that of the deficit country) assumed the entire exchange-rate risk. The first swap arrangements were negotiated in 1962; by late 1967 the total volume of credit available to the United States (and, collectively, to the others) was $7.1 billion, far more than the $1.3 billion of automatic drawing rights then available in the IMF but very small relative to the volume of foreign-currency trading in subsequent decades.[45] The Basle Agreement, first negotiated in 1961, provided a similar source of assistance to Britain.[46]

The Gold Pool arrangements offered short-term credits to stabilize the value of the dollar. Under the Bretton Woods system the U.S. dollar

43. On coordinated intervention in foreign-exchange markets, see Coombs, *Arena of International Finance*, which provides many examples.

44. On swap arrangements in general, see Kenneth W. Dam, *The Rules of the Game: Reform and Evolution in the International Monetary System* (Chicago: University of Chicago Press, 1982), pp. 150–51; Cooper, *Economics of Interdependence*, pp. 48, 212–14; and Strange, *International Monetary Relations*, pp. 85–86, 135–37.

45. Cooper, *Economics of Interdependence*, p. 213.

46. Strange, *International Monetary Relations*, pp. 157–63. Conditions were attached to the 1966 and 1968 renewals of the Basle Agreement to limit credit availability in light of Britain's inability to solve its balance-of-payments problems.

was fixed in terms of gold while other currencies were fixed in terms of dollars. In the early 1960s, investors could speculate against the dollar by selling dollars for gold. Defense of the dollar therefore necessitated intervention in private gold markets, just as defense of other currencies' par values necessitated intervention in private foreign-exchange markets. Britain and the United States reached a bilateral agreement to share the burden of intervention late in 1960. It was replaced in October 1961 by an agreement to establish a multilateral buffer stock of gold called the Gold Pool, which the Bank of England used to stabilize the price of gold at the official level. The United States provided half the gold (worth $135 million) while the Europeans collectively provided the other half.[47] The Gold Pool effectively stabilized gold's private market price at the official price from 1961 to early 1968. It was replaced in March 1968 by the two-tier gold market agreement, discussed as a control on capital mobility earlier in the chapter. Declining confidence in the dollar made European countries reluctant to use their gold reserves to defend the dollar against private speculators.[48]

IMF Lending

The most important mechanisms for providing short-term payments finance to support coordinated intervention in foreign-exchange markets (the swap arrangements and the Basle Agreement) depended upon the existence of longer-term financing to cover imbalances that could not be reversed in the short period in which central bank financing was available.[49] The need for longer-term financing provided an opportunity for attaching conditions to balance-of-payments lending because it was not feasible to negotiate and attach policy conditions to emergency credits.

The IMF provided an enormous volume of international financing for payments imbalances during the period 1956–70. While the fund

47. Ibid., pp. 75–78; IMF, *International Monetary Fund, 1945–1965*, vol. 1, p. 485.

48. Strange, *International Monetary Relations*, pp. 282–89; Margaret Garritsen de Vries, *The International Monetary Fund, 1966–1971: The System under Stress*, 3 vols. (Washington, D.C.: IMF, 1976), vol. 1, 402–4.

49. Richard N. Gardner, *Sterling-Dollar Diplomacy in Current Perspective: The Origins and the Prospects of Our International Economic Order*, expanded ed. with rev. intro. (New York: Columbia University Press, 1980), pp. xviii–xix; Roosa, *Dollar and World Liquidity*, pp. 57–58, 258.

Table 7. Drawings from the IMF, in millions of U.S. dollars

	1956–60	1961–65	1966–70
Canada	—	300	391
France	394	—	1731
Germany	—	—	540
Italy	—	225	133
Japan	125	—	—
Britain	562	3900	2523
United States	—	960	1030
Group of Seven total	1081	5385	6348
All IMF members	2468	7780	9770

SOURCES: IMF, *The International Monetary Fund, 1945–1965: Twenty Years of International Monetary Cooperation.* Volume 2: *Analysis,* by Margaret Garritsen de Vries and J. Keith Horsefield (Washington, D.C.: IMF, 1969), pp. 460–63; Margaret Garritsen de Vries, *The International Monetary Fund, 1966–1971: The System under Stress,* 3 vols. (Washington, D.C.: IMF, 1976), 1: 330–32.

lent little to advanced capitalist states between 1948 and 1955, in 1956 it provided a credit of more than $561 million to help Britain meet a payments crisis set off by the Suez conflict. This credit permitted Britain to weather the crisis without imposing additional trade restrictions, a perfect example of the IMF's intended function.[50] Table 7 lists amounts lent to leading advanced capitalist states and the total amount of IMF lending during this period.

International balance-of-payments lending on this scale represented a significant degree of adjustment policy coordination. Regardless of the intense debates over international monetary system reforms during these years, the IMF's basic lending activities were not seriously questioned by any leading advanced capitalist state. Coordination to change the system proved difficult, but it was extensive within the framework established in the late 1940s and the 1950s.

International debates about balance-of-payments financing in the late 1950s and the 1960s focused on the issue of international liquidity— the volume of international reserves and credit facilities available to cover imbalances in payments positions that threatened the maintenance of fixed exchange rates and trade liberalization.[51] If international liquidity were insufficient, states would be forced to rely more heavily on exchange-rate adjustments, macroeconomic policy adjustments, or

50. IMF, *International Monetary Fund, 1945–1965*, vol. 1, p. 441.
51. Roosa, *Dollar and World Liquidity*, pp. 115–16.

controls on trade and capital flows. Debates about international liquidity reflected the absence of an effective international adjustment mechanism: states were determined to avoid exchange-rate adjustments and
maintain policy-making autonomy, but these positions could be reconciled with increasing openness for trade and capital flows only by
providing an ever-increasing volume of international reserves and
credit for payments imbalances.

During the 1950s international liquidity was increased mainly by
United States payments deficits, which added to the dollar holdings in
the foreign-exchange reserves of central banks outside the United
States. Large American payments deficits permitted most other advanced capitalist states to satisfy their desire for larger foreign reserves
without competing with each other. But by the early 1960s, continuing
American payments deficits were not viewed as an acceptable means
for further increases in international liquidity: they undermined confidence in the dollar and caused the United States to lose gold as foreign states presented their dollar holdings for conversion.

Two broad positions can be identified among the advanced capitalist
states in the debates over liquidity in the late 1950s and the 1960s. The
United States and Britain sought increases that would help them finance their payments deficits, relieve some of the burden of supplying
reserve currencies, and facilitate the continued growth of international
trade. In sharp contrast, continental European states with payments
surpluses did not believe there was any immediate need for expanded
international liquidity, arguing instead for imposing greater balance-of-
payments discipline on deficit states. France articulated this position
most clearly, but in general it was shared by West Germany, the Netherlands, and Belgium. State leaders believed that the dollar's special
status as the world's primary transactions and reserve currency had
given the United States too much freedom to abuse the system by persistently running deficits that forced foreigners to accumulate dollars.
Consequently, they generally opposed proposals to increase the volume
of international liquidity and called for reforms to give creditor states
more power to impose conditions on international debtors.

The United States, Britain, and other deficit states were able to negotiate increases in the volume of international liquidity available
through the IMF but only at the expense of increasing conditionality.
Ironically, the very conditions imposed by creditors discouraged the

United States from relying on the IMF to finance its own deficits, encouraging it to rely instead on ad hoc arrangements and ultimately to adopt the policy of benign neglect.

IMF quotas were increased in 1959, 1965, and 1969 (with much debate in 1965), but the increases failed to keep pace with the growth of international trade. More important were the negotiations surrounding the General Arrangements to Borrow (GAB). By 1961 the United States and Britain had large payments deficits and were concerned about exhausting the IMF's resources of other currencies if they both had to make drawings to meet simultaneous balance-of-payments crises. The United States wanted surplus states to agree to make loans to the IMF if large drawings threatened to exhaust the fund's resources. Surplus states would agree to do so only if they were given greater decision-making powers to prevent the United States and Britain from using their voting power in the IMF to borrow large sums under relaxed conditions. Consequently, under the GAB EEC members were given the power collectively to block the mobilization of any loan; and any state could refuse to participate in a loan of which it disapproved, even if the other states went ahead. Furthermore, the participating states (the Group of Ten) would have to agree among themselves to activate the GAB in response to an IMF request. This meant that borrowers could be pressured to adopt more restrained monetary and fiscal policies under OECD mechanisms of multilateral surveillance. (I discuss this issue later in the chapter.)[52]

The GAB represented a significant instance of negotiated mutual policy adjustment, making available a large volume of conditional credits to finance balance-of-payments deficits and establishing a process of multilateral surveillance of policies in deficit states. But the United States never drew enough from the IMF to necessitate GAB activation, mainly because it rejected the idea of multilateral surveillance over its own macroeconomic policies.

The most prolonged and torturous international liquidity negotiations in the 1960s were those that led to the creation of Special Draw-

---

52. The GAB are discussed in Block, *Origins of International Economic Disorder*, pp. 178–79; IMF, *International Monetary Fund, 1945–1965*, vol. 1, pp. 507–15; and Strange, *International Monetary Relations*, pp. 105–14.

ing Rights (SDR) in 1969. These negotiations were especially intense because they focused on the creation of reserve assets that would be owned by their holders rather than the creation of credit facilities. The SDR negotiations had clear macroeconomic overtones because owned reserve assets could be used as money for settling international payments positions. Therefore, their creation resembled the creation of money, which has traditionally been the preserve of national central banks. In the end, constraints imposed on the creation of SDRs meant they made little contribution to the growth of international liquidity and had little macroeconomic impact.[53]

International discussions about the creation of a new international reserve asset began around 1960, shortly after the appearance of Robert Triffin's widely accepted argument about the inherent instability of a gold-exchange standard. Serious negotiations began in 1965 when the United States began to support the idea of creating a new international reserve asset through the IMF. This asset would relieve the United States of some of the burdens of providing the main international reserve currency and would be available in sufficient volume to finance the continued expansion of a liberalizing international economy. France provided the strongest opposition to the American proposals, advocating instead a return to a gold standard but with the devaluation of the dollar in terms of gold. This was unacceptable to the United States and to other Group of Ten states; it could be both destabilizing and deflationary and would create a major drain on United States gold reserves. Most continental European states agreed that there was a need to make contingency plans for a new international reserve asset but argued that the United States must eliminate its own deficit first. Otherwise, the United States could maintain inflationary policies that many countries felt threatened the stability of the international monetary system.

A compromise was finally reached in 1967–68. It laid contingency plans for a new international reserve asset to be created by the IMF if

53. On the SDR negotiations, see especially de Vries, *International Monetary Fund, 1966–1971*, vol. 1; Strange, *International Monetary Relations*, chaps. 7 and 8; Stephen D. Cohen, *International Monetary Reform, 1964–69: The Political Dimension* (New York: Praeger, 1970). On U.S. policy, see Odell, *U.S. International Monetary Policy*, chap. 3. Here I focus on debates among the advanced capitalist countries and do not deal with the equally intense North-South debates about using SDRs to promote development.

and when it was needed to supplement the owned reserves of member states.[54] SDRs are owned assets with no gold or foreign-exchange backing. Their value rests on the willingness of central banks to accept them in exchange for convertible currencies, up to the limits specified in the SDR agreement. A decision to allocate SDRs (or to increase quotas in the future) required an 85-percent voting majority in the IMF, which was sufficient to give the EEC a collective veto over SDR allocation. In this way, continental European states achieved one of their primary objectives in the negotiations—joint control with the United States over the expansion of international liquidity.[55]

SDRs were barely tested as instruments of international coordination of payments financing during this period. The first decision to allocate them was taken in 1969 at the urging of the United States. Agreement was quickly reached on a three-year allocation, with $9.5 billion allocated in 1970–72.[56] The $3.5 billion allocated in 1970 represented a minor but significant addition to international financing for payments imbalances (compared with $93 billion, the total international reserves of gold and foreign exchange of all IMF members). Nevertheless, any macroeconomic impact that it might have had was overwhelmed by a massive increase in U.S. balance-of-payments deficits in 1970–72. Because foreign governments did not want their currencies to appreciate, dollar outflows from the United States were absorbed into the reserve holdings of foreign central banks, thereby adding to international liquidity as it was then defined. This response again shows that intense negotiations in the 1960s did not produce any meaningful reform in the way the international monetary system functioned. There was no mechanism for coordinating internal policies of adjustment, despite (or because of) elaborate systems for managing symptoms of divergent national monetary, fiscal, and balance-of-payments policies.

54. This description of SDRs draws mainly on Dam, *Rules of the Game*, pp. 151–64.

55. Ironically, the EEC states achieved this objective just as the growth of private international capital markets was about to make official liquidity relatively unimportant.

56. Cohen, *International Monetary Reform*, pp. 152–56; Robert Solomon, *The International Monetary System, 1945–1981* (New York: Harper and Row, 1982), pp. 148–50; Strange, *International Monetary Relations*, p. 254.

Special Arrangements to Finance U.S. Deficits

U.S. payments deficits were a central feature of the Bretton Woods system in the late 1950s and the 1960s. As I have already noted, foreign governments became less willing to automatically absorb American deficits after the early 1960s, but the United States was still able to use its tremendous diplomatic power to negotiate arrangements that insulated it from the constraints that balance-of-payments deficits imposed on less powerful states.

The dollar's special status as the world's primary international reserve and transactions currency meant that until the mid-1960s American payments deficits were often automatically financed by welcome additions to the international reserve holdings of foreign central banks and the working balances of private foreign traders. "Foreign willingness to hold dollar assets amounted to lending to the United States" and meant that U.S. macroeconomic policies could be largely insulated from the external payments position.[57] From 1948 to 1962, foreign central banks added nine billion dollars to their official reserves while foreign banks, businesses, and individuals added six billion dollars to their working balances. As a leading architect of United States policy noted in 1963, "the rest of the world has thus already provided in this way an impressive amount of automatic credit to the United States."[58]

Until the early 1960s, this relationship between the United States and the rest of the world was viewed as beneficial, not exploitative. American payments deficits permitted foreign central banks to achieve desired increases in international reserves without serious competition among themselves that could have restricted trade. All states could not simultaneously achieve payments surpluses and increase their international reserve holdings unless there was an exogenous increase in the supply of international liquidity provided by rapid growth in gold production or American payments deficits.[59]

The dollar's special status also gave the United States a position in

57. Cooper, *Economics of Interdependence*, p. 42.
58. Roosa, *Dollar and World Liquidity*, pp. 117–18.
59. Sidney E. Rolfe and James Burtle, *The Great Wheel: The World Monetary System. A Reinterpretation* (New York: Quadrangle/New York Times Book Company, 1973), pp. xiii–xiv, chap. 6. These authors refer to the period up to 1958 as one of "beneficial disequilibrium."

the IMF that made it possible for the fund to absorb a substantial portion of American payments deficits between 1958 and 1962. When states drew dollars from the IMF in the late 1940s and the 1950s, the United States acquired what was informally called a super gold tranche position in the fund. This position was drawn down automatically when other countries used dollars to repay earlier drawings. From 1958 to 1962, the IMF absorbed $1.3 billion that might otherwise have been presented for conversion at the U.S. Treasury.[60] As the IMF's official history put it, "so long as repurchases were made in dollars, the Fund was in effect absorbing dollar holdings which reflected the adverse balance of payments of the United States."[61]

Foreign central banks were less willing to absorb American payments deficits after 1960. The United States's inability to eliminate its deficit undermined confidence in the dollar and made it a less attractive foreign reserve asset. Washington introduced a variety of measures after 1961 to make it more attractive for foreign central banks to continue holding dollars rather than present them for conversion into gold at the U.S. Treasury. For example, central banks were offered bonds denominated in their own currencies (the so-called Roosa bonds, named after Robert Roosa, treasury undersecretary for monetary affairs). By using dollars to purchase these bonds, foreign central banks could assure themselves that the United States would bear any loss resulting from a devaluation of the dollar or a revaluation of the currency in which the bond was denominated.[62] Washington also tolerated the growth of the Eurodollar market in part because it gave foreign dollar holders an attractive alternative to exchanging their growing dollar holdings for foreign currencies or gold.

The United States negotiated bilateral arrangements with some of its closest allies in which countries agreed to continue accumulating dollars or take other steps to improve the American balance of payments. Washington negotiated a number of agreements with West Germany to offset the drain on the American balance of payments resulting from the troops stationed in West Germany. Perhaps Germany's most important concession in these talks was its commitment in 1967 not to

60. Roosa, *Dollar and World Liquidity*, pp. 150, 191, 200–201.
61. IMF, *International Monetary Fund, 1945–1965*, vol. 1, p. 531.
62. Block, *Origins of International Economic Disorder*, p. 180; Coombs, *Arena of International Finance*, pp. 39–41, 88; Roosa, *Dollar and World Liquidity*, p. 123.

convert anymore dollar holdings into gold.[63] This commitment (and probable similar secret understandings with other American allies in Western Europe) paved the way for de facto dollar-gold inconvertibility after the two-tier gold market agreement was reached in March 1968.

Canada and Japan accounted for substantial shares of American payments deficits in the 1960s because of their borrowing in American capital markets and trade surpluses with the United States. In bilateral deals the United States exempted both countries from some capital controls. Canada agreed, among other things, not to convert its reserves of U.S. dollars into gold or other foreign currencies and to impose a ceiling on its foreign-exchange reserves. "This meant that the Canadians would have to take actions, in certain conditions, deliberately to worsen their balance of payments to assure continued access to U.S. capital markets."[64] In fact, the Bank of Canada had to tolerate a higher-than-preferred rate of inflation to avoid violating the reserve ceiling commitment or the IMF fixed exchange rate commitment, one of the rare cases in the 1960s in which international commitments had a direct impact on national macroeconomic policies.[65] Japan tacitly agreed to maintain its growing international reserves largely in dollars rather than converting more into gold. This willingness to conform to American preferences apparently sheltered Japan from direct pressure to help pay for American defense spending in Asia and from retaliation against its growing bilateral trade surplus.[66]

In this section I have shown that there was extensive international coordination of balance-of-payments financing among the advanced capitalist states in the period 1956–70. Enormous sums were lent to states with payments deficits. Despite heated debates over the future evolution of the international monetary system and increasingly severe mutual recriminations between surplus and deficit states, the system of coordination continued to provide sufficient financing to stabilize exchange rates—including, until 1968, the dollar-gold exchange rate. International coordination did not commit states to positive measures

63. Strange, *International Monetary Relations*, pp. 270–75; Block, *Origins of International Economic Disorder*, pp. 173, 184.

64. Block, *Origins of International Economic Disorder*, p. 184.

65. Michael C. Webb, "Canada and the International Monetary Regime," in A. Claire Cutler and Mark W. Zacher, eds., *Canadian Foreign Policy and International Economic Regimes* (Vancouver: University of British Columbia Press, 1992), p. 163.

66. Strange, *International Monetary Relations*, pp. 275–78.

to promote macroeconomic adjustment, and coordination of payments financing did not lead to coordination of exchange-rate levels. (Instead, it supported exchange-rate rigidity in the face of changing competitive relationships.) Nor did active policy coordination promote adjustment, as I discuss later in the chapter. But coordination to manage the symptoms of incompatible national policies did preserve some national policy-making autonomy at a time when states were relying less on trade and exchange controls to insulate their economies from international influences.

INTERNATIONAL COORDINATION OF INTERNAL POLICIES OF ADJUSTMENT

I have already shown how a relatively low level of international market integration, extensive (and noncoordinated) use of controls on capital flows, and ongoing coordination of symptom-management policies combined to provide governments with considerable policy-making autonomy in the late 1950s and the 1960s. In this section I will show that governments took advantage of this opportunity to formulate policies independently with little consideration for their impact on the balance of payments. The actual level of monetary and fiscal coordination was very low, despite extensive international discussions, American preeminence, and other conditions often considered conducive to policy coordination.

Attempts to coordinate macroeconomic policies took a variety of forms. When advanced capitalist states began borrowing heavily from the IMF in the 1960s, they were generally subject to some form of policy conditionality. Macroeconomic policies were discussed under the auspices of the Organization for Economic Cooperation and Development (OECD), the Group of Ten, and the Bank for International Settlements (BIS), especially in the context of multilateral surveillance of deficit states. There were also attempts in the OECD to formulate explicit guidelines for macroeconomic policy-making. Others have argued that explicit policy coordination was not necessary because of factors that encouraged indirect or implicit coordination of monetary and fiscal policies, including the fixed exchange rate rules of the Bretton Woods regime, U.S. hegemony, and an international consensus in favor of Keynesian macroeconomic policies.

This section reviews each of these possibilities for international co-ordination. I suggest that in practice neither formal mechanisms for coordination nor implicit coordination was a significant factor in macroeconomic policy-making in the late 1950s and the 1960s.

Formal Mechanisms: IMF Conditionality

The potential for formal international policy coordination centered on the IMF. By the beginning of the period, the IMF had evolved policies that made credit access conditional on the borrowing states's adoption of approved macroeconomic adjustment policies. The ability to offer or withhold balance-of-payments financing was supposed to give the IMF considerable leverage to encourage states to pursue restrained monetary and fiscal policies. Debates at Bretton Woods had left the IMF without explicit powers to coordinate national policies through its lending practies; the articles of agreement neither required nor forbade the fund to attach conditions to its loans.[67] Nevertheless, during the 1950s the United States used its veto power in the IMF to ensure that large loans were made only on a conditional basis.[68] As Harry Dexter White, the main American architect of the IMF, stated at the inagural IMF-World Bank meeting, "it has been our belief from the beginning that the Fund constitutes a very powerful instrument for the coordination of monetary policies, for the prevention of economic warfare, and for an attempt to foster sound monetary policies throughout the world."[69] These early conditionality policies were targeted mainly at developing countries, and were even supported by Britain which argued against the principle of conditionality in loans to developed countries.[70]

Thus, when the IMF resumed lending to advanced capitalist countries, American pressure had led to the creation of detailed conditions to be attached to loans of various sizes.[71] The IMF also developed

67. See Chapter 3 of this book and Gardner, *Sterling-Dollar Diplomacy*, especially chaps. 5 and 7.

68. The IMF's official history gives details on the evolution of conditionality guidelines and standby arrangements; see IMF, *International Monetary Fund, 1945–1965*, vols. 1 and 2.

69. Cited in Gardner, *Sterling-Dollar Diplomacy*, p. 261.

70. Regarding Britain, see IMF, *International Monetary Fund, 1945–1965*, vol. 2, p. 485.

71. Ironically, when the United States sought international credits to cover its own payments deficits in the 1960s, it found itself subject to the same conditions it had insisted

standby arrangements that established lines of credit based upon member commitments to pursue IMF-approved policies. By the late 1950s, standby arrangements were the main instrument for imposing conditionality. They were accompanied by letters of intent that committed the borrowing country to the pursuit of certain policies.

Most of the IMF's conditional loans from 1956 to 1970 went to developing countries. Among developed countries only Britain and France were subject to conditionality. The fact that only two of the Group of Ten states were affected, and only for brief periods in each case, testifies to policy conditionality's limited impact. The details of each case are also revealing.

Britain was by far the heaviest user of IMF credits. Between 1956 and 1965, it borrowed nearly $4.5 billion (see table 7) under a series of standby arrangements without any policy conditions beyond the requirement that it consult with the fund about any major shift in policy. This requirement was far less stringent than the quantitative policy commitments demanded from developing-country borrowers and was widely thought to have little effect on British policy.[72]

In November 1967 Britain came to the IMF for yet another standby arrangement. By this time, the IMF and the Group of Ten countries were unwilling to lend Britain any more money unless it accepted more stringent policy commitments and agreed to devalue sterling. In negotiations with creditors, the British government had to commit itself to meeting agreed quantitative targets for government borrowing, domestic demand, and balance of payments; to limiting bank-credit expansion and money-supply growth; and to implementing a price- and income-control policy.[73] When Britain came to the IMF for another loan in 1969, creditors demanded even stricter conditions, including a quantitative limit on domestic credit expansion and a target for a substantial budget surplus.[74]

---

on for other countries in the 1950s. It rejected creditors' demands for conditionality and instead adopted the policy of benign neglect that eventually brought down the fixed exchange rate system.

72. IMF, *International Monetary Fund, 1945–1965*, vol. 1, pp. 428–33, 488, 568, 572; Strange, *International Monetary Relations*, pp. 123–29.

73. See Strange, *International Monetary Relations*, pp. 166–70, which reproduces Britain's 1967 letter of intent to the IMF; de Vries, *International Monetary Fund, 1966–1971*, vol. 1, pp. 340–42.

74. Strange, *International Monetary Relations*, pp. 142–43. The 1969 letter of intent is reproduced on pp. 170–72.

There is no doubt that IMF agreements with Britain involved negotiated mutual adjustment of Britain's macroeconomic policies in return for adjustments in creditor states' lending policies—that is, their agreement to extend further loans to Britain. It is more difficult to assess how different the British government's monetary and fiscal policies were from the course they would have followed without policy coordination. As a deficit country, Britain would have been under strong international market pressure to adopt deflationary policies even without diplomatic pressure from creditor governments. This meant that British policy would have needed to change regardless of adjustments to other countries' policies; it also meant that Britain was in a weak bargaining position vis-à-vis its creditors. The availability of conditional IMF credit probably encouraged the government to rely more on deflation and less on trade restrictions, and IMF demands probably caused London to pay attention to monetary restraint.[75] Certain British officials and ministers favoured the policy adjustments urged by creditors and welcomed IMF pressure for restrictive policies because this pressure assisted them in domestic political debates with expansion-minded government leaders.[76]

France was the only other advanced capitalist state that borrowed from the IMF in sufficient volume to require conditionality. A large drawing in 1956–57 contained no special conditions; however, when France negotiated an additional standby arrangement in 1958, the letter of intent included quantitative limits on public expenditures and the budget deficit as well as commitments to restrict domestic credit and liberalize import controls.[77] As in Britain's case, IMF pressure helped certain French leaders overcome domestic opposition to restrictive policies. At the 1959 annual meeting of the IMF, the governor of the French central bank "gratefully acknowledged the debt due to the Fund for imposing the Fr. 600 billion limit on the budgetary deficit,

75. Ibid., pp. 145–46. Strange also argues that the IMF cared less about influencing British policy than about avoiding international financial crises and maintaining the *appearance* of strictness demanded by creditor states. Strange, *Sterling and British Policy*, pp. 290–94.

76. Russell, "Transgovernmental Interaction," p. 461; Strange, *International Monetary Relations*, pp. 126, 141.

77. IMF, *International Monetary Fund, 1945–1965*, vol. 1, pp. 428, 432; Cooper, *Economics of Interdependence*, p. 215.

and for the help this gave in imposing upper limits on certain categories of public credit.''[78]

A similar situation existed when France negotiated a large standby arrangement in 1969. The country wanted a large IMF credit ($985 million, equivalent to 100 percent of France's quota) to help prevent a further loss of gold to speculators in the wake of the franc's devaluation. Negotiations between the IMF and France proceeded quickly, largely because the government had already announced an extremely restrictive fiscal and monetary program. The letter of intent attached to the standby arrangement was not made public, but it apparently included quantitative performance commitments that matched previously announced government objectives.[79]

Again, it is difficult to determine whether these negotiations had any influence on French macroeconomic policy. The policies that France agreed to pursue were determined largely by the government, which favored restrictive policies to correct its payments deficit and restore confidence in the franc. In 1969, as in 1958, coordination of international adjustment policies between France and the IMF (representing creditor states) did not lead the state to pursue policies that it opposed; instead, it helped the government pursue policies that it preferred in the face of domestic opposition.

No other large advanced capitalist states were subject to IMF conditionality during this period.[80] Overall, the degree of international policy coordination through IMF conditionality was very limited. Conditional lending may have encouraged more restrictive British policies in 1967 and 1969 and French policies in 1958 and 1969, because it supported government leaders who wanted to restrict spending in the face of domestic pressure for increased spending.[81] But this ad hoc coordination

78. Strange, *International Monetary Relations*, p. 54.

79. de Vries, *International Monetary Fund, 1966–1971*, vol. 1, pp. 352–54.

80. Japan borrowed $125 million from the IMF in 1957 and arranged a $350 million stand-by credit (which apparently was not used) in 1961. According to a Japanese official (Toyoo Gyohten), Japan "complied rigorously with the IMF's conditions." At this time Japan was not a major player in international monetary affairs. For the Japanese government, "in those days, the recommendations made by the delegations of IMF officials amounted to almost a voice from heaven. The experience of Allied occupation from 1945 to 1952 had made us extremely respectful of foreign authorities. Furthermore, we were very obedient to the advice of the World Bank and the IMF because we had to borrow from them." Gyohten in Volcker and Gyohten, *Changing Fortunes*, pp. 58 (quotations), 51.

81. Regarding this situation as a general consequence of IMF conditionality, see Dam, *Rules of the Game*, p. 125.

was not an ongoing mechanism of international macroeconomic adjustment. As I make clear in my upcoming discussion of multilateral surveillance, the macroeconomic policies of other states, and even of Britain and France in noncrisis periods, were determined independently—often with little regard for their consequences on international payments equilibrium. This attitude is especially true of the United States, the largest deficit country during the period, which borrowed little from the IMF because it wanted to avoid policy conditionality and was able to persuade its allies to finance its deficits by other means. The governments of surplus states were not subject to IMF pressure to adjust their macroeconomic policies in any way.

Formal Mechanisms: Multilateral Surveillance

Even if formal IMF conditionality had little influence on the macroeconomic policies of advanced capitalist countries in the 1960s, other mechanisms existed for coordination. Perhaps the most important was multilateral surveillance, which was conducted in meetings of the OECD, the Group of Ten, and the BIS. According to some analysts, the macroeconomic policies of leading states were harmonized by these meetings among finance ministers and central bank governors.[82] A careful review of the actual practice, however, suggests that the process had little impact on national policies, with the single exception of Britain in 1967–69.

Multilateral surveillance grew out of the 1961 GAB negotiations in which creditor states successfully demanded that deficit states wanting large balance-of-payments loans submit to detailed international consultations on policies that affected their balance-of-payments positions. These consultations were to be undertaken in Working Party Three of the OECD, whose membership was restricted to the Group of Ten states and whose terms of reference explicitly included responsibility for coordinating macroeconomic adjustment policies.[83]

Early consultations had little substance, and continental European

82. Robert W. Cox, "Social Forces, States, and World Orders: Beyond International Relations Theory,"*Millennium* 10 (Summer 1981), pp. 145–46; see also Robert O. Keohane and Joseph S. Nye, *Power and Interdependence: World Politics in Transition* (Boston: Little, Brown, 1977), pp. 117–19.

83. OECD, *The Balance of Payments Adjustment Process*, Report by Working Party No. 3 of the Economic Policy Committee (Paris: OECD, 1966), p. 8.

states were soon pressing for a more stringent mechanism to force Britain and the United States to alter policies that contributed to persistent deficits. In 1964, the Group of Ten agreed on formal procedures for multilateral surveillance. States would supply the BIS with extensive statistical data on their payments positions and their methods of financing surpluses and deficits. The BIS, in turn, would confidentially supply the data to Group of Ten members. This data would provide the basis for detailed consultations in Working Party Three "with a view to avoiding shortages or excesses in the means of financing existing or anticipated surpluses or deficits . . . and to discussing measures appropriate for each country in accordance with the general economic outlook."[84] By 1966, Working Party Three had instituted an early warning system to identify emerging payments imbalances. States were requested to supply detailed and timely data on both trends in various external accounts and developments in internal conditions and policies. A collective evaluation followed with a goal of recommending appropriate policies (including monetary and fiscal) to be pursued by various countries.[85]

Despite these arrangements, multilateral surveillance had little impact on the macroeconomic policies of advanced capitalist states. In 1967 and 1969 these meetings did determine the policy conditions attached to IMF loans to Britain. Nevertheless, multilateral surveillance had no real impact on British policies before 1967—even though the British situation dominated Group of Ten consultations in the mid-1960s—in part because other Group of Ten states did not agree on the policies that Britain should pursue.[86]

The multilateral surveillance process did not have a direct impact on the macroeconomic policies of any state other than Britain. After the mid-1960s, mutual recriminations among leading surplus and deficit countries became more intense, but there is no evidence that any government changed its policies in response to international criticism. On the basis of extensive interviews with Group of Ten officials, Robert Russell concluded that discussions of monetary and fiscal policies were characterized primarily "by attempts to intellectually rationalize poli-

84. "Statement by the Ministers of the Group of Ten and Annexe Prepared by their Deputies," cited in Strange, *International Monetary Relations*, p. 122. See also IMF, *International Monetary Fund, 1945–1965*, vol. 1, pp. 590–91.

85. OECD, *Balance of Payments Adjustment Process*, pp. 17–18, 27.

86. The best sources on the British experience with multilateral surveillance are Strange, *International Monetary Relations*, chap. 5, and *Sterling and British Policy*.

cies that governments were already intent upon pursuing.'' The participants avoided making specific policy recommendations because they felt that policy-making was the sovereign responsibility of national governments.[87] By early 1968, "European attention was increasingly absorbed by the US deficit—over which no one was attempting to set up any serious machinery for multilateral surveillance.''[88]

Meetings of central bankers in the BIS had an equally small impact on national policies. European central bankers had been meeting regularly at the BIS in Basle, Switzerland, since the interwar period. In the early 1960s, officials of the U.S. Federal Reserve began to participate in these monthly meetings, which played a critical role in coordinating intervention in foreign-exchange markets and the negotiation of short-term credits needed to stabilize exchange rates. They did not, however, coordinate the monetary policies of the Group of Ten states. According to a Federal Reserve official who attended BIS meetings throughout the 1960s, they were "mainly devoted to operational problems in the gold and foreign exchange markets. . . . Little if anything in the way of coordination of national monetary policy was ever accomplished. Each governor reported his problems but rarely forecast policy recommendations.''[89] Outside observers shared this assessment.[90]

The absence of policy coordination was due in part to the fact that in most states such important decisions were made by finance ministers and top political leaders, not by central bankers.[91] According to another interpretation, "central bankers tacitly agreed that the choice of interest rates was a matter of strictly domestic concern, sacrosanct from foreign comment and counsel.'' Allowing foreign pressures to intrude on monetary policy-making could undermine the power and status of individual central banks in domestic policy making processes.[92] For what-

87. For an excellent discussion of Group of Ten meetings, see Russell, "Transgovernmental Interaction"; the quotation is from p. 457. Strange points out that central banks from creditor countries were reluctant to press Britain too hard for changes in monetary policies for fear of undermining the already tenuous principle of central bank policy-making autonomy. Strange, *International Monetary Relations*, p. 163.

88. Strange, *International Monetary Relations*, p. 150.

89. Coombs, *Arena of International Finance*, pp. 28, 198.

90. Russell, "Transgovernmental Interaction," p. 460; Deanne and Pringle, *Economic Cooperation from the Inside*, p. 23. Cooper states that central bankers "avoided candid discussions" in the BIS about pending policy changes. Cooper, *Economics of Interdependence*, pp. 198–99.

91. Deane and Pringle, *Economic Cooperation from the Inside*, p. 23.

92. Strange, *International Monetary Relations*, p. 163.

ever reason, frequent meetings at Basle and the development of personal friendships among central bankers "facing the common enemy of misguided government policy," as a American Federal Reserve offical put it,[93] did not lead to direct coordination of monetary policies or to coordinated bank pressure on governments.

Although the multilateral surveillance process had little direct impact, it may have served an information-sharing function. Close observers and participants agree that the main function of these meetings was to promote mutual understanding of independent state policies. Information-sharing among high-level officials could improve national decision making because well-informed states could avoid policy choices that were incompatible with the known objectives and policies of other states.[94] In support of this hypothesis, there is evidence that senior government officials and political leaders did consult on a number of occasions when reciprocal moves to raise interest rates to prevent capital outflows threatened to trigger an upward spiral of rates. Interest rates did not spiral after these meetings.[95] Neverless, it is virtually impossible to determine whether states would have acted differently without these consultations. Given the small volume of international capital flows and the widespread use of capital controls to deal with unwanted flows before the late 1960s, it seems unlikely that any central bank would have raised interest rates by any significant amount.

More generally, systematic analysis of monetary policy interdependence suggests that governments often moved deliberately to prevent other governments' macroeconomic policy adjustments from having the desired effect on payments imbalances. Monetary policy tended to make parallel shifts in different countries (except in the United States, whose policies did not respond to international influences). It ap-

93. Coombs, *The Arena of International Finance*, p. 58.

94. See Russell, "Transgovernmental Interaction," which notes (p. 456) that the sharing of statistical information alone was of limited value because the data that states provided to each other in Group of Ten meetings were not significantly more detailed or up to date than the information they published. See also Henry G. Aubrey, *Atlantic Economic Cooperation: The Case of the OECD* (New York: Praeger/Council on Foreign Relations, 1967), pp. 40–41, 103, 123–24, 143–45; Roosa, *Dollar and World Liquidity*, pp. 77, 169, 171–73.

95. Mention of such episodes in 1960–61, 1963, and 1967 appears in Roosa, *Dollar and World Liquidity*, p. 55; Aubrey, *Atlantic Economic Cooperation*, pp. 108–9, 195; Cooper, *Economics of Interdependence*, pp. 145, 161–62, 199n31; Strange, *International Monetary Relations*, p. 265.

peared that policy was "directed not at the adjustment of actual imbalances of payments but at the prevention of balance-of-payments movements expected to result from other countries' policies. This, of course, is a pattern of policies which does not conform with the directives of balance-of-payments adjustment: the latter would require two countries which undergo opposite experiences in their balance of payments to undertake policies in opposite directions, rather than to coordinate their policies so that they will move in parallel with each other."[96] Information sharing did not facilitate international adjustment; indeed, it may have increased the ability of decision makers to prevent foreign policies from having their intended impact.

Formal Mechanisms: OECD Policy Guidelines

There were numerous attempts to take multilateral surveillance and the OECD beyond the mere exchange of information toward negotiated policy coordination. The Economic Policy Committee of the OECD established four working parties to formulate international guidelines for various aspects of macroeconomic policy. These attempts failed because most states rejected formal constraints on national policy-making autonomy. Working parties were also established to develop guidelines for national policies that would promote external equilibrium, to formulate policies to accelerate economic growth, and to coordinate price and incomes policies. None of these efforts produced substantial agreements because virtually every government rejected the idea of international diplomatic constraints on policy-making autonomy and because of ideological differences about policies and economic planning.[97]

The OECD's Working Pary Three made extensive efforts to formulate international guidelines for balance-of-payments problems. The working party did facilitate coordination of symptom-management policies and promote mutual understanding of independently determined

96. Michael Michaely, *The Responsiveness of Demand Policies to Balance of Payments: Postwar Patterns* (New York: National Bureau of Economic Research, 1971), p. 57. The findings of this important study are reviewed in greater detail later in the chapter during my discussion of informal mechanisms of policy coordination.

97. The stories of Working Parties One, Two, and Four are briefly recounted in Aubrey, *Atlantic Economic Cooperation*, pp. 42–45, 51–52, 146; and Cooper, *Economics of Interdependence*, pp. 195–96n25.

national policies, but it failed to move beyond crisis management toward ongoing coordination of adjustment policies. In 1963 it undertook a study of the balance-of-payments adjustment process, intending to distill rules to guide national policy-making and improve the process of balance-of-payments adjustment among the advanced capitalist states.[98] Among other things, it explored "whether standards can be formulated on the contribution of monetary and related policies to balance of payments equilibrium, against which the performance of countries could be appraised."[99] If such standards could be formulated, it would be much easier to apply diplomatic pressure to states whose policies threatened international payments equilibrium.[100]

The study, conducted between 1964 and 1966, represented "by far the most ambitious attempt [to that date] to generate a transgovernmental consensus on the use of economic policy instruments to correct balance of payments disequilbria." The resulting report, however, titled *The Balance of Payments Adjustment Process*, represented no more than an international consensus among economists on good advice that governments might be encouraged to follow.[101] The guidelines and recommendations tended to be either exceedingly general or so highly qualified as to justify virtually any policy that a state might choose to pursue.[102]

Attempts to be more precise were defeated by disagreements about the causes of any specific payments imbalances, as had "been clearly apparent from the Working Party's discussions in recent years concerning the United States, the United Kingdom, Germany, and Italy." More fundamentally, the majority of states did not believe that it was possible or appropriate to develop general rules for states facing different cir-

98. Roosa, *Dollar and World Liquidity*, p. 179.

99."Ministerial Statement of the Group of Ten and Annex Prepared by Deputies" (August 1964), cited in OECD, *Balance of Payments Adjustment Process*, p. 7.

100. There were similar efforts to establish such standards in the 1970s and 80s.

101. Russell, "Transgovernmental Interaction," p. 457.

102. OECD, *The Balance of Payments Adjustment Process*. As an example of extremely general recommendations, the section on demand management stated that governments should use "fiscal and monetary policy to maintain demand at a level which is neither excessive nor deficient, and to promote a continuing expansion of total national expenditure in line with the trend growth rate of productive potential" (p. 19). As an example of generous qualifications, see the report's discussion of what should be done by the government of a country experiencing capital outflows and a current account surplus (i.e., the United States) (pp. 21–24).

cumstances.[103] Overall, the report confirmed that few of the Group of Ten states were interested in codifying binding rules of behavior that might constrain their ability to respond independently to circumstances.[104]

None of the OECD attempts to move beyond the management of balance-of-payments crises toward negotiated mutual policy adjustment had a direct influence on the macroeconomic policies pursued by advanced capitalist states. Leading states refused to give the OECD the power to coordinate national policies. Disagreement over how to distribute the burden of adjustment among states, and especially between surplus and deficit states, was another critical obstacle to coordination.[105] States preferred to risk the unpredictable adjustment burdens imposed by international market flows and to manage those burdens unilaterally (supplemented by international borrowing to finance payments deficits) rather than explicitly negotiate the distribution of burdens among states. This preference reflected the fact that international market pressures could be managed by other means, including coordination of symptom-management policies.

Informal Mechanisms: Fixed Exchange Rates

Even if IMF conditionality, multilateral surveillance, and the efforts of OECD working parties had little direct impact on the monetary and fiscal policies of advanced capitalist states, it is possible that other institutions and conditions encouraged informal or indirect policy coordination. Some analysts have argued that explicit coordination was not necessary in the late 1950s and the 1960s because the fixed exchange rate rules of the Bretton Woods regime ensured that countries pursued policies consistent with international stability. For example, a 1988 Group of Thirty report described the Bretton Woods era "as one of significant policy coordination. However, . . . this was achieved not so much by *ad hoc* policy coordination but rather through countries adhering to a set of mutually agreed rules [and] adjusting their policies

103. Ibid., p. 21 (quotation), p. 19.
104. Russell, "Transgovernmental Interaction," p. 457.
105. Aubrey, *Atlantic Economic Cooperation*, p. 143; Russell, "Transgovernmental Interaction," p. 458.

in response to the discipline imposed by the rules."[106] I assess this argument in two ways—first, by looking at how the fixed exchange rate rules might have constrained specific individual states and, second, by examining the degree to which governments adjusted monetary and fiscal policies to eliminate external payments surpluses or deficits that threatened fixed exchange rates.

Regarding the first point, a brief review of the situation indicates that for most leading states the policy-making constraints imposed by the fixed exchange rate rules were weak. The United States was the largest deficit state for most of the period; and had other things been equal, it would have faced intense market pressure to adjust its policies to correct its external imbalance. But the country was in a unique position due to the dollar's role as the primary international reserve and transactions currency. The initial willingness of foreigners to accumulate dollars and their inability to speculate against the dollar without revaluing their own currencies after the U.S. closed the gold window in 1968 insulated the country from external pressure to restrain its macroeconomic policies. External deficits put pressure on the United States only as long as it was willing to sell gold to foreigners on demand. For a brief period in the late 1950s and the early 1960s, the government was willing to do so; and its macroeconomic policies were somewhat sensitive to its external deficit, occasionally discouraging the adoption of an expansionary policy despite relatively high domestic unemployment and low inflation.[107] But by the early 1960s, Washington introduced various measures (described earlier in the chapter) to insulate gold supplies from payments deficits and therefore macroeconomic policies from external deficits.

Other deficit countries did face clear external pressure to adjust their macroeconomic policies. Britain was periodically forced to introduce restrictive policies to eliminate payments deficits despite the availability of enormous volumes of international credit. Canada (in 1962), Italy (in 1963–64), and France (in 1958 and 1968–69) faced similar constraints. But balance-of-payments pressures became more intense after

106. Group of Thirty, *International Macroeconomic Policy Coordination*, p. 8.

107. Cooper, *Economics of Interdependence*, pp. 42, 216–17. Cooper identifies this issue as a concern in the 1959–63 period. Before then, restrained U.S. policies were viewed as a source of international disequilibrium, as they made it more difficult for foreign states to avoid deficits in their trade with the United States.

fixed exchange rates were abandoned in the early 1970s, as I will show in later chapters.

Surplus states in Western Europe and (after the mid-1960s) Japan were, like the United States, relatively unconstrained by their payments imbalances. Surplus states could avoid unwanted domestic expansion as long as they could sterilize additions of dollars to their foreign-reserve holdings by reducing their central bank reserves of domestic currencies. The ability to sterilize, combined with the desire to increase international reserve holdings, gave most states considerable room to pursue relatively restrictive macroeconomic policies despite external surpluses.

Aggregate analysis confirms that the fixed exchange rate rules did not seriously reduce policy-making autonomy. If the Bretton Woods era was "one of significant policy coordination . . . achieved . . . through countries adjusting their policies in response to the discipline imposed by the rules," then governments must have adjusted monetary and fiscal policies to eliminate external payments surpluses or deficits that threatened fixed exchange rates. But careful study indicates that in most cases governments did not. In *The Responsiveness of Demand Policies to Balance of Payments*, Michael Michaely identified periods of payments imbalance for the Group of Ten countries and assessed whether monetary and fiscal policies shifted as economic theory prescribes—that is, deficits met with more restrictive policies, and surpluses with more expansionary policies. He found that in each country fiscal policy "was not responsive to the requirements of the balance of payments."[108] Monetary policy was also not generally responsive, but there were exceptions. Japan and Britain consistently relaxed monetary policy when in surplus and restrained monetary policy when in deficit. Belgium, France, and the Netherlands tightened monetary policy when they were faced with payments deficits but did not relax during periods of payments surpluses, which included most of the 1960s. Monetary policy in the United States, Germany, and Sweden was "consistently nonresponsive to the needs of the balance of payments position."[109]

Together, Michaely's findings and my review of specific circumstances suggest that in practice adherence to fixed exchange rate rules

108. Michaely, *Responsiveness of Demand Policies*, pp. 30 (quotation), 31–33.
109. Ibid., pp. 42–43.

did not lead to indirect policy coordination. The United States and overseas surplus states clearly had considerable freedom to set independent monetary and fiscal policies regardless of their external payments positions. The relatively low level of international market integration, the widespread use of capital controls, and the extensive network of coordinated policies to manage the symptoms of macroeconomic policy differences meant that most states did not have to coordinate macroeconomic policies in order to maintain stable currency values. Deficit countries other than the United States occasionally did have to pursue deflationary policies after exhausting international financial support, but this condition existed even after the fixed exchange rate system was abandoned in the early 1970s. Therefore, the fixed exchange rate rules did not force deficit governments to pursue macroeconomic policies much different from what they would have been otherwise.

Informal Mechanisms: Keynesian Consensus?

Monetary and fiscal policies could conceivably have been harmonized in the 1960s if all countries had followed the same approach to macroeconomic management. It is often thought that policy-making in the advanced capitalist countries during this period was guided by Keynesian ideas about fiscal-demand management and that this intellectual consensus ensured that policies of different countries were consistent. Furthermore, some analysts have attributed the spread of Keynesian macroeconomic thinking to American hegemony, especially given the supposed influence of Marshall Plan advisors over economic policy-making in Western Europe and Japan.[110]

Both parts of this argument are suspect. The influence of Keynesian ideas on countercyclical demand management varied widely among countries. They had almost no influence on policy in West Germany or Japan before the late 1960s; both countries focused more on supply-side management than on demand stimulus and emphasized monetary

110. Peter A. Hall, "Conclusion: The Politics of Keynesian Ideas," and Albert O. Hirschman, "How the Keynesian Revolution Was Exported from the United States, and Other Comments," in Peter A. Hall, ed., *The Political Power of Economic Ideas: Keynesianism Across Nations* (Princeton: Princeton University Press, 1989).

rather than fiscal policy.[111] American policies were inspired by Keynesian ideas only for a brief period in the Kennedy and Johnson years.[112] The ideas were influential in Britain throughout the 1950s and 1960s, but this situation reflected domestic political dynamics much more than American advice. Such advice did contribute to the adoption of Keynesian demand management in France, but that country also devoted considerable attention to supply-side policies.[113]

Overall, there never was a strong consensus in favor of Keynesian macroeconomic management among the governments of advanced capitalist countries in the 1950s and 60s. It is more accurate to characterize the consensus as one in favor of a broader notion of government responsibility for domestic stability, as John Gerard Ruggie has done.[114] This notion captures the wide variety of monetary and fiscal policies actually pursued during these years. But—and this is my key point—the consensus on domestic stabilization was too vague to ensure that national policies were consistent enough to prevent destabilizing international market flows.

Informal Mechanisms: United States Hegemony

One argument about implicit coordination in a hegemonic system focuses on the hegemon as a focal point that others can use independently to coordinate their policies. Game theory analysis suggests that in a system in which one player is much larger than any other, independent action can generate an equilibrium in which welfare is greater than it is under the Nash equilibrium achieved by independent play among myopic and more equal players. This argument has been applied to international monetary relations in the 1950s and 1960s. The United States was so much larger than other countries (and interna-

111. Christopher S. Allen, "The Underdevelopment of Keynesianism in the Federal Republic of Germany," and Eleanor M. Hadley, "The Diffusion of Keynesian Ideas in Japan," in Hall, ed., *Political Power of Economic Ideas*.

112. Walter S. Salant, "The Spread of Keynesian Doctrines and Practices in the United States," and Margaret Weir, "Ideas and Politics: The Acceptance of Keynesianism in Britain and the United States," in Hall, ed., *Political Power of Economic Ideas*.

113. Pierre Rosanvallon, "The Development of Keynesianism in France," in Hall, ed., *Political Power of Economic Ideas*.

114. John Gerard Ruggie, "International Regimes, Transactions, and Change: Embedded Liberalism in the Postwar Economic Order," in Stephen D. Krasner, ed., *International Regimes* (Ithaca: Cornell University Press, 1983).

tional trade was of relatively little importance to the American economy)[115] that it could set its own macroeconomic policy without regard for external consequences. Then this exogenous policy provided a focus for the policies of other countries. According to one proponent of this view, "the essential role of . . . the U.S. after 1944 was not so much to force other countries to alter their policies as to provide a focal point for [implicit] policy harmonization."[116]

The United States was relatively larger at this time than in subsequent decades, and the Japanese economy grew dramatically over the same period. West Germany replaced Britain as the largest European economy, but its share of total OECD output has been relatively stable since the 1960s. The relative decline of the United States and rise of Japan might suggest that the U.S. was less able to serve as a focal point for implicit policy coordination in the 1980s than it was in the 1960s. But even at its smallest, the American economy still accounted for almost 40 percent of total OECD GDP and was still more than twice as large as the Japanese economy.[117] This raises a crucial question: when is a country big enough to be called hegemonic? By almost any measure, the United States is still the dominant country in the world economy, even if it is not quite as dominant as it was in the 1950s and 60s. In the absence of strong theoretical reasons for claiming that a country can serve as the focal point for implicit coordination when it accounts for 50 percent of total OECD economic output (as in the mid-1960s) but not when it accounts for 40 percent (as in the 1980s), the argument comes dangerously close to tautology.

Proponents of the focal point argument need to show how actual macroeconomic policies were affected by this dynamic. American policies have been the focal point for international economic diplomacy since 1945. At all times European countries and Japan have tried to benefit from American payments deficits caused by stimulative fiscal policies and military spending abroad while simultaneously trying to shelter themselves from the harmful effects (for example, imported

115. The degree of insulation is a separate variable from hegemony; the two need not covary.

116. Barry Eichengreen, "Hegemonic Stability Theories of the International Monetary System," Discussion Paper No. 193 (London: Centre for Economic Policy Research, 1987), p. 36.

117. Michael C. Webb and Stephen D. Krasner, "Hegemonic Stability Theory: An Empirical Assessment," *Review of International Studies* 15 (April 1989).

inflation in the 1960s and high American interest rates in the early 1980s). If American preeminence was insufficient to cause informal policy coordination in the 1970s and 80s, there is no reason to expect that it was sufficient in the late 1950s and the 1960s—especially with so much evidence of foreign opposition to American policies, disagreement about coordination, and divergence in policies actually pursued.

Informal Mechanisms: Comparison to the 1980s

One way to assess these arguments is to compare divergence among monetary and fiscal policies in the 1960s with divergence in the 1980s. It is often argued that in contrast to the 1960s, informal mechanisms for policy coordination were entirely lacking in the 1980s and 90s. For most of the 1980s, interstate diplomacy appeared conflictual, exchange rates fluctuated wildly, and theoretical and ideological disputes about the global economy and appropriate policies were severe among governments and macroeconomists.[118]

Although reliable data are controversial and difficult to find, we can examine three crude measures of the relative expansiveness of monetary and fiscal policies in the largest advanced capitalist countries: the money-supply growth rate (annual percentage rate of change in M1), inflation rates (annual percentage rate of change in consumer price index), and fiscal balance (central government budget surplus or deficit as a percentage of GDP). If the fixed exchange rate rules, the purported Keynesian consensus, American hegemony or some combination caused governments to harmonize their macroeconomic policies in the late 1950s and the 1960s, we ought to see greater crossnational variability in the 1980s (when these factors supposedly were absent) than in the Bretton Woods years.

A comparison of tables 8, 9, and 10 (in this chapter) with 13, 14, and 15 (in Chapter 6) reveals mixed evidence. With regard to the money supply, rates of growth were more divergent in the Bretton Woods period than in the 1978–92 period, as indicated by the greater

118. On theoretical disputes as an obstacle to policy coordination in the 1980s, see Jeffrey A. Frankel, *Obstacles to International Macroeconomic Policy Coordination*, Princeton Studies in International Finance No. 64 (Princeton: Department of Economics, Princeton University, December 1988); Richard Cooper, "International Economic Cooperation: Is It Desirable? Is It Likely?" *Bulletin of the American Academy of Arts and Sciences* 39 (November 1985).

Table 8. Money-supply growth rate (annual rate of change of M1, in percent), G5 countries

	1956	1957	1958	1959	1960	1961	1962	1963	1964	1965	1966	1967	1968	1969	1970	1956–70
United States	1.1	−0.6	4.3	0.1	−0.4	2.9	2.1	2.8	4.1	4.3	4.6	3.9	7.0	5.9	3.8	
Japan	16.4	4.1	12.8	16.5	19.1	19.0	17.1	26.3	16.8	16.8	16.3	13.4	14.6	18.4	18.3	
Germany	7.2	12.1	13.1	11.8	6.8	14.8	6.6	7.4	8.3	8.9	4.5	3.3	7.6	8.2	6.4	
France	10.3	8.6	6.4	11.4	13.0	15.5	18.1	16.7	10.3	9.0	8.9	6.2	5.5	6.1	−1.3	
Britain	1.0	2.7	3.0	4.6	−0.8	3.2	4.4	0.3	5.0	2.7	2.6	3.2	6.0	0.4	6.4	
G5 mean	7.2	5.4	7.9	8.9	7.5	11.1	9.7	10.7	8.9	8.3	7.4	6.0	8.1	7.8	6.7	8.1
G5 standard deviation	5.8	4.5	4.2	5.8	7.7	6.7	6.6	9.6	4.5	4.9	4.9	3.9	3.3	5.9	6.4	5.6

SOURCE: Federal Reserve Bank of St. Louis, *International Economic Conditions*, June 1985, as reported in Ronald I. McKinnon, "The Dollar Exchange Rate and International Monetary Cooperation," in R. W. Hafer, ed., *How Open Is the U.S. Economy?* (Lexington, Mass.: D. C. Heath, 1986), pp. 216–17.

Table 9. Inflation rates (annual rate of change in consumer price index, in percent), G5 countries

	1956	1957	1958	1959	1960	1961	1962	1963	1964	1965	1966	1967	1968	1969	1970	1956–70
United States	1.4	3.6	2.7	0.9	1.6	1.1	1.1	1.2	1.3	1.6	3.1	2.8	4.2	5.4	5.9	
Japan	0.0	3.2	–0.3	0.9	3.8	5.4	6.6	7.8	3.7	6.7	4.9	4.1	5.3	5.3	7.6	
Germany	2.5	2.0	2.2	0.9	1.5	2.3	2.9	3.0	2.3	3.2	3.6	1.6	1.6	1.9	3.4	
France	4.2	–0.6	15.3	5.7	4.2	2.4	5.2	5.1	3.1	2.7	2.6	2.8	4.6	6.1	5.9	
Britain	4.3	3.2	2.8	0.6	1.0	3.5	4.2	2.0	3.3	4.8	3.9	2.5	4.7	5.5	6.4	
G5 mean	2.5	2.3	4.5	1.8	2.4	2.9	4.0	3.8	2.7	3.8	3.6	2.8	4.1	4.8	5.8	3.5
G5 standard deviation	1.6	1.5	5.5	2.0	1.3	1.4	1.9	2.4	0.9	1.8	0.8	0.8	1.3	1.5	1.4	1.7

SOURCES: 1956–59 data from IMF, *International Financial Statistics Yearbook, 1979* (Washington, D.C.: IMF, 1979), p. 58; 1960–70 data from IMF, *International Financial Statistics Yearbook, 1988* (Washington, D.C.: IMF, 1988), pp. 116–17.

Table 10. Fiscal balance (central government surplus or deficit as a percentage of national GDP), G5 countries

	1956	1957	1958	1959	1960	1961	1962	1963	1964	1965	1966	1967	1968	1969	1970	1956–70
United States	1.1	0.3	−1.6	−1.6	0.0	−0.7	−1.3	−0.8	−0.9	−0.2	−0.5	−1.1	−1.8	0.6	−1.2	
Japan	0.7	0.4	−0.8	−0.1	0.7	1.2	−0.3	−0.8	−0.2	−0.9	−1.6	−1.4	−1.0	−0.6	−0.4	
Germany	0.6	−2.3	−0.2	−1.7	−0.6	−1.0	−0.4	−0.8	−0.3	−0.5	−0.5	−1.7	−0.7	0.3	−0.1	
France	−5.3	−4.9	−2.8	−2.3	−1.4	−1.4	−1.7	−2.0	−0.3	0.0	−0.4	−1.1	−1.5	−0.5	0.5	
Britain	−0.2	−0.8	−0.4	−0.6	−1.2	−0.8	0.3	−0.5	−1.3	−1.7	−1.4	−2.9	−1.7	1.9	1.3	
G5 mean	−0.6	−1.5	−1.2	−1.3	−0.5	−0.5	−0.7	−1.0	−0.6	−0.7	−0.9	−1.6	−1.3	0.3	0.0	−0.8
G5 standard deviation	2.4	2.0	0.9	0.8	0.8	0.9	0.7	0.5	0.4	0.6	0.5	0.7	0.4	0.9	0.8	0.9

SOURCES: Data for United States, Germany, France, and Britain from IMF, *International Financial Statistics Yearbook, 1979* (Washington, D.C.: IMF, 1979); data for Japan from OECD, *Economic Survey: Japan* (July 1977). p. 44.

standard deviation from the mean G5 increase in the money supply (compare tables 8 and 13). These data do not support the argument that because governments adhered to the rules of a strong international monetary regime, explicit policy coordination was not required in the 1960s. They are consistent with my argument that the relative insulation of national capital markets in the 1960s permitted governments to pursue different macroeconomic policies without generating enormous international payments imbalances.

Inflation rates since the late 1970s have been more divergent than in the 1960s (compare tables 9 and 14). It is more difficult to maintain fixed exchange rates when inflation rates diverge because divergence causes changes in international competitiveness that can contribute to trade imbalances. However, annual data reveal that inflation rates were no more divergent after 1984 than for much of the 1960s, yet exchange rates were extremely unstable in the later period. This suggests that capital mobility rather than greater macroeconomic policy divergence underlies recent international instability.

With regard to fiscal policy data, deficits were substantially larger on average in the 1980s than in the Bretton Woods period; the standard deviation from the mean G5 deficit was also larger in the 1980s (compare tables 10 and 15). There was less divergence among fiscal policies in the earlier period. As I have already shown, this was not because of policy coordination; governments did not tailor fiscal policy to the requirements of the balance of payments in the 1960s. Instead, the difference is a consequence of the secular trend toward larger fiscal deficits, which has been more pronounced in some countries (especially the United States) than in others.(See Chapter 6 for a more detailed discussion of this trend.)

CONCLUSIONS

In the late 1950s and the 1960s, when the volume of trade flows was moderate and capital flows were relatively minor, macroeconomic policies were made independently, and international coordination focused on symptom-management policies. This pattern is consistent with the economic-structural model developed in Chapter 2. Coordination of trade restrictions and exchange controls did limit states' reliance on external strategies of adjustment. (The spread of currency convertibility was especially important in this respect.) Nevertheless, states used trade controls to insulate their economies much more in the 1960s than in subsequent decades. The trend was toward negotiated liberalization, although the character of trade policies was substantially more protectionist than in later years. In contrast, controls on short-term capital flows were universally used as instruments of adjustment, and policy-making was unilateral. Attempts to coordinate exchange-rate changes to facilitate international adjustment failed (with the single exception of the devaluation of sterling in 1967), and states unilaterally decided whether to alter currency values or (more often) resist market pressures for adjustment.

Macroeconomic policies were also made independently. Extensive international consultations on adjustment problems generally avoided explicit reference to specific monetary and fiscal policy adjustments, as all governments were reluctant to discuss what they still considered internal policies. Britain in 1967 and 1969 and France in 1958 and 1969 were the only cases in which international diplomacy influenced the national policies of deficit countries seeking large IMF credits. In some of these cases, the borrowing government did have to make specific commitments regarding monetary and fiscal policies. Nevertheless, because market pressures would have forced both governments to deflate regardless of international diplomatic pressure, these negotiated policy adjustments did not involve substantial departures from the likely course of unilateral policies. International financial support and diplomatic pressure probably had their greatest impact in the area of trade policy, discouraging France and Britain from relying on trade protectionism as a central instrument of adjustment. In contrast to these cases and to examples of negotiated mutual policy adjustments in subsequent decades, there were no cases in which the governments of key surplus countries agreed to pursue more stimulative monetary or fiscal policies in order to reduce international imbalances.

Independent policy-making was reconciled with increasing international market integration by extensive coordination of symptom-management policies. Coordinated intervention in foreign-exchange markets backed by short-term lending among central banks stabilized exchange rates in the face of payments imbalances. These imbalances were often managed for extended periods with longer-term lending through the IMF and special understandings between the United States and its allies that financed the American payments deficit.

Different countries faced different degrees of international market pressure for policy adjustments because of variation in national openness to international trade and capital flows. The most open countries were the United States and Britain. The U.S. was sheltered by the relatively minor role that international transactions played in the huge American economy, the dollar's special status, and the government's ability to persuade foreign states to finance its deficits. Initially, the American capital market was far more open than foreign ones, but Washington brought American practice closer to foreign practices with the capital controls introduced in 1963 and tightened in subsequent years.

Because of a much smaller economy and a weaker bargaining position, Britain could not ignore international market pressures. The government's desire to establish London as the leading international financial center made it unwilling to impose severe restrictions on speculative capital movements. Consequently, British macroeconomic policy was influenced by international market pressures more than other leading countries were.[119]

The Japanese and French economies were much less open to international market pressures, especially capital flows. Both governments used extensive capital controls to protect administered national credit systems from international pressures. Therefore, both were able to shelter relatively inflationary policies from international deflationary pressures. Tables 8 and 9 reveal that money-supply growth rates and inflation rates were often much higher in Japan and France than in other leading countries.[120]

Germany's economy was more open than those of Japan and France, though generally less than the United States and Britain. Nevertheless, its position as a surplus country meant that it could better insulate its policies from international pressures. In addition, the government proved adept at finding administrative measures to block speculative capital inflows—at least until the early 1970s, when the growth of international market linkages began to overwhelm administrative controls (see Chapter 5).

As my summary suggests, macroeconomic adjustment policy coordi-

119. Strange, *International Monetary Relations*, p. 120.
120. As noted earlier, France's inflationary policies were also sheltered from potential trade deficits by substantial currency devaluation in the late 1950s.

nation in the late 1950s and the 1960s focused on managing imbalances rather than promoting adjustment. Coordinated adjustment was blocked by states' determination to select exchange-rate levels and formulate monetary and fiscal policies independently. Governments preferred to risk unpredictable burdens of adjustment imposed by market forces and to manage those burdens with a combination of unilateral and coordinated measures of insulation and symptom management rather than directly negotiate adjustments to policies that had generated the market imbalances in the first place. No single state or group of states was powerful enough to force others to adjust policies or exchange-rate levels, except in the case of creditor states vis-à-vis Britain. Continental European countries were unable to persuade the United States to devalue the dollar, pursue more restrained macroeconomic policies, or accept balance-of-payments policies that would increase international market pressure for devaluation or deflation. Perhaps this is not surprising; according to most analysts today, the United States continued to occupy a hegemonic position until the late 1960s. But Washington was unable to persuade its allies to revalue their currencies within the existing system or to reflate their economies. Some analysts have argued that the United States never really tried to use its international power to correct imbalances in the 1960s because of divisions within the American government itself.[121] This argument is difficult to assess, relying as it does on inevitably controversial counterfactual hypotheses. A simpler explanation is the fact that given the relatively insular structure of the international economy in the 1960s, states did not have to coordinate macroeconomic policies to stabilize exchange rates while liberalizing trade; instead, they could rely on symptom-management policies. Thus, the absence of macroeconomic policy coordination is less a consequence of the distribution of power than of the structure of the international economy.

To reiterate, national autonomy in macroeconomic policy-making was compatible with fixed exchange rates and growing international market flows only because states were willing and able (given moderate levels of market integration) to coordinate exchange-rate intervention and international lending to offset the market flows that resulted from noncoordinated monetary and fiscal policies. Extensive efforts were

121. Henry R. Nau, *The Myth of America's Decline: Leading the World Economy into the 1990s* (New York: Oxford University Press, 1990), p. 132.

made, particularly by various OECD bodies, to devise a system that would promote adjustment. These efforts failed because all leading states preferred to formulate their own policies even though they wanted to influence policy-making in foreign countries. In addition, surplus and deficit countries could not agree on how to share the burdens of policy adjustment to achieve international equilibrium, and a viable alternative strategy—symptom management——was available.

My findings are not consistent with much of the literature on international economic cooperation in the 1960s. Most interpretations have focused too much on the stability of exchange rates and the coordination of international financing of payments imbalances and have paid too little attention to the independent nature of macroeconomic policy-making and the absence of coordination to promote rather than impede adjustment. The international economy was relatively stable in the late 1950s and the 1960s, but not because states coordinated macroeconomic policies. Stability reflected the ability to manage the symptoms of noncoordinated policies. As subsequent chapters will show, negotiated mutual adjustment of national policies was not substantially lower in the 1970s and the 1980s than in the 1960s; in fact, it was more extensive in the late 1980s than in any preceding period. Nevertheless, the international economy was much less stable because market integration was more extensive. Rising market integration meant that policy coordination had to become more extensive simply to maintain the stability of the late 1950s and the 1960s.

The growth of the Euromarkets during the 1960s meant that by the later part of the decade international capital flows stimulated by cross-national policy differentials were larger than could be managed by coordinated foreign exchange market intervention and international financing of payments imbalances. The negotiated devaluation of sterling in 1967, the de facto closing of the gold window in 1968, and unilateral changes in the exchange rates for the French and German currencies in 1969 all relieved some pressure on the system. But the most important circumstance was the special status of the dollar. Foreigners continued to be willing to absorb part of the U.S. deficit because of the dollar's usefulness as the world's primary reserve and transactions currency and the United States's role as leader of the anti-Soviet alliance. Political-military relations were particularly important in persuading West Germany and Japan to hold dollars rather than convert them into gold (which they had the legal right to do until 1971).

The bipolar structure of security relations was critical to the pattern of international adjustment policy coordination in the late 1950s and the 1960s. The importance that all advanced capitalist states attached to the anti-Soviet alliance made them willing to tolerate the presumed economic abuses of their allies. Most Western European states as well as Japan and Canada tolerated American payments deficits and avoided putting intense payments pressure on the United States because of its heavy contributions to the common defense. The United States for its part tolerated what it viewed as foreign abuses of the system (in particular, Western European and Japanese payments surpluses and countries' unwillingness to revalue their currencies) because of the overriding importance it attached to political unity in the anti-Soviet alliance. Bipolarity also accounts for heavy American military spending in Western Europe, which generated payments surpluses for most of these states. Surpluses permitted states to relax trade and exchange controls without jeopardizing national macroeconomic objectives. Military spending abroad accounted for a large share of American payments deficits and therefore was an important cause of international imbalances, but it also enabled the United States to achieve a liberal trading system among its Western allies and Japan.

Coordination of balance-of-payments lending and foreign exchange market intervention was a successful strategy in the late 1950s and the 1960s. But this strategy could not be sustained in the face of rising international capital mobility. In the early 1970s, states chose to abandon fixed exchange rates rather than policy-making autonomy, ushering in a period of low-level coordination of international macroeconomic adjustment policies.

CHAPTER FIVE

Flexible Exchange Rates and the Search for Policy Autonomy, 1971–77

The 1970s were years of considerable economic instability and diplomatic disharmony as governments sought to reassert policy-making autonomy in the new context of capital mobility and growing trade-market integration. The decade began with the abandonment of fixed exchange rates by most large advanced capitalist countries in 1970–73. Many analysts have interpreted this as a breakdown of the Bretton Woods system and have explained it as a consequence of declining American hegemony. This chapter challenges both elements of the conventional interpretation, arguing that international coordination remained extensive and that the key reason for instability was a change in the structure of the international economy—namely, rising capital mobility. Capital mobility fundamentally changed the environment for international adjustment policies. It meant that macroeconomic policy coordination was necessary to maintain the level of stability achieved in the 1960s through coordination of symptom-management policies.

According to the argument I developed in Chapter 2, the policies subject to coordination are shaped primarily by the degree of international market integration for goods, services, and capital. Given the relatively high degree of international capital mobility existing by the early 1970s, the most appropriate and effective government strategy would have been to coordinate monetary and fiscal policies. As we shall see, however, such coordination was no greater in the 1970s than it had been in the 1960s; international diplomacy influenced macroeconomic policies only in countries whose payments deficits were so large that they were forced to borrow from foreign governments and the IMF.

The dominant tendency in the 1970s was for governments to reassert policy-making independence. By the end of the 1960s, many governments felt constrained by the need to maintain fixed exchange rates in the face of growing speculative capital flows. Fixed exchange rates were abandoned in the early 1970s as governments sought to free themselves from exchange-rate constraints on monetary and fiscal policies. States hoped that flexible exchange rates would adjust gradually and moderately to crossnational differences in price trends and interest rates, thereby permitting them to achieve domestic objectives while trade and capital flowed relatively freely across national borders. Only later did policymakers and their economic advisors realize that short-term international capital flows had become far more important than trade balances as determinants of exchange rates and payments positions and that these capital flows had direct, often adverse, effects on national policies and conditions.[1]

Thus, most states opted for an external strategy of adjustment—flexible exchange rates—to avoid coordinating monetary and fiscal policies. Many also attempted to use capital controls, another external strategy, to insulate national policy-making from international influences; but these controls were not effective amid extensive private international financial networks. Symptom management was no longer viable in an environment of international capital mobility. In fact, states continued to borrow and lend on roughly the same scale as in the 1960s (although coordinated intervention in foreign exchange markets was not as systematic), but these activities were overwhelmed by capital flows through private international markets.

The dominant domestic problem for macroeconomic policy-making in the 1970s was stagflation, the combination of serious inflation and unemployment. It would have been extremely difficult to maintain fixed exchange rates in this environment. The inflationary and recessionary oil price shock of 1973–74, and the fact that it had varying impacts on different states, was bound to have some effect on exchange rates. Although I will not include a full explanation of the rise in infla-

1. Ronald I. McKinnon, *An International Standard for Monetary Stabilization*, Policy Analyses in International Economics No. 8 (Washington, D.C.: Institute for International Economics, March 1984).

tion in advanced capitalist countries, I will identify one central feature.[2] During the late 1960s and the 1970s, most states chose to use inflation as a means for avoiding rather than resolving distributional conflicts: "inflation has served as a vent for distributional strife, an escape hatch through which excess demands are automatically channelled."[3] This political function is closely related to a central macroeconomic policy objective identified in Chapter 2—creating conditions conducive to internal political stability. Inflationary "monetary policies . . . respond to political and social forces not merely or necessarily in escape from responsibility or rationality, but to accommodate pressures that threaten or appear to threaten the broad political and constitutional fabric, and economic-financial stability in consequence."[4] Fixed exchange rates were not politically viable in the face of such powerful inflationary pressures.

But divergent macroeconomic policies after 1973 cannot explain the abandonment of fixed exchange rates in 1971–73. This point is crucial for understanding the role of capital flows in the demise of fixed exchange rates. Policies and inflation rates diverged sharply only *after* fixed exchange rates were abandoned; logically, therefore, the abandonment could not have been caused by the erosion of a purported commitment to adjust policies to maintain exchange-rate stability. This can be seen by comparing the indicators of macroeconomic policy divergence in table 11 with those in tables 8, 9, and 10. Inflation rates across the G5 countries were relatively consistent before 1974, and it is hard to see how the abandonment of fixed exchange rates could be blamed on American inflation. Only Germany had inflation rates consistently lower than the United States during the 1960s; indeed, if divergent inflation rates were the cause of exchange-rate changes, the U.S. dollar ought to have been revalued, not devalued. The American budget deficit did exceed those of other governments by a significant margin in 1970 and 1971 (although not in the late 1960s), but only

2. For excellent discussions of the various causes of inflation in the 1970s, see Fred Hirsch and John H. Goldthorpe, eds., *The Political Economy of Inflation* (Cambridge, Mass.: Harvard University Press, 1978); and Leon N. Lindberg and Charles S. Maier, eds., *The Politics of Inflation and Economic Stagnation* (Washington, D.C.: Brookings Institution, 1985).

3. Fred Hirsch, "The Ideological Underlay of Inflation," in Hirsch and Goldthorpe, *Political Economy of Inflation*, p. 270.

4. Ibid., p. 275. In a similar vein, James O'Connor explained inflation as a consequence of state efforts to meet the somewhat contradictory functions of accumulation and legitimation necessary for the reproduction of a capitalist system; *The Fiscal Crisis of the State* (New York: St. Martin's Press, 1973).

Table 11. Money-supply growth rates, inflation rates, and fiscal balances, G5 countries

Money supply (annual rate of change in M1, in percent)

	1971	1972	1973	1974	1975	1976	1977	1971–77
United States	6.7	7.1	7.2	5.0	4.5	5.6	7.7	
Japan	25.5	22.0	26.2	13.1	10.3	14.2	7.0	
Germany	11.9	13.6	5.8	3.7	16.3	10.5	8.3	
France	13.8	13.1	10.0	9.7	10.4	17.7	7.9	
Britain	12.9	15.2	8.5	5.5	20.8	15.0	14.4	
G5 mean	14.2	14.2	11.5	7.4	12.5	12.6	9.1	11.6
G5 standard deviation	6.2	4.8	7.5	3.5	5.6	4.2	2.7	4.9

Inflation rates (annual change in consumer price index, in percent)

	1971	1972	1973	1974	1975	1976	1977	1971–77
United States	4.3	3.3	6.2	11.0	9.1	5.8	6.5	
Japan	6.3	4.9	11.6	23.2	11.8	9.4	8.2	
Germany	5.2	5.5	7.0	7.0	5.9	4.3	3.7	
France	5.5	6.2	7.3	13.7	11.8	9.6	9.4	
Britain	9.5	7.1	9.2	15.9	24.3	16.6	15.8	
G5 mean	6.2	5.4	8.3	14.2	12.6	9.1	8.7	9.2
G5 standard deviation	1.8	1.3	1.9	5.4	6.2	4.3	4.0	3.6

Fiscal balance (central government budget surplus or deficit as a percentage of national GDP)

	1971	1972	1973	1974	1975	1976	1977	1971–77
United States	−2.3	−1.5	−0.6	−0.8	−3.6	−4.5	−2.7	
Japan	−0.9	−1.1	0.0	−1.8	−4.2	−4.5	−5.5	
Germany	−0.2	−0.4	−0.3	−1.0	−0.7	−2.8	−2.1	
France	−0.4	0.6	0.7	0.3	−2.6	−1.0	−1.2	
Britain	−1.1	−2.5	−3.2	−4.2	−4.6	−5.7	−3.4	
G5 mean	−1.0	−1.0	−0.7	−1.5	−3.1	−3.7	−3.0	−2.0
G5 standard deviation	0.7	1.0	1.3	1.5	1.4	1.6	1.5	1.3

SOURCES:

Money-supply growth rates: Federal Reserve Bank of St. Louis, *International Economic Conditions,* June 1985, as reported in Ronald I. McKinnon, "The Dollar Exchange Rate and International Monetary Cooperation," in R. W. Hafer, ed., *How Open Is the U.S. Economy?* (Lexington, Mass.: D. C. Heath, 1986), pp. 216–17.

Inflation rates: IMF, *International Financial Statistics Yearbook, 1988* (Washington, D.C.: IMF, 1988), pp. 116–17.

Fiscal balance: 1971–74 data for U.S., Germany, France, and Britain from IMF, *International Financial Statistics Yearbook, 1979* (Washington, D.C.: IMF, 1979); 1975–77 data for U.S., Germany, France, and Britain from IMF, *International Financial Statistics Yearbook, 1989* (Washington, D.C.: IMF, 1989), p. 156; 1971–77 data for Japan from OECD, *National Accounts, 1964–81.* Volume 2: *Detailed Tables* (Paris: OECD, 1983), pp. 31, 38.

in 1971 did it exceed levels that had been common among G5 countries in the 1960s. Large American payments deficits inflated money-supply growth rates in Germany and Japan in 1971 and 1972 because these governments were trying to prevent their currencies from appreciating by purchasing dollars in foreign-exchange markets. Nevertheless, only Germany pursued monetary policies that were less inflationary than American policies in the late 1960s and early 1970s (see tables 8, 9, and 11).

Divergence in macroeconomic policies in the late 1960s and the early 1970s was not large enough to undermine fixed exchange rates among economies linked by international trade alone, as was the case before the mid-1960s. What changed was not so much macroeconomic policies as the freedom of private agents to speculate on the future course of monetary and fiscal policies and currency levels through private international capital markets. Stimulative American fiscal and monetary policies during the late 1960s and early 1970s did worsen the American trade balance, but it remained positive before 1971. The more important source of international payments imbalance was speculative capital flows responding to expectations of higher U.S. inflation in the future, flows that would not have been possible earlier when international capital market linkages were less well developed. Only later did divergent policy choices (in response to the 1973–74 oil price shock) make restoring fixed exchange rates impossible.

By the late 1970s, most advanced capitalist states had learned that exchange-rate flexibility did not provide policy-making autonomy in an open capital-market environment. Flexible exchange-rates proved to be highly volatile, and market-driven exchange rate fluctuations had unanticipated adverse impacts on domestic macroeconomic conditions. States were not able to achieve independent objectives simply by abandoning their obligation to maintain fixed exchange rate parities. Flexible exchange rates were also blamed for stimulating protectionist pressures and for other ills that beset advanced capitalist states.

Therefore, attitudes toward coordination of internal adjustment policies changed in most governments. Many leaders recognized that some policy coordination, matched by cooperative efforts to manage foreign-exchange markets, was necessary to enable states to achieve internal and external objectives.[5] Consequently, later years were characterized by a substantial degree of international coordination (see Chapter 6).

5. This changing attitude is discussed in a first-hand account of international discussions during these years written by two key policymakers from the United States and Japan; see Paul Volcker and Toyoo Gyohten, *Changing Fortunes: The World's Money and the Threat to American Leadership* (New York: Times Books, 1992), pp. 136–37, 152, 162.

The 1970s were a transitional period in which states (and economists) learned that international capital-market integration severely reduced the effectiveness of independent national policy-making, even when exchange rates were not fixed.

In this chapter I argue that the growth of international capital mobility explains the changing pattern of coordination between the 1960s and the 1970s. Therefore, I look in some detail at 1970s trends in international capital markets and the forces encouraging greater capital flows. By the end of the 1960s, Eurocurrency markets had become very active, and private channels for quickly moving short-term capital in and out of currencies were well established (see Chapter 4). The opportunities for risk-free currency speculation provided by the fixed exchange rate system also fueled the development of short-term capital markets in the late 1960s and early 1970s.

This growth continued during the 1970s, in part because of the increasing technological ease with which private market operators could identify and take advantage of international financial opportunities. But, as in the 1960s, the actions of the advanced capitalist states imparted a powerful impetus to international integration of national short-term capital markets. Most important, states encouraged petrodollar recycling through private markets. OPEC countries were encouraged to deposit their vast new payments surpluses in private Western banks, which were then able after 1973 to lend large sums to states wanting to finance payments deficits inflated by high prices for oil and other primary commodities. Petrodollar recycling meant that states did not have to increase the scale of intergovernmental balance-of-payments lending through the IMF and made it possible for deficit countries to avoid severe trade restrictions.

Diplomatic conflicts also stimulated the growth of private short-term capital flows. As it became increasingly apparent that a return to a stable exchange-rate structure was unlikely, investors and businesses became more involved in currency speculation. When currency traders were confident that a return to stable parities would eventually occur, some had been willing to engage in equilibriating speculation—that is, they had been willing to take currency positions in anticipation of an eventual return to values suggested by economic fundamentals and government statements. But when government intentions were unclear and official intervention in foreign-exchange markets was inconsistent, few traders were willing to take such positions. Once a shift in or out of a particular currency began, no one wanted to be left holding a depreciating currency at its old rate, or miss out on the appreciation of a strong one.[6]

Thus, the private capital flows that led to the 1973 abandonment of fixed exchange rates were caused in part by the apparent breakdown of interstate agreement about the international monetary system. It is critical to remember, however, that the emergence of international markets for short-term capital had itself contributed to that apparent breakdown by necessitating a higher degree of coordination to achieve the stability that had existed in earlier decades. States would have had to coordinate macroeconomic policies to discourage speculation against fixed exchange rates in the 1970s, and speculation on this scale did not even exist before the late 1960s. In other words, even had coordination of foreign exchange market intervention been as extensive in the early 1970s as it was in the mid 1960s, fixed exchange rates could not have been maintained unless leading states had also coordinated macroeconomic policies.

In the long run, the encouragement that state policies gave to private balance-of-payments lending strengthened international integration of national capital markets. This integration increased both the vulnerability of each national market to developments in foreign markets and the volume of capital flows triggered by crossnational policy differentials, thereby making independent national policies even less effective for achieving favorable national conditions.

At the same time, international capital and trade flows were not as high in the early and mid-1970s as they became in the mid-1980s (see Chapter 2). While it is difficult to be precise about thresholds, this point does indicate that states were somewhat less constrained by international market flows in the 1970s. Thus, it appears that international market pressures for policy coordination were not as intense in those years as they became in subsequent decades.

The widespread belief that fluctuating exchange rates would automatically and smoothly adjust to compensate for different national macroeconomic policies encouraged governments to reject explicit coordination of monetary and fiscal policies. The attempt to pursue

6. John S. Odell, *U.S. International Monetary Policy: Markets, Power, and Ideas As Sources of Change* (Princeton: Princeton University Press, 1982), pp. 299–305.

autonomous policies in an international economic structure characterized by rising capital mobility undoubtedly contributed to the severe
economic instability of the 1970s.

This chapter reviews international coordination of the three types of
international macroeconomic adjustment policies in the 1970s: external, symptom management, and internal. Economic diplomacy among
the advanced capitalist countries was marked by intense, conflictual debates about reforms to the IMF-centered international monetary system.
Although I review these debates, I focus primarily on negotiated mutual
adjustments of actual policies. As we shall see, states often found it possible to coordinate policies to deal with specific problems even when they
disagreed strongly on proposals for general guidelines or rules. The importance of particular international institutions as forums for coordinating adjustment policies changed significantly over the course of the
decade. The IMF, the OECD, and the Group of Ten all became less central, while two newer, smaller, and less formal institutions—the Group of
Five (G5) finance ministers and the Group of Seven (G7) economic summit meetings—became much more important.

INTERNATIONAL COORDINATION OF EXTERNAL POLICIES
OF ADJUSTMENT

The shift to flexible exchange rates in the early 1970s meant that
states were relying more heavily on an external strategy of adjustment.
Unilateral policy-making predominated, but exchange-rate adjustments
occasionally were coordinated internationally. Trade controls were
rarely used as instruments of international adjustment after the 1971
U.S. import surcharge. Many states did attempt to use capital controls
as an instrument of adjustment, introducing measures intended to
block the speculative capital flows that interfered with policy-making
autonomy. As in the past, capital controls generally were not coordinated, but unilateral controls became largely ineffective. Consequently,
a number of states called for international coordination to limit speculative capital flows. These efforts, however, were blocked by severe
technical problems and U.S. opposition.

Trade Controls

Many states experienced large trade deficits in the 1970s, but few states imposed or seriously considered trade restrictions to reduce balance-of-payments deficits. The most dramatic case occurred in 1971 when the United States imposed a 10-percent tariff surcharge on imports of manufactured goods. This decision is often interpreted as a dramatic break from the Bretton Woods system, but in many respects it was consistent with international understandings that emerged in the 1960s. Canada and Britain had both temporarily used tariff surcharges to reduce trade deficits caused in part by expansionary macroeconomic policies. The American tariff surcharge was temporary, modest, and nondiscriminatory; the rhetoric that accompanied it was more shocking than the measure itself. For the Nixon administration, the surcharge was primarily a bargaining tool intended to force surplus states in Western Europe and Japan to revalue their currencies, lower trade barriers, and increase their share of defense spending. These changes would reduce the American payments deficit, thereby reducing external pressure for less expansionary U.S. policies. Other advanced capitalist countries loudly criticized the import surcharge and associated American demands, but a compromise was reached in the Smithsonian agreement of December 1971. The United States withdrew the surcharge in return for modest currency revaluations by other leading states.[7]

Among other leading countries, only Britain and Italy seriously considered using wide-ranging import restrictions to reduce massive trade and payments deficits. In both cases, diplomatic pressure from other countries and the fact that IMF credits depended on a borrowing state's commitment to trade liberalization ensured that the restrictions were temporary and minor.[8]

In general, there was a trend toward freer trade among advanced capitalist states despite payments deficits, the oil crisis, and high un-

7. Ibid., chap. 4.

8. See Robert D. Putnam and Nicholas Bayne, *Hanging Together: The Seven-Power Summits* (London: Heinemann Educational Books for the Royal Institute of International Affairs, 1984), pp. 33–34, for a discussion of Britain's consultations with its economic summit partners; D. C. Kruse, *Monetary Integration in Western Europe: EMU, EMS, and Beyond* (London: Butterworths, 1980), p. 238, on EEC pressure on Italy; Margaret Garritsen de Vries, *The International Monetary Fund, 1972–1978: Cooperation on Trial*, 3 vols. (Washington, D.C.: IMF, 1985), vol. 1, p. 322 on conditions attached to borrowing from the IMF, specifically the oil facility.

employment. The growing interdependence of national economies and the transnationalization of industries made protectionism less attractive as a response to payments deficits. Negotiated policy adjustments were therefore less important in explaining the limited use of trade controls to insulate national policy making from international influences than were changes in the structure of the international economy that reflected the success of past measures of trade-policy coordination.

Capital Controls

As in earlier periods, there was virtually no coordination of capital controls for purposes of international macroeconomic adjustment. Controls on international short-term capital flows had proliferated during the 1960s, as deficit and surplus states tried to limit payments imbalances and maintain macroeconomic policy-making autonomy. (I describe these controls in Chapter 4.) The Nixon shock of August 1971 and the attempt to maintain fixed exchange rates in the tumultuous period that followed encouraged many states outside North America to impose new restrictions on short-term capital flows, especially on speculative inflows that threatened central-bank efforts to prevent currency revaluation. Unfortunately, they did not work. Japan, West Germany, and others found that even a wide array of partial controls could not prevent huge inflows of speculative capital. For example, the Japanese government was confident in August 1971 that it could hold the value of the yen unchanged because it exercised extensive controls over international capital flows; but in August alone, Japanese companies sold $4.5 billion to the Bank of Japan, making revaluation inevitable and creating a substantial loss for the central bank.[9] In mid-1972, "despite the imposition of additional capital controls by a number of countries, strong speculative pressures against the dollar led to massive flows of funds into various European countries and Japan. Between June 28 and July 14, the inflows came to $6 billion."[10]

Similarly, capital controls imposed by deficit states in Western Europe (Britain, Italy, and France) failed to halt speculative capital outflows that forced these states to abandon European currency stabi-

9. Odell, *U.S. International Monetary Policy*, pp. 227, 276.
10. Robert Solomon, *The International Monetary System, 1945–1981* (New York: Harper and Row, 1982), p. 223. This amount seemed large at the time but pales in comparison to the *daily* volume of speculative flows in the 1980s and early 1990s (see Chapter 6).

lization arrangements. By 1973 most Western European states agreed with the Bundesbank's view "that even stronger administrative action against capital flows from foreign countries ... does not suffice when speculative expectations run particularly high."[11] Controls aimed at speculative capital flows proved easy to evade as long as trade and trade-related financial flows remained liberalized. The international financial linkages developed since the 1960s, along with increasing trade flows, provided investors with a wide range of channels through which to move their funds.[12]

The ineffectiveness of unilateral capital controls left two alternatives for states that wanted to insulate policy-making from speculative international market pressures. One was to reintroduce comprehensive trade and exchange controls. But autarky was not an attractive option because a country that imposed comprehensive controls would not have been able to participate in the international division of labor. (I develop this argument further later in the chapter.)

The second alternative was to coordinate capital control policies with other states. In theory, coordinated controls on outflows from deficit countries, inflows into surplus countries, and firms participating in the Eurocurrency markets should be more effective than unilateral controls. Therefore, continental Western European states called repeatedly for coordination of controls on speculative short-term capital flows, most prominently during the 1972–74 IMF Committee of Twenty debates about international monetary reforms.[13]

Proponents of coordinated controls faced three major obstacles. A technological obstacle was the inability to create a system of partial controls that could distinguish between undesirable speculative flows

11. Cited in Kruse, *Monetary Integration in Western Europe*, p. 130. See also Solomon, *International Monetary System*, p. 247.

12. See Kruse, *Monetary Integration in Western Europe*, chap. 6; and Loukas Tsoukalis, *The Politics and Economics of European Monetary Integration* (London: George Allen and Unwin, 1977), chap. 6. Both authors include chronologies of European attempts to use controls to block speculative capital flows and investors' ability to find ways around the controls.

13. Kenneth W. Dam, *The Rules of the Game: Reform and Evolution in the International Monetary System* (Chicago: University of Chicago Press, 1982), pp. 248–49; Eric Helleiner, "From Bretton Woods to Global Finance: A World Turned Upside Down," in *Political Economy and the Changing Global Order*, Richard Stubbs and Geoffrey R. D. Underhill, eds. (Toronto: McClelland and Stewart, 1994), pp. 166–68. The outline for reform agreed upon in 1974 managed to sanction both this European view and the American view that controls were to be avoided.

and desirable ones related to trade and productive investment. Modest coordinated controls failed to defend fixed exchange rates within the European Community from speculative pressures. The critical political obstacle to coordination of capital controls was U.S. opposition. The United States was opposed to controls that would relieve pressure on surplus states to revalue, and prominent American leaders opposed controls on ideological grounds.[14] Britain opposed regulation of Eurocurrency markets because of the purported benefits of concentrating Euromarket activity in London, although British Labour governments were ideologically predisposed to favor controls and sought to insulate the domestic capital market from Euromarket influences. A third obstacle was the fact that most states wanted to encourage petrodollar recycling and balance-of-payments lending through private international capital markets.

Because no agreement was possible, individual states pursued whatever approach they independently believed was appropriate. By 1974 the United States had eliminated all capital controls imposed in the 1960s. The dominant trend in other states was to relax controls introduced in the early 1970s, although many remained in place.[15] Thus, the overall trend was toward greater capital mobility. The American veto on coordination was a key factor because of the dynamic of competitive liberalization (see Chapter 2). In sharp contrast to the trade situation, the structure of incentives in the case of capital favored liberalization when international agreement could not be reached: all things being equal, states that treated capital more leniently could expect to receive an inflow of international investment capital and stimulate the growth of financial service industries within their borders. In practice, other states had to follow the U.S. lead or risk losing financial industries and investment capital.

14. Helleiner, "From Bretton Woods to Global Finance," pp. 166–68; Susan Strange, *International Monetary Relations*, vol. 2 of Andrew Shonfield, ed., *International Economic Relations of the Western World, 1959–1971* (London: Oxford University Press for the Royal Institute of International Affairs, 1976), p. 193; Odell, *U.S. International Monetary Policy*, pp. 306, 310.

15. See M. S. Mendelsohn, *Money on the Move: The Modern International Capital Market* (New York: McGraw-Hill, 1980), for a description of controls in place in various states in the 1970s.

Exchange Rates

Exchange-rate fluctuations were one of the most important instruments of international macroeconomic adjustment in the 1970s. As I discussed earlier, most states abandoned fixed exchange rates in a search for greater policy-making autonomy. Consequently, exchange rates were volatile, especially in comparison with the rigidity of earlier decades, and attempts to coordinate adjustments were largely unsuccessful.[16] I argue that fixed exchange rates were abandoned because they were incompatible with autonomy in the new environment of international capital mobility, not because of a decline in American hegemony. In this section I highlight the attempts made to coordinate exchange-rate adjustments and the reasons for their failure.

The commitment to maintain fixed exchange rates broke down in 1970–73. Canada permitted its dollar to float in May 1970 and never restored a fixed parity. Germany permitted the mark to float in May 1971, a move the Netherlands soon followed. Most significant, the United States announced in August 1971 that it would no longer exchange foreign dollar holdings for treasury gold. The United States had never committed itself to maintaining the dollar's value in terms of other convertible currencies, so it could not renounce the maintenance of a fixed exchange rate except by refusing to defend the dollar-gold exchange rate and suspending the swap arrangements that had supported coordinated foreign exchange market intervention. Japan initially sought to hold the yen at its previous parity, but the central bank was forced to let the yen float upward after Japanese corporations sold large dollar holdings to the central bank in anticipation of the dollar's devaluation.

In all these cases, states were trying to avoid external constraints on macroeconomic policy-making. Canada, West Germany, the Netherlands, and Japan permitted their currencies to fluctuate in order to avoid having to buy dollars to prevent currency appreciation because an indefinite commitment to purchase dollars threatened to fuel domestic inflation. The United States made the dollar officially inconvertible in August 1971 to avoid balance-of-payments pressure to adopt a less inflationary macroeconomic policy. Washington would no longer

16. Recall from Chapter 4 that states were unable to coordinate exchange-rate adjustments even in the golden years of the Bretton Woods system.

exchange foreign dollar holdings for gold. At the same time, it refused to exchange such holdings for other convertible currencies, as most other advanced capitalist states agreed to do when they adopted formal currency convertibility in 1958. The United States did not maintain reserves of foreign currencies, and in any case the volume of dollars held overseas was enormous.[17]

Dollar inconvertibility was a critical assertion of American autonomy in macroeconomic policy-making.[18] In practice, foreign states could continue to convert their dollar holdings into other currencies through private markets, but this action would necessarily involve a depreciation of the dollar, the outcome sought by the United States. Therefore, surplus states could not avoid some combination of currency appreciation and inflation; if they intervened in foreign-exchange markets to purchase dollars and prevent appreciation, they would add to the money supply in their economies, thereby fueling inflation.[19] Thus, nonconvertibility insulated American policies from balance-of-payments pressures and gave Washington greater power to persuade foreign states to agree to American proposals for changes in the international monetary system.[20]

IMF obligations were violated by all states that abandoned fixed exchange rates. These governments put policy-making autonomy first, suggesting that obligations had been upheld in earlier years only because they did not seriously intrude upon autonomy. The American decision to suspend dollar-gold convertibility received the greatest criticism, but the Nixon administration simply ignored it as well as IMF attempts to resolve the disputes.[21]

Despite the heated rhetoric of 1971, the common assumption was that international negotiations would determine a new structure of fixed exchange rates, although the United States (almost alone) also wanted mechanisms for periodic exchange-rate adjustments that would allow it to pursue policies that foreign states believed were inflationary.

17. Dam, *Rules of the Game*, p. 188.
18. Joanne Gowa, *Closing the Gold Window: Domestic Politics and the End of Bretton Woods* (Ithaca: Cornell University Press, 1983).
19. Strange, *International Monetary Relations*, p. 339.
20. Odell, *U.S. International Monetary Policy*, pp. 250–63.
21. Margaret Garritsen de Vries, *The International Monetary Fund, 1966–1971: The System under Stress*, 2 vols. (Washington, D.C.: IMF, 1976), vol. 1, chaps. 25 and 26, pp. 533–34; Dam, *Rules of the Game*, pp. 187–88; Odell, *U.S. International Monetary Policy*, pp. 272–73.

Consequently, the December 1971 Smithsonian agreement did establish new fixed exchange rates for all Group of Ten countries except Canada.[22] The United States agreed to devalue the dollar in terms of gold, and most other states agreed to maintain the gold value of their currencies or to increase it, thereby effecting a real revaluation against the dollar. Broader foreign-policy concerns clearly shaped the agreement. The economic conflict of interest was intense, but the United States decided to back down from its initial refusal to devalue the dollar because of its desire to avoid a serious split in the anti-Communist alliance.[23]

Through the Smithsonian agreement, the United States successfully persuaded foreign states to revalue their currencies, an objective that had eluded American efforts in the 1960s. Nevertheless, leading states soon demonstrated their unwillingness to subordinate macroeconomic policies to the maintenance of the new fixed rates. The first state to abandon the Smithsonian rates was Britain. In March 1972, the British budget statement commented that "the lesson of the international balance-of-payments upsets of the last few years is that it is neither necessary nor desirable to distort domestic economies to an unacceptable extent in order to maintain unrealistic exchange rates, whether they are too high or too low."[24] The government subsequently made a "dash for growth" fueled by expansionary monetary policy. When this led to an exchange crisis in June 1972, Britain followed its own advice and permitted sterling to float—or, rather, to sink.[25]

Fixed exchange rates among other leading countries finally broke down in March 1973 because of powerful speculative pressures that had not been reduced by negotiated exchange-rate adjustments in February.[26] States were unwilling to intervene to maintain rates in the face

22. The negotiations leading up to the Smithsonian agreement are reviewed in detail in Volcker and Gyohten, *Changing Fortunes*, chap. 3; Solomon, *International Monetary System*, chap. 12; Strange, *International Monetary Relations*, chap. 11; and Odell, *U.S. International Monetary Policy*, pp. 271–88. Regarding the exemption won by Canada, see Michael C. Webb, "Canada and the International Monetary Regime," in A. Claire Cutler and Mark W. Zacher, eds., *Canadian Foreign Policy and International Economic Regimes* (Vancouver: University of British Columbia Press, 1992), p. 167.

23. Odell, *U.S. International Monetary Policy*, pp. 272, 280–83.

24. Cited in Solomon, *International Monetary System*, p. 221.

25. Robert O. Keohane, "The International Politics of Inflation," in Lindberg and Maier, *Politics of Inflation*, p. 85.

26. Odell, *U.S. International Monetary Policy*, pp. 313–24; Volcker and Gyohten, *Changing Fortunes*, chap. 4.

of large-scale speculative capital flows. The volume of speculation in 1973 was undoubtedly stimulated by loud public disagreements about the international monetary system. More narrowly, U.S. refusal to support coordinated foreign exchange market intervention directly encouraged private speculation.[27] But the underlying problem was the incompatibility of national macroeconomic policies; fixed exchange rates were simply not feasible in a context of open capital markets and divergent national policies.[28] U.S. Treasury Secretary George Shultz summarized this unwillingness to coordinate policies when he stated in the spring of 1973 that "American policy for interest rates and domestic liquidity will only be determined in accordance with the needs of the United States economy, excluding any other international concerns."[29] Although American policy had always focused on domestic concerns, this approach could no longer be reconciled with fixed exchange rates.

The questions of fixed-versus-fluctuating exchange rates and mechanisms for exchange rate adjustment were central to the 1972–74 international monetary reform negotiations. Most Western European states and Japan sought a return to fixed exchange rates, both for the stability this would bring to international commerce and as a way to enforce international market discipline on expansionary policies in the United States and Britain. The United States would consider returning to fixed exchange rates only if other states agreed to establish a mechanism for periodic rate adjustments to pressure persistently surplus countries to revalue their currencies or reflate. Such a mechanism would correct what Washington saw as the main asymmetry in the existing system: states experiencing payments deficits faced market pressures to devalue or deflate while surplus states could avoid adjustment by simply increasing their foreign-reserve holdings.[30]

27. Odell, *U.S. International Monetary Policy*, pp. 299–302.

28. Analysts who argue that fixed exchange rates could have been maintained implicitly assume that divergences among the policies of leading states would have been less substantial than they actually were. See, for example, Charles A. Coombs, *The Arena of International Finance* (New York: John Wiley and Sons, 1976); and Susan Strange, *Casino Capitalism* (Oxford: Basil Blackwell, 1986), pp. 37–40. Coordinated foreign exchange market intervention could have worked in the 1970s only if macroeconomic coordination was more extensive than it had been in the 1960s.

29. Cited in Tsoukalis, *Politics and Economics of European Monetary Integration*, p. 127.

30. Surplus states focused on a different asymmetry in which the United States, by virtue of the reserve currency role of the dollar, was able to pursue inflationary policies

In 1972 the United States proposed that the IMF adopt a reserve indicator scheme in which states whose foreign reserves exceeded (or fell below) appropriate levels would face coordinated pressures to adjust exchange rates or macroeconomic policies. In particular, surplus states that failed to revalue or reflate when their reserves grew above specified levels would be subject to coordinated trade restrictions. Aside from the scheme's formidable technical difficulties, there was no chance that surplus states would agree to a mechanism that would obviously constrain their own freedom of action, just as the United States would not agree to a return to fixed exchange rates without some mechanism to pressure surplus states to bear a greater share of international adjustment. Predictably, negotiations in the Committee of Twenty in 1972–74 failed to agree on the use of exchange rates as a mechanism of international adjustment.[31]

Rapid inflation in 1972–74 and the enormous increase in international payments imbalances caused by the 1973–74 oil price shock made even ardent advocates of fixed exchange rates (such as the French government) realize that conditions were too turbulent to permit them to be maintained. By 1973 U.S.-government support for fluctating exchange rates had also increased because of the growing ideological influence of free-market supporters within the Nixon administration[32] and because fluctuating exchange rates promised to lead to the appreciation of surplus states' currencies, thereby improving the international competitive position of American industry. After much debate, the IMF articles of agreement were amended in January 1976 to grant members the freedom to choose any exchange-rate system they wished, leaving open the possibility of a return to fixed rates if all states concurred in the future. The package also provided for multilateral surveillance of exchange-rate practices and asked states to pursue economic policies compatible with exchange-rate stability. (Neither provision was implemented until 1978, as I discuss in Chapter 6.)[33]

---

that produced large payments deficits without facing the discipline that deficits imposed on other states.

31. See Dam, *Rules of the Game*, pp. 222–35; de Vries, *International Monetary Fund, 1972–1978*, vol. 1, chaps. 9–14; and Solomon, *International Monetary System*, chap. 14. For an account of the discussions surrounding the reserve indicator scheme from the perspective of one of its authors (Paul Volcker), see Volcker and Gyohten, *Changing Fortunes*, pp. 119–23.

32. Odell, *U.S. International Monetary Policy.*

33. This amendment was based on a bilateral Franco-American compromise reached

In the face of multilateral instability, European Community countries attempted to stabilize exchange rates among themselves. But the "snake in the tunnel" arrangements they introduced in 1972 quickly fell apart for essentially the same reasons as the IMF-centered system failed. States were unwilling to coordinate macroeconomic policies, and coordinated market intervention was insufficient to offset speculative flows. Some coordinated capital controls were introduced at the insistence of France and Italy; but they were ineffective, and Germany opposed more stringent controls.[34]

While the general picture of 1971–77 shows little international coordination of exchange rates, it is important to note that relations did not become competitive. None of the leading states adopted the much-feared policy of competitive depreciations designed to improve balance-of-payments positions at the expense of trading partners.[35] Some analysts suggest that the norm proscribing competitive exchange-rate manipulation was applied less effectively after 1971,[36] but this interpretation is difficult to sustain. Before 1971 surplus states used the fixed exchange rate system and mechanisms of coordinated foreign exchange market intervention to maintain currencies that were clearly undervalued. After 1971, it was far more difficult to maintain exchange rates that private markets believed were either overvalued or undervalued, despite state efforts to block capital flows that pushed exchange rates away from desired levels.

Thus, states continued to achieve one of the primary objectives of the Bretton Woods system even though the specific mechanism (fixed parities) adopted in 1944 was no longer acceptable. They avoided exchange-rate competition that could lead to the adoption of mercantilistic and autarkic trade policies. Flexible exchange rates were seen as a new way to reconcile national macroeconomic objectives with international economic liberalism—that is, as a new manifestation of the

---

before the November 1975 Rambouillet economic summit meeting. Dam, *Rules of the Game*, pp. 256–59; Putnam and Bayne, *Hanging Together*, pp. 30–32; Solomon, *International Monetary System*, pp. 307–12.

34. Kruse, *Monetary Integration in Western Europe*, chaps. 5–7; Tsoukalis, *Politics and Economics of European Monetary Integration*, chap. 6.

35. Louis W. Pauly, "The Political Foundations of Multilateral Economic Surveillance," *International Journal* 47 (Spring 1992), pp. 319n44.

36. Keohane, "International Politics of Inflation," p. 58.

embedded liberalism that motivated the Bretton Woods agreements.[37]

INTERNATIONAL COORDINATION OF SYMPTOM-MANAGEMENT POLICIES

Symptoms of macroeconomic policy divergence were much worse in the 1970s because the rise of international capital mobility vastly increased the volume of private market flows generated by national differences in interest rates and economic expectations. The basic causes of international payments imbalances remained the same (crossnational differences in macroeconomic policy and American military spending overseas), but the symptoms were much worse. Payments imbalances and pressures on exchange rates were both larger in the 1970s. In fact, states continued to borrow and lend on roughly the same scale as in the 1960s (although coordinated intervention in foreign-exchange markets was not as systematic), but these activities were overwhelmed by capital flows through private international markets. Thus, the international economic instability of 1970s was primarily due to the change in the structure of the international economy, not a breakdown of policy coordination. In this section I review the coordination of two types of symptom-management policies—foreign exchange market intervention and IMF lending—and look at the growth of state borrowing and lending through private international capital markets.

Exchange-rate Stabilization

Despite state decisions to rely on fluctuating exchange rates as a primary instrument of international adjustment, central banks continued to intervene heavily in foreign-exchange markets. Much of this intervention took the form of dollar purchases by strong currency states (led by West Germany and Japan) seeking to limit currency appreciation without altering relatively restrictive policies. Deficit states often tried to intervene to limit currency depreciations, but these efforts tended to be short-lived because of enormous central bank losses when spec

37. John Gerard Ruggie, "International Regimes, Transactions, and Change: Embedded Liberalism in the Postwar Economic Order," in Stephen D. Krasner, ed., *International Regimes* (Ithaca: Cornell University Press, 1983).

ulation forced depreciation. More generally, central banks intervened to try to dampen short-term currency fluctuations. Consequently, the total volume of central bank intervention in foreign-exchange markets was actually much larger after 1971 than it had been during the years of the fixed exchange rate system.[38] Although states were not willing to adjust macroeconomic policies to maintain rates, they also were not willing to permit markets alone to determine them.

International coordination of exchange-rate intervention was less consistent in the 1970s than in preceding years, a reflection of the abandonment of fixed exchange rates and the clear intervention guidelines that formal par values provided. A more specific reason for inconsistent coordination was U.S. refusal to participate on a regular basis. Some analysts have pointed to the growing influence in Washington of free-market ideology as the reason for this refusal to intervene.[39] But the American government's actual behavior suggests that narrow, concrete economic interests were more important. Officials did not support coordinated intervention that helped surplus states avoid currency revaluation and even appeared to favor speculative capital flows that put pressure on those states to revalue or reflate. Nevertheless, when market forces pushed the dollar higher or lower than American leaders believed was appropriate, they set aside their belief in the superiority of market decisions in favor of coordinated intervention in foreign-exchange markets with like-minded central banks. In July 1972, July 1973, the first half of 1975, and the first few months following the November 1975 economic summit meeting, the Federal Reserve joined with foreign central banks to curb extreme speculative activity and exchange-rate volatility—in particular, to support the value of the dollar.[40] The Federal Reserve also led a number of cooperative ventures to make large short-term credits available to foreign deficit states whose currencies were under strong speculative pressures. The main borrowers were Italy in 1973 and 1974–75 and Britain in 1976–77.[41] These

38. Robert Z. Aliber, *The International Money Game*, 4th ed. (New York: Basic Books, 1983), p. 4; Dam, *Rules of the Game*, p. 197, and citations therein.

39. Odell, *U.S. International Monetary Policy*, develops this ideological explanation.

40. Coombs, *Arena of International Finance*, pp. 226–32, 236–37; Kruse, *Monetary Integration in Western Europe*, p. 147.

41. Luigi Spaventa, "Two Letters of Intent: External Crises and Stabilization Policy, Italy, 1973–77," and Malcolm Crawford, "High Conditionality Lending: The United Kingdom," both in John Williamson, ed., *IMF Conditionality* (Washington, D.C.: Institute for International Economics, 1983); Benjamin J. Cohen (in collaboration with Fabio Bas-

American actions are all puzzling from an ideolgical perspective. They suggest that a belief in free markets was a less important reason for American reluctance to intervene than was the hope that nonintervention would lead to the revaluation of foreign currencies, thereby improving the international competitive position of American industry. Washington might have supported a return to fixed exchange rates if foreign governments had been willing to agree to American ideas about the need for periodic currency realignments (for example, the reserve indicator proposals I discussed earlier).

Once it became apparent that a return to fixed exchange rates was unlikely, states involved in international monetary reform negotiations began seriously to consider creating guidelines for intervention in foreign-exchange markets and mechanisms for multilateral surveillance of national exchange-rate policies. It proved impossible, however, to agree on any measures that would constrain state freedom to determine when and how to intervene despite a number of short-lived agreements for more extensive consultations and coordinated intervention.[42] The IMF never regained a central role in exchange rate policy coordination among the advanced capitalist countries, and the extensive coordination that has existed since the late 1970s has been organized in smaller groups on a much less formal basis (see Chapter 6).

IMF Lending

In the 1970s the IMF lent to advanced capitalist states at roughly the same rate as in the 1960s, but its contribution to financing payments deficits was much less significant. The three largest borrowers were Britain, Italy, and the United States. Average annual lending to the G7 states amounted to 1.1 billion SDRs in 1971–73 and 1.6 billion in 1974–77, compared with 0.2 billion in 1956–60, 1.1 billion in 1961–65, and 1.3 billion in 1966–70.[43] In other words, IMF lending increased

---

agni), *Banks and the Balance of Payments: Private Lending in the International Adjustment Process* (Montclair, N.J.: Allanheld, Osmun, 1981), p. 196; Kruse, *Monetary Integration in Western Europe*, p. 236.

42. One example is the agreement reached at the November 1975 economic summit meeting, which formed the basis of the 1976 amendment to the IMF articles of agreement. De Vries, *International Monetary Fund, 1972–1978*, vol. 1, pp. 297–302, vol. 2, pp. 837–38; Putnam and Bayne, *Hanging Together*, pp. 31–33.

43. Until 1971, one SDR equaled one U.S. dollar; after 1971, the value of the SDR in terms of any one currency fluctuated with the values of the currencies that made up

in nominal terms in the 1970s, contrary to the usual picture of a break-down in cooperation after August 1971.

The IMF's smaller contribution to financing payments deficits did not result from any erosion of international cooperation but rather from two factors related to changes in the structure of the international economy. First, the demand for lending increased very sharply. With hindsight we can see that the needs fulfilled by the IMF in the 1960s were modest.[44] Contrary to the hopes of many, flexible exchange rates after 1971 did not eliminate payments imbalances; and massive speculative capital flows and the oil price shock created much larger deficits.[45] Second, an alternative source of credit emerged—the Euromarkets[46]—the same markets that contributed to deficit growth and a greater need for balance-of-payments financing.

Efforts were made to increase the IMF's lending capacity to meet the increased demand for balance-of-payments credits. If the fund were to continue to play a central role in financing international payments imbalances, it would have to increase members' quotas. In addition, given the sharp increase in payments deficits relative to trade flows, it would have to "increase ... members' access to Fund resources beyond the strict limit set by their quotas."[47] But agreements to increase the IMF's lending capacity were slow in coming and modest in impact. Quotas were increased by 32 percent in 1976, two years after an increase was first proposed. The United States, West Germany, and Japan opposed the increase of 70–100 percent that developing countries and deficit states demanded, claiming that it would be inflationary and that most members could borrow on private markets rather than from the IMF.[48]

Special oil facilities were established in 1974 and 1975 to help countries cope with the immediate effects of the oil-price increase.[49] The IMF managing director took this initiative in hopes of asserting the

the SDR valuation basket. 1956–70 data are calculated from table 7. 1971–77 data are calculated from Margaret Garritsen de Vries, *The International Monetary Fund, 1966–1971*, vol. 1, pp. 330–32, and *International Monetary Fund, 1972–1978*, vol. 2, pp. 433–38.

44. Benjamin J. Cohen, "Balance-of-Payments Financing: Evolution of a Regime," in Krasner, *International Regimes*, pp. 327–29, 334.

45. Aliber, *International Money Game*, p. 196; Strange, *Casino Capitalism*, pp. 8–9.

46. Cohen, "Balance-of-Payments Financing," provides a good discussion of the shift from IMF to private balance-of-payments financing.

47. Ibid., p. 328.

48. De Vries, *International Monetary Fund, 1972–1978*, vol. 1, chap. 27.

49. The following discussion is based on ibid., vol. 1, chaps. 17 and 18.

fund's leadership role in managing the payments consequences of the oil price shock. The initial proposal was made in January 1974; but the facility was not activated until September (long after many members began to suffer payments deficits due to higher oil prices), and the amount of available assistance was modest. Furthermore, creditor states were only willing to lend to the fund to support the oil facility at market interest rates, which seriously undermined the IMF's appeal to potential borrowers.[50] Italy and Britain were the only advanced capitalist states that borrowed from the IMF oil facility, although the amounts they borrowed were substantial (1.5 and 1.0 billion SDRs, respectively).

Aside from the oil facility, to which they had unconditional access, states generally drew on the IMF for balance-of-payments finance only when shut out of Euromarket borrowing. For example, both Britain and Italy borrowed heavily on the Euromarkets until private lenders lost confidence in the governments' ability to manage payments crises. The countries then turned to the IMF, the United States, the EC, and Germany, all of which insisted they adopt restrictive macroeconomic policies as a condition for official credits.[51]

These episodes show how much the IMF's role had changed since the 1960s. From being a major source of international finance for payments imbalances, it had become a fallback for countries shut out of private international capital markets. Because most advanced capitalist states had ready access to private international capital markets, the IMF became increasingly detached from policy coordination.

The privatization of international balance-of-payments lending also made debates about international liquidity and reserve assets largely irrelevant. The Committee of Twenty meetings in 1972–74 devoted a great deal of attention to the roles of gold, SDRs, dollars, and other currencies as reserve assets and to proposals for their international management.[52] By the middle of the decade, however, liquidity creation had been taken over by private credit markets. These markets recycled the reserves of surplus countries into financing for deficit countries, with the volume of liquidity limited only by the willingness of deficit states to pay higher interest rates on ever-larger credits and

50. A subsidy was eventually arranged for low-income borrowers.

51. Cohen, *Banks and the Balance of Payments*, pp. 195–97, 221–23; Mendelsohn, *Money on the Move*, pp. 96–97.

52. These debates are reviewed in Solomon, *International Monetary System*; Dam, *Rules of the Game*; and de Vries, *International Monetary Fund, 1972–1978*, vol. 1.

by lenders' perceptions of state creditworthiness. As the 1977 Mc-Craken report to the OECD noted, "since governments can now borrow so freely from the international financial markets to finance payments imbalances and influence exchange-rate movements, official reserve stocks have become a comparatively minor element of international liquidity."[53]

Private International Capital Markets and Balance-of-Payments Financing

The declining importance of IMF lending was intimately linked to the growth of government borrowing on private capital markets to finance payments deficits. Advanced capitalist states and oil-importing developing states borrowed heavily on the Euromarkets to finance enormous deficits that otherwise would have had drastic effects on employment, output, and exchange rates. International borrowing promised to permit gradual adjustments to higher energy prices, thereby helping governments avoid unpopular deflationary policies and protectionism.

From the perspective of deficit states, an especially attractive feature of private-market borrowing was the fact that no policy conditions were attached.[54] As I discussed in Chapters 3 and 4, few advanced capitalist states borrowed from the IMF in sufficient volume during the 1950s and 60s to activate the conditionality requirement. But the huge deficits that many states faced after 1973 meant that IMF credits would have been conditional on specific courses of state action. Private banks were not able to attach policy conditions to their loans,[55] although their willingness to loan large amounts was dependent on their collective judgment about the creditworthiness of the borrowing state.

The ability of private lenders to meet the strong demand for loans reflected Euromarket growth in the 1960s and 70s. By the early 1970s, well-established markets were able to offer large credits to deficit states long before the IMF increased the volume of credit it could offer. The volume of available funds increased enormously once the Organization of Petroleum Exporting Countries (OPEC) began to deposit payments

---

53. OECD, *Towards Full Employment and Price Stability* (McCracken Report) (Paris: OECD, 1977), pp. 129–30.
54. Dam, *Rules of the Game*, p. 296.
55. Ibid., p. 300.

Table 12. Payments imbalances and method of financing, selected groups of countries, 1974–76, in billions of dollars (cumulative flows)

	Current account	Net foreign direct investment	Total	Financial flows	Change in reserves	Source of loans	
						Official	Banks
G10 deficit[a]	−54	−5	−59	58	−1	9	41
Non-G10 OECD[b]	−49	5	−45	40	−5	5	26
G10 surplus[c]	27	−6	22	−13	9		
United States	11	−13	−2	6	4		

SOURCE: OECD, "The Adjustment Process since the Oil Crisis," *OECD Economic Outlook* 21 (July 1977), p. 95.
[a]Britain, Canada, France, Italy, Sweden
[b]All non-G10 OECD countries were in deficit during this period.
[c]Germany, Japan, Belgium, the Netherlands, Switzerland.

surpluses into the Euromarkets.[56] Eurobanks also received substantial deposits from advanced capitalist countries with balance-of-payments surpluses (see table 12) because of high deposit rates and the freedom from taxation and government regulation. Most governments, surplus or deficit, encouraged private banks to extend loans to deficit countries (developing and developed) because private lending reduced the demand for intergovernmental lending through the IMF and allowed deficit states to avoid drastic import restrictions. Private banks actively offered balance-of-payments lending to advanced capitalist states and certain developing countries, considering it a safe, lucrative opportunity to use the growing funds at their disposal.

Table 12 provides data on the relative contribution of private and official international lending to financing payments imbalances among advanced capitalist countries. For Britain, Canada, France, Italy, and Sweden as a group, private international borrowing financed four times as much of the total deficit in the years 1974–76 as did the IMF and other official institutions (compare "source of loans," table 12). The table also indicates the degree to which states were able to lend foreign currency surpluses to deficit states through the Euromarkets, thereby reducing the need to revalue their currencies or inflate their economies to establish external payments equilibrium. Of the current account surplus (after investment outflows) of twenty-one billion dollars

56. Cohen, "Balance-of-Payments Financing," p. 329.

accumulated by the surplus countries in the Group of Ten (Germany, Japan, Belgium, the Netherlands, and Switzerland), only nine billion dollars were added to foreign-exchange reserves, while the bulk (thirteen billion dollars) was recycled through short-term capital outflows. (Figures do not subtract to zero due to rounding.)

The decline in the relative importance of IMF lending was not due to any erosion of cooperation among advanced capitalist countries. Nevertheless, the fact that deficit states preferred to borrow from private lenders rather than from the IMF or other states manifests the drive for policy-making autonomy that characterized 1971–77. Freedom from the IMF obligation to maintain fixed exchange rates did not free states from balance-of-payments and exchange-rate pressures, especially after the oil price shock of 1973–74. But states responded to the need to finance payments deficits in the most unilateral manner possible by borrowing on private international capital markets.

INTERNATIONAL COORDINATION OF INTERNAL POLICIES OF ADJUSTMENT

As I emphasized earlier, macroeconomic policy-making in most advanced capitalist countries during this period was characterized by a desire for freedom from international constraints. Attempts to control short-term capital flows, the shift to fluctuating exchange rates, and large-scale borrowing and lending on private international capital markets were all manifestations of this search for autonomy. Thus, it is not surprising that there was little international coordination of macroeconomic policies. As in the 1960s, the only states whose policies were influenced by international diplomacy were those forced to turn to the IMF for loans to finance large payments deficits. Extensive international consultations during negotiations about reforming the IMF and at the first three economic summit meetings (1975, 1976, and 1977) had little impact on national policies. The shift to fluctuating exchange rates appeared to give governments greater freedom to pursue independently determined national policies, but international market pressures continued to constrain policy-making despite the absence of a fixed exchange rate commitment.

Direct Mechanisms: IMF Conditionality

States with payments deficits preferred to borrow from private international lenders rather than the IMF, in large part because of a desire to avoid IMF conditionality. Thus, there was little opportunity for the IMF to influence the macroeconomic policies of most advanced capitalist states through its lending policies. Nevertheless, two leading states did borrow from the IMF in sufficient volume to require policy conditions. Italy arranged very large standby credits in early 1974 and again in 1977, while Britain arranged a modest standby credit in 1975 and a much larger one in 1977. Both states turned to the IMF only when private lenders lost confidence in goverment ability to restore payments balances and refused to continue lending. The IMF and key creditor governments (the United States and Germany) demanded detailed, specific commitments regarding monetary and fiscal restraint from both countries. For example, the British government had to agree to quantitative limits on public-sector borrowing, and the Italian government had to agree to modify wage-determination practices that creditors believed were inflationary. Both governments were deeply divided themselves over how to respond to external deficits, with strong factions arguing for and against restraint. International diplomatic pressure and the offer of IMF financial aid appears to have helped supporters of restraint win internal battles.[57] Conditional borrowing from the IMF clearly involved explicit, negotiated adjustments to macroeconomic policies. Both governments would have faced severe international market pressure to deflate, even in the absence of international diplomatic pressure; but the policies they actually pursued undoubtedly would have been different had policy-making been unilateral. In that case, expansionist factions in both governments may have defeated colleagues who supported restraint, and in Britain the alternative of intensified trade and capital controls was seriously considered.

Even though IMF lending was not important relative to the volume of payments imbalances, conditionality continued to have as great an impact on macroeconomic policies in the 1970s as it had in the pre-

---

57. These cases are reviewed in detail in Spaventa, "Two Letters of Intent"; Crawford, "High Conditionality Lending"; de Vries, *International Monetary Fund, 1972–1978*, vol. 1, chaps. 23 and 24.

ceding period. Only two leading states were subject to policy conditionality (Britain and France in 1956–70 and Britain and Italy in 1971–77), and the conditionality's impact on the policies of borrowing states was more substantial in the 1970s than in the 1960s. Thus, the degree of policy coordination achieved through IMF conditionality did not decline.

Direct Mechanisms: IMF Reform Negotiations

The international monetary negotiations that led to the 1976 adoption of the Second Amendment to the IMF Articles of Agreement dealt extensively with issues of macroeconomic policy—without results. States were unable to agree on either substantive rules and guidelines for macroeconomic policies or specific policy adjustments. The reserve-indicator scheme proposed by the United States (intended to pressure surplus states to revalue or reflate) was rejected by the governments that would have been affected. The same fate met French initiatives to pressure deficit states to adjust by restoring fixed exchange rates and dollar-gold convertibility. No government wanted to give up the freedom to determine policies that they believed had been achieved by fluctuating exchange rates and, in the case of the United States, by dollar inconvertibility. Most governments still hoped that fluctuating exchange rates and private international borrowing and lending would accommodate policy differences. Consequently, no one was motivated to press for proposals that met stiff foreign opposition.

Direct Mechanisms: Multilateral Surveillance and the Economic Summits

During the 1960s, the Group of Ten and the OECD established a system of multilateral surveillance of national policies that they hoped would coordinate the macroeconomic policies of advanced capitalist states. As I explained in Chapter 4, this practice did not influence national policies. Discussions focused mainly on exchange rates and balance-of-payments financing rather than monetary and fiscal policies, an emphasis that continued into the 1970s. By 1973–74, the adoption of fluctuating exchange rates and the growth of private balance-of-payments lending eliminated much of the rationale for OECD Working Party Three meetings in which the Group of Ten states discussed balance-of-payments issues. Participating states continued to disagree about which types of policies were legitimate subjects for international discussion and which were purely domestic. In the IMF reform negotiations of 1974–76 there was much discussion of multilateral surveillance to ensure that the shift to fluctuating exchange rates was not accompanied by manipulation of currency values to gain unfair competitive advantage; but the agreed-upon provisions for surveillance were weak and never fully implemented.[58]

After the early 1970s, the focus for international coordination shifted to the annual economic summit meetings and associated meetings of the finance ministers of the G5 countries (the United States, Germany, Japan, Britain, and France), occasionally joined by Italy and Canada (the smallest of the G7).[59] Unlike the OECD multilateral surveillance consultations, these meetings have considerable potential for policy coordination. The number of states represented is relatively small, they are the most important states in the system, and the individuals who attend the meetings are top political leaders who have the power to implement international agreements.

The advent of the economic summit meetings reflected a shared need to discuss international economic turmoil in the wake of the oil price shock and the abandonment of fixed exchange rates. Consequently, the first three meetings were dominated by macroeconomic policy and exchange-rate issues. Debate focused on how to respond to the recessionary and inflationary consequences of much higher oil prices. Britain argued consistently for coordinated reflation to promote growth and reduce unemployment. Its preferred strategy, also advocated by the OECD Secretariat, called for low-inflation surplus countries to adopt expansionary policies. This approach would support world growth and allow deficit countries such as Britain to focus on fighting inflation, with export-led growth ensuring that anti-inflationary policies did not cause recession and high unemployment.[60]

58. Pauly, "Political Foundations of Multilateral Economic Surveillance," pp. 310–24.

59. The origins of the economic summit meetings are discussed in Putnam and Bayne, *Hanging Together*.

60. On summit-related discussions of macroeconomic policy in 1975–76, see ibid., pp. 29–42; George de Menil and Anthony M. Solomon, *Economic Summitry* (New York: Council on Foreign Relations, 1983), pp. 18–20; Robert D. Putnam and C. Randall Henning, "The Bonn Summit of 1978: A Case Study in Coordination," in Richard N. Cooper et al., *Can Nations Agree? Issues in International Economic Cooperation* (Washington, D.C.: Brookings Institution, 1989), pp. 21–27; and I. M. Destler and Hisao Mitsuyu, "Locomotives on Different Tracks: Macroeconomic Diplomacy, 1977–79," in I. M. Destler and Hideo

Attitudes towards coordinated reflation varied widely. German chancellor Helmut Schmidt urged the United States to provide more fiscal stimulus in 1974–75 to match expansionary fiscal policies in Germany, at the same time encouraging other European countries to focus on containing inflation. By late 1975, however, the German government was focusing on the need to fight inflation; and it consistently opposed coordinated reflation until 1978. The Ford administration in the United States and the Japanese government generally opposed the idea of coordinated reflation, focusing more on the dangers of inflation. Nevertheless, President Ford suggested at the 1976 economic summit that surplus countries should help to establish international equilibrium by letting their external payments positions deteriorate. Occasional support for reflation came from the Italian and French governments, although France was more often concerned about the dangers of inflation emanating from countries such as Britain and the United States.

These differences meant that neither the first summit at Rambouillet in 1975 nor the second in Puerto Rico in 1976 generated agreements to coordinate macroeconomic policies. The first focused mainly on reforms to the IMF (ratifying the Franco-American agreement on fluctuating exchange rates), international trade, and North-South relations. The 1976 summit put greater emphasis on the need to restrain inflation.

Macroeconomic discussions at the 1977 London economic summit were dominated by President Carter's attempt to persuade surplus states (Germany and Japan) to join the United States in reflating their economies, thus providing a locomotive for economic growth throughout the world. Carter's stance was consistent with the approach long advocated by the British Labour government and the OECD secretariat. But Germany rejected the locomotive theory, arguing instead that inflation was already too high and needed to be reduced before full employment and economic growth could be restored. This view was incorporated into the summit communiqué, which declared that "inflation does not reduce unemployment. On the contrary, it is one of its major causes." Japan generally (if quietly) supported the German

Sato, eds., *Coping with U.S.-Japanese Economic Conflicts* (Lexington, Mass.: Lexington Books, 1982).

position. These differences could not be resolved, and the summit was widely perceived as a failure.[61]

Nevertheless, the London summit did produce an important precedent. In the course of the debates, German and Japanese leaders defended their policies by projecting that their economies would grow rapidly over the coming year and needed no additional stimulation. American and British leaders then sought to extract commitments from these countries to achieve specific growth targets and to take remedial action if their actual performance fell below the targets. In the summit communiqué, the participants agreed "to commit our governments to stated economic growth targets," although German and Japanese leaders refused to include specific figures in the communiqué.[62] Both states also indicated that they would consider additional measures if actual growth rates fell below those projected. Consequently, when it became apparent that the projections had been optimistic, Germany and Japan came under strong pressure from the United States, Britain, and smaller OECD countries to take action to meet their commitments. No public agreements were reached during the remaining months of 1977; but by the end of the year the Japanese government conceded the need to stimulate fiscal policy to meet previously announced growth targets, and Germany's agreement followed in 1978 (see Chapter 6).[63]

Indirect Mechanisms: Exchange-rate Systems

Many analysts argue that a system of fixed exchange rates indirectly coordinates macroeconomic policies by forcing states to adopt those that minimize external payments imbalances. Chapter 4 showed that in practice the fixed exchange rate system of the 1950s and 60s did not operate in this fashion. Some deficit states restrained monetary policies to reduce payments deficits and maintain exchange-rate stability, but others (including the United States) did not; and surplus states did not alter monetary policies to prevent currency appreciation.

Certainly, if states had been committed to maintaining fixed exchange rates, macroeconomic policies would not have diverged so

61. Putnam and Bayne, *Hanging Together*, pp. 68–75; de Menil and Solomon, *Economic Summitry*, pp. 21–23.
62. Cited in Putnam and Bayne, *Hanging Together*, p. 75.
63. Ibid., pp. 71, 75, 79; Destler and Mitsuyu, "Locomotives on Different Tracks."

sharply after 1973—especially given the degree of capital mobility that existed by that time. When compared with tables 8, 9, and 10, table 11 reveals that policies were more divergent after 1973 than in the preceding period (1956–70). However, this is not the appropriate way to frame the relationship. As Chapters 3 and 4 showed, states did not choose the exchange-rate system first and then shape macroeconomic policies to maintain it; rather, fixed exchange rates could be maintained *without* preventing governments from pursuing policies tailored to domestic political requirements.

Other evidence suggests that international market constraints on national policies remained just as important after the commitment to maintain fixed exchange rates was abandoned. In the 1960s and 70s states pursuing expansionary policies (excluding the United States in the 1960s, as I explained in Chapter 4) experienced downward pressure on their currencies that forced them to adopt more restrained policies. In the 1970s this category included Britain, Italy, France, and (after 1977) the United States. Surplus states faced less severe market pressures than deficit states because of their greater ability to conduct sterilized foreign exchange market intervention to prevent currency appreciation and domestic inflation. But the greater volume of speculative capital flows in the 1970s meant that international market pressures on surplus states were greater in the 1970s—a key reason explaining why surplus states abandoned fixed exchange rates.

Thus, the shift to fluctuating exchange rates did not shelter either deficit or surplus states from growing international market pressure to adjust macroeconomic policies to eliminate external payments imbalances. States did try to reassert policy-making autonomy in the 1970s, which (in combination with the varying effects of and responses to the oil price shock) did generate greater divergence in macroeconomic policies. But the ensuing international economic instability was far worse than proponents of fluctuating exchange rates had anticipated, and macroeconomic policies have been much less divergent since 1984 (see tables 13, 14, and 15) despite the absence of fixed exchange rates. The choice of fixed or fluctuating exchange rates is therefore best seen as a consequence of national macroeconomic policy choices and the structure of the international economy, not as a determinant of those choices.

CONCLUSIONS

In the 1970s international macroeconomic adjustment strategies were dominated by state attempts to reassert policy-making autonomy in the face of rising capital mobility, growing trade imbalances, and severe economic shocks. The search for autonomy led many states to abandon fixed exchange rates and finance payments deficits or surpluses through private international capital markets. The pursuit of independently determined policies generated considerable international economic instability, but policy coordination did not break down. Coordination of external policies of adjustment (trade and capital controls, exchange-rate adjustments) continued to be extensive and helped to ensure that the search for autonomy did not degenerate into competitive trade protectionism or manipulation of exchange rates. The symptom-management strategies developed in the 1960s persisted into the 1970s (although coordinated foreign exchange market intervention was less extensive) but were no longer very effective in the face of large international payments imbalances generated by capital flows.

Changes in the structure of the international economy—especially the development of active capital markets—help to explain why states abandoned adjustment strategies that included fixed exchange rates, but the pattern of coordination is not fully consistent with the model in Chapter 2. According to that model, the most effective way for states to achieve their national macroeconomic objectives in a context of relatively open international capital markets is to coordinate policies; yet states were reluctant to do so, and the overall level of monetary and fiscal coordination was no higher than it was in the 1960s.

As in the 1960s, the only states whose macroeconomic policies were subject to international coordination were those forced to request payments financing from the IMF. Britain and Italy both adopted restrained policies as a condition for access to official credits. But in all other cases, states hoped that flexible exchange rates combined with borrowing and lending on private international capital markets would automatically reconcile divergent national policies without a need for autarkic trade and capital controls.

Governments of surplus and deficit countries regularly demanded that others adjust their macroeconomic policies to reduce international imbalances, but none had the combination of power and interest necessary to persuade foreign states to adjust. American leaders did not insist on reflation abroad because they believed that in the absence of policy coordination, international market pressures would force surplus states to revalue or reflate. Thus, the belief in exchange-rate changes as useful instruments of international adjustment reduced interest in direct policy coordination, just as the medium-term viability of symptom-management strategies in the late 1950s and the 1960s had also lessened interest. States other than the United States often did express strong interest in monetary and fiscal policy adjustments among the G5 countries, but these governments usually were divided among themselves and lacked effective ways to pressure the United States.

Overall, international coordination of adjustment policies remained extensive in the 1970s, with the exception of significantly less coordination of foreign exchange market intervention. But international coordination was much less successful in reconciling independent national objectives with international economic stability because the structure of the economy had changed. Most important, increasing international flows of short-term capital meant that the external imbalances caused by divergent macroeconomic policies were much larger than before, and external imbalances emerged as soon as market participants perceived such divergences. The role that short-term capital flows played in exacerbating the problem was apparent even before the first oil price increase. By mid-1973, most of the major advanced capitalist states had abandoned fixed exchange rates in attempts to free national macroeconomic policies from constraints imposed by a commitment to maintain such rates in the face of volatile, large-scale, short-term capital flows. The oil crisis made an existing problem even more intractable, but it did not cause the problem.

My analysis differs from hegemonic stability theory. According to that view, there was a breakdown of international economic cooperation in the early 1970s caused by a decline in American power relative to its European and Japanese rivals. But my analysis shows that there was no breakdown of international coordination. It remained at a level similar to 1960s conditions, if one defines coordination in terms of the degree of departure from unilateralism in the adjustment policies of leading states.

Assertions about the decline of international coordination fail to distinguish between policy coordination defined as negotiated mutual adjustment of national policies and the success of that coordination in achieving desired international economic outcomes. As in the 1970s, coordination may remain at a relatively constant level, but its success may deteriorate because of a change in the nature of the problems it addresses. When international market integration increases, the degree of coordination (measured as departures from unilateralism in policy-making) must also increase. Otherwise, international economic instability will also increase.

But policy coordination did not become more extensive in response to international capital market integration. Instead of coordinating monetary and fiscal policies, states hoped that fluctuating exchange rates and private balance-of-payments financing would absorb the market flows generated by divergent macroeconomic policies, thus preserving national policy-making autonomy.

Prominent economic theories of the 1960s led states to hope that fluctuating exchange rates would smoothly and gradually adjust to accommodate different national policies. On the assumption that national economies were linked primarily by international trade in goods and services, analysts argued that exchange rates should be permitted to fluctuate freely to compensate for changes in competitiveness caused by varying rates of price inflation in different economies. The link between domestic macroeconomic conditions and external equilibrium was assumed to follow this pattern:[64] monetary stimulus (or fiscal stimulus accommodated by monetary policy) would increase output and then prices; increased demand at home would stimulate imports while higher domestic prices would discourage exports, thereby worsening the trade balance; the deterioration of the trade balance would cause a corresponding depreciation in the exchange rate to maintain real parity between domestic and international prices; and exchange-rate depreciation would stimulate exports and discourage imports, thereby restoring the trade balance.

It is essential to note that this pattern focuses entirely on international markets for goods and services, which adjust relatively slowly to actual changes in prices. These characteristics (the reliable but gradual response to real price changes) permit gradual exchange-rate changes to maintain competitiveness and external equilibrium. If international markets did behave this way, fluctuating exchange rates would indeed

64. This section draws heavily on McKinnon, *International Standard for Monetary Stabilization*, esp. pp. 15–18, 25–27.

provide policy making-autonomy. States would be freed from the need to adjust policies to ensure external payments equilibrium, and different states could choose different inflation-unemployment trade-offs that reflect national political preferences.[65] According to a leading advocate of fluctuating exchange rates,

> the fundamental argument for flexible exchange rates is that they would allow countries autonomy with respect to their use of monetary, fiscal and other policy instruments, consistent with the maintenance of whatever degree of freedom in international transactions they choose to allow their citizens, by automatically ensuring the preservation of external equilibrium.[66]

Intellectual arguments in favor of fluctuation found empirical support in the experiences of Canada and West Germany. In the case of Canada, the exchange rate was permitted to fluctuate between 1950 and 1962 and behaved in a stable and equilibriating fashion.[67] This stability, however, was due to the fact that the government prevented its monetary policy from departing significantly from that of the United States as well as to other special characteristics of the integration between the Canadian and U.S. economies. When Germany permitted the mark to float to a new, higher value in 1969, it did so in a manner that calmed the worst fears of those opposed to flexible exchange rates. "It demonstrated that the markets could be trusted with deciding exchange rates without serious disruption of trade and international investment decisions. . . . Academic advocates of floating were heartened to press for it harder, especially in the United States."[68] Market pressures gave the German government a convenient indication of the exchange rate that private operators felt was appropriate, and the float to a new rate seemed to dampen speculation and reduce Germany's payments imbalance.[69]

65. Economists have become increasingly skeptical that there is such a trade-off beyond the very short term.

66. Harry G. Johnson, writing in 1969, cited in McKinnon, *International Standard for Monetary Stabilization*, p. 16.

67. For an argument that the Canadian experience supported the academic argument for fluctuating exchange rates, see Leland B. Yeager, *International Monetary Relations: Theory, History, and Policy* (New York: Harper and Row, 1966), chap. 24.

68. Strange, *International Monetary Relations*, p. 330.

69. Odell, *U.S. International Monetary Policy*, pp. 179, 228–29; Solomon, *International Monetary System*, pp. 163–64, 171.

After a few years' experience with generalized floating, advanced capitalist states learned that when short-term capital was permitted to flow relatively freely across national borders, exchange rates tended to interfere with the achievement of national macroeconomic objectives. Fluctuating exchange rates were extremely volatile: they reacted in an immediate and exaggerated way to any change in expectations about the future course of economic policy. These fluctuations can be harmful in themselves, and the need to adjust monetary policies in response to adverse exchange-rate movements undermines any autonomy that might have been gained by fluctuating rates in an environment of limited capital mobility.[70]

The decision of many states to reject international policy coordination was also motivated, at least initially, by a belief that capital controls could be used to block speculative flows that interfered with national objectives. Most Western European states and Japan imposed new capital controls in the early 1970s in the hope of blocking these flows, but the controls were universally unsuccessful. Private banks and investors were always able to find ways to evade them. In fact, controls tended to trigger exactly the types of international capital flow they were designed to block. For example, when Italy sought to discourage capital outflows in early 1973, its action resulted in capital flight as investors tried to get their money out while they still could. German and Swiss monetary authorities introduced controls on capital inflows that seemed to encourage investors to shift funds to those countries before controls became restrictive. As I noted earlier, by 1973 the German Bundesbank concluded that administrative controls were not effective in the face of strong speculative pressures. The IMF Committee of Twenty, meeting in the spring of 1973, also concluded that recent experience demonstrated "the impotence or, at best, limited effectiveness of capital controls in the face of strong speculative incentives to move funds."[71] Macroeconomic policy differentials were, of course, one of the main reasons why speculative expectations were high.

No advanced capitalist state was willing to consider autarky as a route to policy-making autonomy. If partial capital controls were ineffective,

---

70. For an acount by officials involved in international discussions during the 1970s that makes some of these points, see Volcker and Gyohten, *Changing Fortunes*, chaps. 4 and 5.

71. Solomon, *International Monetary System*, p. 247.

the only effective alternative was to introduce comprehensive trade and exchange controls; but all states considered that the costs of autarky would far exceed the benefits. Although some economists called for controlled disintegration of national capital and goods markets, there is little doubt that such a move would have constricted international trade and created severe adjustment problems. Given the networks of international trade and investment that had developed by the mid-1970s, powerful corporations and banks in all advanced capitalist states would have strongly opposed a shift toward autarky. It is difficult to imagine that any of these states would have been strong enough to overcome such opposition and survive the ensuing domestic political turmoil:

> Indeed, so difficult is it to envisage quite how "controlled disintegration" could be brought about, that it raises the question whether, in fact, it is possible in the 1980s to put the clock back 30 years or more. More damage to confidence and enterprise would result from this strategy . . . than would be gained in the long run.[72]

In the first half of the 1970s, states sought to use flexible exchange rates, controls on speculative capital flows, and private borrowing on international capital markets to regain the policy-making autonomy lost with the growth of short-term capital markets in the late 1960s and early 1970s. By the middle of the decade, states learned that any autonomy so gained was illusory. They might now be able to choose policies without violating an international commitment to maintain a fixed exchange rate, but this option did not increase their ability to achieve national objectives in the face of growing international market pressures. After 1977, states turned to greater explicit policy coordination. Thus, the model in Chapters 1 and 2 is confirmed, although with a time delay attributable to a lag in learning by certain leading governments.

72. Strange, *Casino Capitalism*, p. 168.

CHAPTER SIX

Macroeconomic Conflict
and Coordination, 1978–94

Macroeconomic policy coordination has been a central issue in international economic diplomacy since the late 1970s. By that time, many government leaders and economists in advanced capitalist countries realized that exchange-rate flexibility did not provide national policy-making autonomy when capital was internationally mobile. The mobility of short-term capital caused private foreign-exchange markets to overreact to differences in economic policy, performance, and prospects. Exchange rates were volatile and often severely overvalued or undervalued, interfering with government attempts to achieve domestic economic objectives and encouraging them to adjust policies unilaterally to address exchange-rate problems.

Thus, even though open economy macroeconomic theory suggests that monetary policy is more effective in achieving independently determined national objectives when capital is internationally mobile, governments are not willing to tolerate the extreme exchange-rate volatility associated with policy-making focused solely on domestic conditions.[1] In the 1970s they continued to intervene heavily in foreign-exchange markets, and by 1977 there was growing interest in coordinating monetary and fiscal policies to reduce international payments imbalances and exchange-rate volatility and misalignment. Many economists and

1. Wendy Dobson, *Economic Policy Coordination: Requiem or Prologue?* Policy Analyses in International Economics No. 30 (Washington, D.C.: Institute for International Economics, April 1991), p. 13.

officials believed that "both the inflation of 1973–1974 and the recession of 1974–1975 were aggravated by the failure of policy makers in each country to take adequate account of the cumulative effects of developments and policies in other countries."[2]

Despite widespread interest and extensive international debate, coordinated adjustments to monetary and fiscal policies were difficult to achieve. The experience of the past fifteen years reveals that when capital is mobile, macroeconomic policy coordination is necessary for international economic stability. But macroeconomic policies are inherently more difficult to coordinate than symptom-management policies or external policies of adjustment. Monetary and fiscal policies are a government's most important influence over domestic economic conditions; therefore, domestic political considerations are central to macroeconomic policy-making. As I emphasized in Chapter 2, this fact explains why governments have preferred to use external policies of adjustment and symptom-management policies to insulate monetary and fiscal policies from international influences. By the 1970s, however, those approaches no longer sufficed to reconcile national macroeconomic objectives with international market pressures because capital mobility made pressures so intense. Yet the obstacles to coordinating monetary and fiscal policies were very high and were overcome only when fears of an international economic crisis became widespread. The weakness of macroeconomic policy coordination meant that international payments imbalances were large, exchange-rate volatility was severe, and coordination of symptom-management policies was extensive if sporadic.

In the late 1970s, the 1980s, and the early 1990s, most key issues concerning international macroeconomic coordination arose from policy divergence between the United States on the one hand and Japan and Germany on the other. These divergences varied substantially over the years, but for much of the period the United States pursued more expansionary policies and demanded that Japan and Germany stimulate their economies to reduce U.S. trade deficits and discourage capital outflows (or encourage capital inflows). Japan and Germany,

2. Brookings Institution, "Economic Prospects and Policies in the Industrial Countries: A Tripartite Report," 1977, cited in I. M. Destler and Hisao Mitsuyu, "Locomotives on Different Tracks: Macroeconomic Diplomacy, 1977–1979," in I. M. Destler and Hideo Sato, eds., *Coping With U.S.-Japanese Economic Conflicts* (Lexington, Mass.: Lexington Books, 1982), p. 244.

occasionally joined by other G7 governments, demanded instead that the United States pursue more restrained policies. In the early 1980s, very restrictive American anti-inflationary monetary policies (combined with a stimulative fiscal policy) contrasted with more moderately restrictive monetary policies in most foreign countries, generating enormous capital inflows that drove the dollar up and exacerbated trade imbalances. Throughout the period, most G7 countries faced large fiscal deficits, and international diplomatic conflicts also arose over the priority that should be attached to deficit reduction versus further fiscal stimulus. The recession that began in several G7 countries in 1989–90 coincided with inflationary pressures, and this combination triggered overlapping domestic and international debates about how to respond and with what instruments. The tight monetary policies of Germany's central bank, pursued in response to the Bonn government's stimulative reunification policies, exacerbated these debates in 1991–93, especially between Germany and other European countries.

Although the political debates surrounding these policy differences were intense, it is importatnt to note that after 1984 macroeconomic policies were not significantly more divergent than they had been for much of the 1950s and 60s, when debates were less intense. Tables 13, 14, and 15 present data on money-supply growth rates, inflation rates, and fiscal deficits (compare to similar tables in Chapters 4 and 5).

Divergence in money-supply growth rates and inflation rates, measured as the standard deviation of rates for each G5 country around the G5 mean, was roughly the same after 1984 as in the late 1950s and the 1960s and lower than the 1970s. Fiscal deficits were more divergent in the 1980s and early 1990s because all countries were experiencing larger deficits than in the 1960s, although divergence would have been greater without the fiscal policy coordination in the late 1980s (mainly Japanese and German reflation) that I describe later in this chapter. Nevertheless, greater international capital mobility means that macroeconomic policy differentials of roughly the same magnitude as those in the 1960s today generate more serious market imbalances and diplomatic controversy.

In this chapter I seek to understand both the pressures for and obstacles to policy coordination. First, I examine the continuing growth of capital mobility after the late 1970s and its implications for macroeconomic adjustment policy coordination. Then I focus on interna-

Table 13. Money-supply growth rate (annual rate of change of M1, in percent), G5 countries

	1978	1979	1980	1981	1982	1983	1984	1985	1986	1987	1988	1989	1990	1991	1992	1978–92
United States	8.2	7.7	6.2	7.4	6.6	11.1	7.1	9.0	13.5	11.6	4.2	0.6	4.2	8.0	14.3	
Japan	10.8	9.9	0.8	3.9	7.0	3.0	3.0	4.6	7.4	9.0	7.8	0.1	4.2	12.2	3.7	
Germany	13.3	7.5	2.4	1.2	3.5	10.3	3.2	4.2	10.0	8.9	9.7	4.6	n.a.	7.3	10.7	
France	n.a.	12.9	8.9	11.5	11.8	9.8	10.6	9.0	7.9	4.4	2.5	7.3	1.7	-2.3	0.6	
Britain	20.4	10.9	4.0	8.5	6.5	10.0	8.3	3.5	11.3	9.7	12.6	-5.4	-4.6	1.2	0.9	
G5 mean	13.2[a]	9.8	4.5	6.5	7.1	8.8	6.4	6.1	10.2	8.7	7.4	1.4	1.4[a]	5.3	6.0	6.8
G5 standard deviation	4.5[a]	2.0	2.8	3.6	2.7	3.0	3.0	2.4	2.2	2.4	3.7	4.3	3.6[a]	5.2	5.5	3.4

SOURCES: 1978–88 data from Federal Reserve Bank of St. Louis, *International Economic Conditions*, July 1991; 1989–92 data from Federal Reserve Bank of St. Louis, *International Economic Conditions*, August 1993.

[a]Four countries. M1 growth in Germany in 1990 was 23.9 percent, reflecting unification rather than monetary policy.

Table 14. Inflation rates (annual rate of change in consumer price index, in percent), G5 countries

	1978	1979	1980	1981	1982	1983	1984	1985	1986	1987	1988	1989	1990	1991	1992	1978–92
United States	7.6	11.3	13.5	10.4	6.2	3.2	4.3	3.6	1.9	3.7	4.0	4.8	5.4	4.2	3.0	
Japan	4.2	3.7	7.7	4.9	2.7	1.9	2.3	2.0	0.6	0.0	0.7	2.3	3.1	3.3	1.7	
Germany	2.7	4.1	5.4	6.3	5.3	3.3	2.4	2.2	−0.1	0.2	1.3	2.8	2.7	3.5	4.0	
France	9.1	10.8	13.3	13.4	11.8	9.6	7.4	5.8	2.5	3.3	2.7	3.5	3.4	3.2	2.4	
Britain	8.6	13.4	18.0	11.9	8.6	4.6	5.1	6.1	3.4	4.1	4.9	7.8	9.5	5.9	3.7	
G5 mean	6.4	8.7	11.6	9.4	6.9	4.5	4.3	3.9	1.7	2.3	2.7	4.2	4.8	4.0	3.0	5.2
G5 standard deviation	2.5	4.0	4.5	3.3	3.1	2.7	1.9	1.7	1.3	1.8	1.6	2.0	2.5	1.0	0.8	2.3

SOURCES: 1978–85 data from IMF, *International Financial Statistics Yearbook, 1988* (Washington, D.C.: IMF, 1988), pp. 116–17; 1986–88 data from IMF, *International Financial Statistics*, June 1990, p. 73; 1989–92 data from IMF, *International Financial Statistics*, August 1993, p. 59.

Table 15. Fiscal balance (central government surplus or deficit as a percentage of national GDP), G5 countries

	1978	1979	1980	1981	1982	1983	1984	1985	1986	1987	1988	1989	1990	1991	1992	1978–92
United States	−2.8	−1.5	−2.9	−2.7	−4.1	−6.2	−4.9	−4.5	−4.7	−3.3	−2.8	−2.3	−3.0	−3.7	−4.9	
Japan	−4.9	−5.8	−5.5	−5.3	−5.2	−4.9	−4.1	−3.7	−3.2	−2.2	−1.3	−1.2	−0.5	−0.3	−0.9	
Germany	−2.1	−2.0	−1.8	−2.4	−2.0	−2.0	−1.8	−2.5	−1.2	−1.4	−1.7	−0.9	−1.8	−1.9	−1.3	
France	−1.4	−1.5	0.0	−2.7	−3.1	−3.6	−2.7	−3.3	−2.8	−2.2	−2.0	−1.6	−1.4	−2.0	−3.3	
Britain	−5.2	−5.7	−4.7	−4.8	−3.5	−4.4	−3.2	−2.3	−2.0	−1.0	1.2	1.2	−1.2	−2.5	−6.0	
G5 mean	−3.3	−3.3	−3.0	−3.6	−3.6	−4.2	−3.3	−3.3	−2.8	−2.0	−1.3	−1.0	−1.6	−2.1	−3.3	−2.8
G5 standard deviation	1.5	2.0	2.0	1.2	1.1	1.4	1.1	0.8	1.2	0.8	1.4	1.2	0.8	1.1	2.0	1.3

SOURCES: 1978–84 data for United States, Germany, France, and Britain from IMF, *International Financial Statistics Yearbook, 1989* (Washington, D.C.: IMF, 1989); 1978–84 data for Japan from OECD, *National Accounts 1976–1988.* Volume 2: *Detailed Tables* (Paris: OECD, 1990), pp. 61, 69; 1984–92 data from IMF, *World Economic Outlook,* May 1993, p. 148.

tional coordination of external mechanisms of adjustment and find that during these years governments did not seriously consider using trade controls as instruments of international macroeconomic adjustment, international coordination contributed to the virtual elimination of capital controls, and states continued to rely heavily—if often by default—on exchange-rate fluctuations. Coordination of exchange-rate adjustments was sporadic yet had a greater impact than in most earlier periods. I review international coordination of symptom-management policies, finding that intergovernmental lending and coordinated intervention in foreign-exchange markets were extensive (though again sporadic) as governments sought to manage the international problems caused by divergent national policies. Next, I examine international coordination of monetary and fiscal policies. Leading governments did coordinate macroeconomic policies on a number of important occasions, with the policy adjustments of various states reflecting the international distribution of power (especially U.S. power) more than the calculations of global welfare emphasized in economists' models. Governments were frequently unable to coordinate policies, and attempts to create ongoing mechanisms of coordination floundered, just as they had in the past. I conclude the chapter by focusing on why governments find it so difficult to coordinate monetary and fiscal policies even though noncoordinated policy-making generates serious international and domestic problems when capital is internationally mobile.

CAPITAL MOBILITY AND INTERNATIONAL MARKET PRESSURES

International market integration continued to grow in the late 1970s and the 1980s, particularly among capital markets. As in the past, integration was driven by a combination of economic and technological incentives and state policies. Improvements in international communications enhanced knowledge about conditions in foreign markets and encouraged businesses and wealthy individuals to borrow and invest funds outside their national capital markets. Communications and computer technologies reduced transactions costs, which further encouraged international flows.[3] As a consequence, "financial instruments denominated in different currencies and issued by borrowers in

3. BIS, *Recent Innovations in International Banking* (Basle: BIS, April 1986).

different nations became less imperfect substitutes in the portfolios of increasingly sophisticated investors."[4] A central factor was the growth of transnational corporations, which directly increased the volume of international financial transactions and provided additional channels through which private actors could evade government attempts to control international capital movements.[5]

The growth of private international financial markets and transnational corporations directly undermined governments' ability to restrict capital movements by using controls. Thus, the liberalization of capital controls reflected, in part, their declining effectiveness.[6] Many states, however, saw positive reasons to liberalize controls—for example, to encourage private financing of payments imbalances. Japan in 1979–80 and Germany in 1981 liberalized controls in the hope of attracting inflows that would limit currency depreciation in the wake of the second oil shock.[7] The United States introduced a number of tax and regulatory changes in 1984 to encourage capital inflows to finance its budget and trade deficits.[8] In 1983–85, the United States pressed Japan to liberalize its capital controls. One American motive was to make it easier for private Japanese investors to buy American government and corporate bonds, thereby financing U.S. deficits. American pressure coincided with the Japanese financial industry's growing interest in international finance and generated an important bilateral agreement to liberalize Japanese capital controls.[9] Capital liberalization helped both governments avoid adjusting fiscal policies: private capital inflows from Japan made it easier for the United States to avoid politically difficult budget cuts and easier for Japan to deflect international and domestic pressure for fiscal stimulus.[10] Overall, the American government's reliance on international borrowing to finance its huge budget deficits was

4. Ralph C. Bryant, *International Financial Intermediation* (Washington, D.C.: Brookings Institution, 1987), pp. 65 (quotation), 64.

5. John B. Goodman and Louis W. Pauly, "The Obsolescence of Capital Controls? Economic Management in an Age of Global Markets," *World Politics* 46 (October 1993).

6. Ibid.

7. Ibid, p. 62; Jeffrey A. Frankel, *The Yen/Dollar Agreement: Liberalizing Japanese Capital Markets* (Washington, D.C.: Institute for International Economics, 1984), pp. 19–20.

8. I. M. Destler and C. Randall Henning, *Dollar Politics: Exchange Rate Policymaking in the United States* (Washington, D.C.: Institute for International Economics, 1989), pp. 28–30.

9. Frankel, *Yen/Dollar Agreement.*

10. Ibid.; Robert Gilpin, *The Political Economy of International Relations* (Princeton: Princeton University Press, 1987), esp. pp. 332–37.

one of the most important causes of the rapid growth in international financial flows in the 1980s.[11]

The dynamic of competitive deregulation also encouraged states to reduce border controls on the flow of capital. As it became easier for corporations and individuals to shift operations and investments internationally in search of looser government regulation and lower taxes, states with high levels of regulation and taxation faced the prospect that national financial services industries would lose business to lower-cost foreign competitors.[12] Controls on short-term capital flows were also seen as obstacles to desirable flows of long-term investment in the national economy.[13]

These international competitive pressures contributed to a significant liberalization of capital controls that began in the late 1970s. In particular, barriers were reduced between national capital and Euro-currency markets, and national regulations relaxed to match low-level Euromarket regulations.[14] The timing of capital liberalization and deregulation varied slightly across countries, but the trend was clear. By the late 1980s, most governments had eliminated restrictions on foreign deposit taking and lending in domestic currencies and domestic deposit taking and lending in foreign currencies and had removed or reduced withholding taxes on foreign purchases of domestic securities and bonds. France and Italy were the last of the large advanced capitalist countries to rely on capital controls to shelter national macroeconomic conditions from international market pressures, but both countries relaxed controls in the late 1980s as part of the European Community's plan to move toward a Single European Market by 1992.[15] All governments also relaxed restrictions on the establishment of foreign-owned banking offices in national markets.[16] This trend was

11. "Survey of the World Economy: Fear of Finance," *Economist*, 19 September 1992, p. 12.

12. Edward J. Kane, "Competitive Financial Reregulation: An International Perspective," in Richard Portes and Alexander K. Swoboda, eds., *Threats to International Financial Stability* (Cambridge: Cambridge University Press, 1987); Eric Helleiner, "From Bretton Woods to Global Finance: A World Turned Upside Down," in *Political Economy and the Changing Global Order*, Richard Stubbs and Geoffrey R. D. Underhill, eds. (Toronto: McClelland and Stewart, 1994), pp. 168–70.

13. Goodman and Pauly, "Obsolescence of Capital Controls?"

14. This is a central theme of BIS, *Recent Innovations.*

15. Goodman and Pauly, "Obsolesence of Capital Controls?", pp. 70–78.

16. See Louis W. Pauly, *Opening Financial Markets: Banking Politics on the Pacific Rim* (Ithaca: Cornell University Press, 1988).

especially important because transnational banks are particularly sensitive to crossnational differences in interest and exchange rates.[17]

The virtual elimination of capital controls represented a sharp turn from the autarkic view of capital that predominated in the 1940s and 50s—that international capital flows should be tightly controlled to prevent speculation from interfering with national macroeconomic policy-making and trade liberalization.[18] In contrast to decisions that permitted Euromarkets to develop in the 1960s, decisions to liberalize capital flows in the 1980s were made with the knowledge that liberalization would restrict national policy-making autonomy.

The technological changes and state policies I have described generated a remarkable expansion of international capital flows in the 1980s.[19] Long-term data presented in Chapter 2 reveal that by the mid-1980s international capital flows had become far larger than in any previous period. Statistics have become much better in the past decade, and they reveal the growth of international lending in greater detail. Table 16 shows that net new international lending increased by more than 500 percent between the mid-1970s and the late 1980s, although the pace slowed with the spread of recession in the early 1990s.

Another measure of the volume of international capital flows is the daily volume of trading on leading foreign-exchange markets. Data on this have been collected only recently, but they indicate that the volume is enormous and growing rapidly. As I reported in Chapter 2, central bank surveys estimated the *daily* volume of foreign-exchange trading at $218 billion in April 1986, $431 billion in April 1989, and $880 billion in April 1992. During the crises in the European Monetary System (EMS) in 1992–93, observers frequently spoke of one trillion dollars in daily foreign trades. The total foreign exchange reserves of the industrialized countries have grown much more slowly, from $259 billion in 1986 to $453 billion in 1989 and $487 billion in 1992 (see Chapter 2). By the late 1980s, then, private trading in foreign exchange *on only*

17. BIS, *Recent Innovations,* p. 150.

18. Helleiner, "From Bretton Woods to Global Finance"; Bryant, *International Financial Intermediation,* pp. 61–62, 70.

19. Capital mobility is highest in the case of financial assets such as bonds, bank deposits, and loans; equity capital (stocks) and direct investments are significantly less mobile: Jeffry A. Frieden, "Invested Interests: The Politics of National Economic Policies in a World of Global Finance," *International Organization* 45 (Autumn 1991), p. 429. Financial assets respond most easily and quickly to investor comparisons of crossnational profit opportunities, thereby linking macroeconomic policies in different countries.

Table 16. Volume of average annual international lending, in billions of U.S. dollars

	1975–76	1977–78	1979–80	1981–82	1983–84	1985–86	1987–88	1989–90	1991	1992
Bank loans[a]	55	83	143	130	88	150	290	438	80	195
Bond financing[b]	25	30	28	46	70	142	124	154	170	118
Euronotes[c]	0	0	0	0	3	12	22	19	33	38
Total[d]	77	107	163	168	138	235	375	533	245	280

SOURCE: Bank for International Settlements, *Annual Report* (Paris: BIS), various issues.

[a]New international bank lending, net of redepositing among banks.

[b]New bond financing, net of redemptions and repurchases.

[c]Net new Euronote placements.

[d]Net of double counting of bonds taken up by banks and bonds issued by banks to underpin lending.

one day exceeded the entire volume of foreign reserves held by the central banks of these countries. National reserves would have quickly been exhausted in any attempt to fight strong market sentiment against particular currency values.

The trend toward greater capital mobility and larger volumes of foreign-exchange trading has generated increasing criticism in recent years, especially in response to the role of speculation in the EMS currency crises. For most of the 1980s, governments and international finance specialists generally believed that increasing capital mobility was both inevitable (due to technology) and beneficial (promoting the efficient use of capital). Critics who pointed to currency volatility's detrimental impact on the real economy and policy-making autonomy were not taken seriously.[20] The massive speculative attacks on the British pound, Italian lira, Spanish peseta, French franc, and other currencies in the Exchange Rate Mechanism (ERM) of the EMS caused many European officials to reconsider the liberalization of capital controls. Attention focused on the possibility of imposing a small tax on foreign-exchange transactions to reduce the incentives for short-term currency speculation without unduly interfering with capital movements associated with investments and trade in the real (as opposed to financial) economy.[21]

There are two problems with a tax on foreign exchange market transactions that undermine its usefulness as an instrument for restoring policy-making autonomy. First, in order to be effective, a tax needs to be introduced simultaneously in every major trading center. Otherwise, traders can simply shift their business to tax-free markets. Pressures for competitive deregulation to attract financial services industries and the commitment to market liberalization on the part of the United States, Britain, and Germany rule out such an alternative today.

Second, even a universal transactions tax that slows speculation cannot insulate macroeconomic policies from international capital market pressures. Much stronger capital controls did not insulate French, American, or British policies from capital market pressures in the 1970s and 80s. A transactions tax low enough not to interfere with capital

---

20. Eric Helleiner, "Liberalization and After: A Changing Pattern of Financial Relations among Advanced Industrial States?" (Paper prepared for the 1993 Annual Meeting of the American Political Science Association, Washington, D.C.), pp. 7–8.

21. Ibid.; pp. 9–10; *Economist*, 3 October 1992, p. 71.

movements related to trade and long-term investment might also have little effect during a crisis in foreign-exchange markets.[22]

In any case, key European leaders have rejected the options of renewed capital controls or a transactions tax.[23] Governments have been unable to devise a way to control speculative capital movements effectively without interfering with extensive (and valued) international trade and investment linkages.

Data in table 2 (Chapter 2) suggest that international integration of markets for goods and services has not grown as rapidly since the late 1970s as integration of short-term capital markets. Imports as a proportion of gross domestic product declined slightly for most leading advanced capitalist states after 1980, due mainly to a sharp decline in the price of oil. Overall, international trade flows achieved by the late 1970s remained at the same moderate level in the 1980s. This level of trade integration, combined with the willingness of private investors and central banks to lend enormous amounts to finance trade deficits, generated large spillover and feedback effects from divergent national macroeconomic policies. Consequently, most leading countries experienced large, persistent trade imbalances in the 1980s and the early 1990s. These imbalances complicated state efforts to achieve satisfactory long-term macroeconomic performance and threatened the liberal trading system.

Increasing international integration of national capital markets forced economists and policymakers to reconsider the problem of international macroeconomic adjustment. Before the shift to fluctuating exchange rates in the early 1970s, most observers believed that exchange rates were determined primarily by international trade balances, which in turn were determined by relative prices of internationally traded goods. This belief encouraged the shift to fluctuating exchange rates because it suggested that states could reassert policy-making independence simply by permitting exchange rates to adjust to compensate for different national rates of inflation. Observers assumed that the adjustment would be gradual and moderate (see Chapter 5).

After a few years' experience with generalized floating, economists

22. *Economist*, 23 October 1993, p. 26.
23. *Globe and Mail*, 16 September 1993, p. B10; *Economist*, 21 August 1993, p. 37.

and policy-makers realized that earlier models had been wrong. Exchange rates were no longer determined by the supply of and demand for a country's imports and exports of goods and services but rather by supply and demand in international money markets for financial assets denominated in different currencies.[24] The supply of and demand for national financial assets depend primarily on national monetary policies and investors' expectations about future exchange and interest rates. Thus, exchange rates are now determined directly by monetary and fiscal policies and by expectations about their future course. Small changes in policies (especially in interest rates) or expectations can immediately trigger large speculative capital flows, causing sharp exchange-rate movements. Exchange rates inevitably overshoot appropriate levels: currencies frequently appreciate or depreciate far more than crossnational differences in inflation rates justify. This problem imposes enormous costs of adjustment on domestic industries and workers, especially when currencies become overvalued.[25] Currency movements can also have direct adverse effects on macroeconomic policies, as when rapid currency depreciation stimulates inflation through higher import prices.[26]

Thus, the shift to fluctuating exchange rates in the early 1970s has not brought autonomy in macroeconomic policy-making. Amid rising international capital mobility, fluctuating exchange rates have been extremely volatile, and severe misalignments have persisted. Fluctuating exchange rates not only failed to produce macroeconomic autonomy but also brought new problems. The symptom-management policies that maintained international economic stability in the late 1950s and the 1960s (coordinated intervention in foreign-exchange markets and balance-of-payments lending) have been unable to cope with the volume of recent international capital flows.

24. This is the basis for the monetary approach to the exchange rate; Francisco L. Rivera-Batiz and Luis Rivera-Batiz, *International Finance and Open Economy Macroeconomics* (New York: Macmillan, 1985), chap. 15.

25. Richard C. Marston, "Exchange Rate Policy Reconsidered," in Martin Feldstein, ed., *International Economic Cooperation* (Chicago: University of Chicago Press, 1988), pp. 88–96.

26. The United States was sheltered from some of this inflationary impact in 1985–89 because a large proportion of its imports were priced in dollars and oil prices had collapsed.

Macroeconomic policy coordination offers governments an opportunity to avoid international economic instability and currency volatility when capital is internationally mobile. Although policy-oriented economists devoted considerable attention to the issue in the 1980s, their models are not terribly helpful for understanding actual policy coordination; the assumptions are unrealistic and the models were dismissed by policymakers. It seems more productive to return to the political motives for coordination that I introduced in Chapter 2.

Economists who favor policy coordination argue that it could increase national and global welfare by accounting for the spillover effects (or externalities) of national macroeconomic policies.[27] Coordination could ensure that the combined effect of various national policies is neither excessively inflationary nor deflationary, a situation that some people believe existed in the 1970s and 80s.[28]

Coordination could improve the ability of all countries to achieve their macroeconomic objectives, even if states differ among themselves on the priorities of price stability, growth, and employment.[29] It could also ensure that when all states believe that macroeconomic expansion is desirable, stimulus emanates from countries with low inflation. Conversely, when restriction is desirable, high-inflation countries would be responsible for the greatest policy shift.[30] In other circumstances, policy coordination could promote convergence among national policies to reduce exchange-rate volatility.

Other economists have challenged the view that macroeconomic policy coordination would increase national and global welfare. They advance three main counterarguments, each pointing to serious flaws in economistic interpretations of policy coordination and emphasizing the need for political interpretation. First, they claim that inter-

27. This literature is summarized in Michael Artis and Sylvia Ostry, *International Economic Policy Coordination*, Chatham House Paper No. 30 (London: Routledge and Keegan Paul, 1986); and Michael Devereux and Thomas A. Wilson, "International Coordination of Macroeconomic Policies: A Review," *Canadian Public Policy* 15, supp. (February 1989).

28. Destler and Mitsuyu, "Locomotives on Different Tracks," p. 244; Sylvia Ostry, "The World Economy in 1983: Marking Time," *Foreign Affairs* 62 (1984), p. 560.

29. A good explanation of this argument is given in Artis and Ostry, *International Economic Policy Coordination*, pp. 12–17.

30. Ronald I. McKinnon, *An International Standard for Monetary Stabilization*, Policy Analyses in International Economics No. 8 (Washington, D.C.: Institute for International Economics, 1984), pp. 67–70.

national spillover effects are relatively small; therefore, the potential gains from coordination would be equally small or even negative.[31] However, these calculations neglect the costs of trade protectionism that could easily result from persistent international trade imbalances caused by noncoordinated macroeconomic policies.[32] When Japan and Germany negotiated a fiscal and monetary stimulus after 1985, they clearly intended to defuse the threat of U.S. congressional protectionism. Empirical estimates that purport to reveal small or negative gains from coordination are also based on unrealistic assumptions about policy-making. For example, an important 1984 paper by Gilles Oudiz and Jeffrey Sachs assumed that the macroeconomic policies of each leading government accurately reflected the country's long-run social welfare function. This conclusion is doubtful at best; for example, U.S. policies at the time were clearly unsustainable—the unintended consequence of a political impasse between the president and Congress unrelated to any protagonist's conception of the national interest.[33]

The second counterargument is that greater welfare gains could be achieved if states independently chose optimal macroeconomic policies. International coordination could even reduce welfare by permitting governments to evade international market discipline. Coordinated expansion could enable all governments to avoid the balance-of-payments deficits that normally accompany expansionary policies, thereby making it easier for them to pursue inflationary policies.[34] If so—and the experience of the late 1980s offers some confirmation—this normative argument against coordination may help to explain why certain governments want to persuade foreign states to adopt more stimulative macroeconomic policies.

The third counterargument focuses on problems of uncertainty.[35]

31. Gilles Oudiz and Jeffrey Sachs, "Macroeconomic Policy Coordination among the Industrial Economies," *Brookings Papers on Economic Activity* 1 (1984).

32. Devereux and Wilson, "International Coordination," p. S33.

33. Oudiz and Sachs, "Macroeconomic Policy Coordination." Stephen Marris raises the issues of national preferences and sustainability in his comments on the Oudiz and Sachs paper in the same volume, pp. 68–71.

34. Martin Feldstein, "International Economic Cooperation: Introduction," in Feldstein, *International Economic Cooperation;* Henry R. Nau, *The Myth of America's Decline: Leading the World Economy into the 1990s* (New York: Oxford University Press, 1990), p. 349.

35. Jeffrey A. Frankel, *Obstacles to International Macroeconomic Policy Coordination,* Princeton Studies in International Finance No. 64 (Princeton: Department of Economics, Princeton University, December 1988).

Uncertainty about the current state of the economy, the true social welfare function, and especially the nature of international policy multipliers means that international macroeconomic coordination could make some or all states worse off.[36] More generally, some economists argue that intellectual consensus is a prerequisite for any international economic cooperation. From this perspective, the absence of international consensus about macroeconomic theory posed a serious obstacle in the 1980s to prospects for coordination, whether or not such coordination was desirable.[37] Nevertheless, history does not support the argument. Later in the chapter I show that governments did coordinate macroeconomic policies in the late 1970s and after the mid-1980s despite deep disagreements about optimal policies and considerable uncertainty about the exact nature of international linkages. The political power of the United States was the decisive factor, not intellectual consensus among economists. Policymakers also did not use econometric models to guide coordination. According to a participant in G7 finance ministers' meetings in 1987–89,

> most senior treasury officials have made little use of the results [of econometric simulations of proposed measures of coordination] when they were brought to their attention, and they remain skeptical of the value and relevance of quantitative research to the problem at hand, preferring to rely on firsthand experience and back-of-the-envelope judgments about linkages.[38]

For all these reasons, econometric calculations of welfare-maximizing policies do not provide a good explanation for international macroeconomic policy coordination. The critical political argument is that coordination can help governments pursue preferred policies (which may or may not have anything to do with welfare maximization) in the face of adverse international market pressures and domestic political ones. Coordinated foreign exchange market intervention and balance-of-payments lending served this purpose in the 1960s (See Chapter 4)

36. Frankel, *Obstacles to International Macroeconomic Policy Coordination.* He uses the estimates for national social-welfare functions developed by Oudiz and Sachs, "Macroeconomic Policy Coordination."

37. Richard N. Cooper, "International Economic Cooperation: Is It Desirable? Is It Likely?" *Bulletin of the American Academy of Arts and Sciences* 39 (November 1985).

38. Dobson, *Economic Policy Coordination*, p. 72.

but were overwhelmed by private capital flows in the 1970s, 80s, and 90s. Because those techniques no longer work, some governments now favor macroeconomic policy coordination to reduce payments imbalances and currency misalignment that threaten domestic economic stability and the liberal trading system. Coordination of this sort could easily become the coordinated inflation that some economists fear–that is, if inflation serves political interests of leading governments.

Finally, macroeconomic coordination could help states pursue perferred policies in the face of domestic political constraints and international market pressures. Usually governments are internally divided about what policies to pursue, and coordination may allow them to choose policies that benefit foreign countries as well as themselves. For example, the promise of greater foreign-government stimulation could make it easier for a deficit country to restrain its own policies, allowing exports to offset the deflationary impact of restraint and demonstrating to domestic constituents that other countries are sharing the burdens of international adjustment.[39]

Still, domestic political obstacles are often more significant than possible domestic benefits. Other strategies of international adjustment may no longer be viable, but that reality does not ensure that macroeconomic policies will now be coordinated. If they are not, international economic instability is the predictable result.

INTERNATIONAL COORDINATION OF EXTERNAL POLICIES OF ADJUSTMENT

Trade and Capital Controls

Trade controls were not used as instruments of macroeconomic adjustment in the 1980s,[40] but this situation reflected harmony, not conflict, among advanced capitalist countries (see Chapter 1). The absence of comprehensive controls certainly did not result from the absence of international market pressures; on the contrary, trade deficits were enormous, particularly in the United States but also in Britain, France, and

39. For a general argument about two-level games involving international and intra-governmental bargaining, see Robert D. Putnam, "Diplomacy and Domestic Politics: The Logic of Two-level Games," *International Organization* 42 (Summer 1988).

40. Japan did liberalize import restrictions in response to American demands that it reduce its payments surplus.

other countries. Industries and workers threatened by import penetration demanded protection, which often resulted in temporary sectoral restrictions intended to assist particular industries but not to insulate national macroeconomic policies from international influences. International adjustment was avoided or pursued by means of other types of policies. Even in the United States, where trade deficits caused by expansionary policies generated the strongest protectionist pressures, leaders sought to insulate the liberal international trading system from international macroeconomic adjustment problems.

Restrained use of trade restrictions reflects the success of earlier trade-policy coordination. Liberalization led to the creation of an international economic structure that now discourages states from reintroducing comprehensive trade controls. Selective controls are still imposed to deal with sectoral threats, but comprehensive ones would interfere with the globalized production structures that now dominate the economies of all advanced capitalist countries. International barriers that interfere with leading national industries would be extremely costly, even in the absence of foreign retaliation. Thus, in contrast to earlier decades, there is little incentive for individual states to defect from cooperative international trade liberalization. Nevertheless, specific threats of trade protection—especially when the U.S. Congress threatens to block Japanese imports—have been powerful bargaining levers in macroeconomic policy negotiations.

I have already detailed the trend in the 1980s toward liberalizing capital controls and the significant contribution that international coordination made to the process. In fact, liberalization was frequently used as an instrument of international macroeconomic adjustment: governments liberalized controls to stimulate private capital inflows or outflows to finance payments imbalances. Capital controls were no longer favored because of their accompanying political and economic costs. No one has yet devised a system that would block only undesirable speculative capital movements while permitting desirable trade and investment-related flows to continue. International financial linkages are highly developed, and investors have proven adept at finding ways around partial controls. Thus, any attempt to control capital flows would inevitably restrict international trade flows, which most advanced capitalist states believe would be harmful. In addition, comprehensive controls would face powerful domestic opposition from key industries that depend on multinational trade and financial networks' functioning within open international capital markets. Such opposition would make it extremely difficult for any state to reintroduce comprehensive exchange controls.

Exchange-rate Fluctuations

Exchange-rate changes were an important mechanism of international macroeconomic adjustment, if often by default. Governments occasionally tried to adjust exchange rates either unilaterally or in coordination with other governments to reduce payments imbalances. But more often they were forced to permit exchange rates to fluctuate because they were unable either to maintain stable exchange rates through coordinated foreign exchange market intervention or to agree on macroeconomic policy adjustments. Exchange rates among the key currencies—the American dollar, the Japanese yen, and the German mark (and associated European currencies)—fluctuated sharply in response to capital movements and trade imbalances. Keeping market-driven exchange-rate changes in mind, I will examine government efforts to alter exchange rates in order to promote international macroeconomic adjustment. I focus here on attempts to manipulate exchange rates without altering monetary and fiscal policies: that is, on exchange-rate policy as an external adjustment strategy intended to reduce pressures for internal policy adjustment. Specific instruments include foreign exchange market intervention and declaratory policy, either of which can be attempted in a unilateral or coordinated way. Later in the chapter I consider government efforts to block fluctuations symptomatic of macroeconomic policy differences among countries.[41]

The G5's coordinated intervention to lower the dollar from early 1980s heights began in January 1985 when the finance ministers agreed that the dollar was grossly overvalued. All agreed that a decline in the dollar's value would help reduce the massive American trade deficit and persuade Congress not to adopt a protectionist solution. American assent to coordinated intervention represented a sharp change from the Reagan administration's earlier approach, and resulted from growing concern in private industry, Congress, and

---

41. Admittedly, the distinction between coordination to encourage adjustment and coordination to prevent adjustment through currency fluctuations is sometimes difficult to draw.

branches of the administration about the problems an overvalued dollar posed for American industry. Reportedly, the personal intervention of British Prime Minister Margaret Thatcher also helped persuade President Reagan of the need for government intervention.[42] Bundesbank-led intervention in February and March 1985 had little immediate impact, although it did introduce uncertainty into the market and may have triggered the decline that began in March 1985.[43] Nevertheless, the dollar began to rise again in foreign-exchange markets in August and September despite a relaxation of American monetary policy.[44] In order to combat this rise, the G5 agreed in the Plaza Accord of 22 September 1985, that nondollar currencies should appreciate and that States would coordinate appropriate intervention.[45]

This announcement and the coordinated intervention that followed had a decisive impact on foreign-exchange markets, bursting the speculative bubble that had pushed up the dollar in 1984–85 and triggering a sustained decline in its value. Apparently, such an announcement persuaded the markets to pay attention to the fundamentals, and little actual intervention was needed to push down the dollar.[46] Furthermore, the announcement was consistent with macroeconomic policy adjustments: Congress had recently adopted the Gramm-Rudman-Hollings deficit cutting policy, and the Federal Reserve had recently relaxed monetary policy.[47]

On two occasions since 1985, the American government has unilaterally caused the dollar to fall in order to reduce its trade deficit and pressure foreign governments to stimulate their economies with relaxed monetary and fiscal policy. For much of 1986 and early 1987, senior American officials "talked down" the dollar, pressuring Japan and Germany to reflate simply by declaring that their currencies were

42. Destler and Henning, *Dollar Politics*, chap. 3; regarding Margaret Thatcher's role, see Paul Volcker's account in Volcker and Toyoo Gyohten, *Changing Fortunes: The World's Money and the Threat to American Leadership* (New York: Times Books, 1992), p. 240

43. Robert D. Putnam and Nicholas Bayne, *Hanging Together: Cooperation and Conflict in the Seven-power Summits*, rev. and enlarged ed. (London: Sage, 1987), p. 199.

44. Maurice Obstfeld, "Floating Exchange Rates: Experience and Prospects," *Brookings Papers on Economic Activity* 2 (1985), p. 413.

45. Marston, "Exchange Rate Policy Reconsidered," p. 103.

46. Kathryn M. Dominguez and Jeffrey A. Frankel, *Does Foreign Exchange Intervention Work?* (Washington, D.C.: Institute for International Economics, September 1993), pp. 10–14, 136, 139.

47. Yoichi Funabashi, *Managing the Dollar: From the Plaza to the Louvre* (Washington, D.C.: Institute for International Economics, 1988), p. 63.

undervalued and that the United States would not intervene to keep the dollar from falling.[48] Foreign-exchange markets responded as American officials had hoped, and the United States joined in coordinated efforts to halt the dollar's decline only after foreign governments agreed to consider more stimulative domestic policies. In the context of bilateral negotiations to reduce Japan's trade surplus, President Clinton and Treasury Secretary Lloyd Bentsen called for a higher yen to make Japanese exports less competitive and put pressure on the Japanese government to relax import barriers in the spring and summer of 1993 and again in early 1994. These comments pushed the dollar to record lows against the yen and encouraged the Japanese government to adopt the stimulative fiscal policy demanded by Washington. But the sinking dollar and the Clinton administration's initial indifference to it undermined market confidence in American policy, pushed up long-term interest rates, and destabilized U.S. financial markets. Eventually the Clinton administration was forced to intervene to support the dollar in August 1993 and May–June 1994. Unilateral American efforts to adjust exchange rates to reduce international trade imbalances thus had high costs for foreign countries and for the United States.[49]

Efforts have also been made to coordinate exchange-rate adjustments in the EC. Exchange rates among the countries participating in the ERM were remarkably stable from the early 1980s until 1992, due mainly to coordination of monetary policies, an internal strategy of adjustment. Coordination of foreign exchange market intervention (a symptom-management strategy) was extensive but less important. Adjustments to ERM exchange rates have been frequent and sometimes substantial. At first some changes were announced unilaterally, but between 1982 and 1987 all adjustments were negotiated. In the ERM's early years adjustments were made in cases of persistent payments imbalances to accommodate divergent national inflation rates. The ability of the EC states to coordinate exchange-rate adjustments in the mid-1980s contrasts sharply with their inability to do so in the 1950s and 60s (see Chapters 3 and 4).

Nevertheless, the ERM countries were unable to coordinate

48. Funabashi, *Managing the Dollar*, describes this strategy in some detail.
49. *New York Times*, 29 April 1993, p. D2; 2 May 1993, p. IV:7; 20 August 1993, pp. D1, D4; 5 May 1994, pp. A1, D20; *Globe and Mail*, 22 April 1993, p. B4; 23 August 1993, p. B3; 5 May 1994, pp. B1, B2; 25 June 1994, pp. B1, B5.

exchange-rate adjustments after 1987, which contributed to a serious weakening of the mechanism in 1992–93. Exchange rates were very stable between 1987 and 1992, encouraging the view that the ERM would serve as a transitional fixed exchange rate predecessor to an eventual monetary union and single European currency. The British government's decision to take sterling into the ERM in 1990 seemed to support this view. But Britain unilaterally determined the rate at which the pound entered the ERM, preferring a high rate to signal its commitment to pursue anti-inflationary monetary policies. The Bundesbank in particular felt that the rate was too high in light of high British inflation rates.[50] This failure to coordinate exchange-rate levels helped set the stage for sterling's departure from the ERM in September 1992.

There was some discussion of realignment in early 1991 when German interest rates rose sharply to contain the inflation expected to follow reunification. The mark's revaluation would directly dampen inflationary pressures, thereby reducing the need to raise German interest rates, and might help other ERM countries avoid following those rates up.[51] But other ERM governments feared that devaluation would undermine market confidence in their economic policies, and there was little market pressure for realignment because the mark was generally weak due to lack of market confidence in German government policies.

The German central bank proposed currency realignments again in September 1992 during the first massive speculative attack on the ERM. Specifically, the Bundesbank offered to reduce interest rates (reportedly by one percentage point) if Britain, Italy, and other governments with currencies under attack would agree to devalue their currencies in the ERM. Such a package might well have met the economic concerns of each government: revaluing the mark would have dampened inflation in Germany even while interest rates were lowered, while lower currency values and interest rates would have helped other countries' economies recover from recession.[52] But British leaders rejected the proposal, blaming Germany for the crisis because of its high interest rates. In addition they feared losing political and economic credi-

50. *New York Times*, 23 September 1992, p. A16.
51. *Economist*, 23 February 1991, p. 65; *Globe and Mail*, 1 February 1991, p. B10.
52. On the other hand, there were fears that devaluation would force governments to raise interest rates to offset a presumed loss of anti-inflationary credibility.

bility if they agreed to devalue after declaring publicly that they would never do so. These concerns would have been reduced if the French franc and other EC currencies had also been devalued, as the British government proposed; but neither the French government not the Bundesbank believed that franc devaluation was appropriate.[53] This inability to agree on exchange-rate adjustments beyond a small devaluation of the lire led the Bundesbank to make a modest cut of one-quarter of a percentage point in interest rates, which was not sufficient to change the incentives for speculators. The pound was soon forced to depreciate outside the ERM without the benefit of a significant decline in German interest rates.

Although we have witnessed some negotiated exchange-rate adjustments since 1978, there continue to be significant obstacles to international coordination. Important obstacles include the domestic political importance of the exchange rate as a measure of confidence in government policies (particularly in European countries) and American willingness to manipulate the value of the dollar as a unilateral bargaining tool. Underlying all these obstacles is declining government ability to influence exchange rates without altering monetary and fiscal policies.

INTERNATIONAL COORDINATION OF SYMPTOM-MANAGEMENT POLICIES

International capital mobility and moderate levels of trade-market intervention generated enormous payments imbalances and exchange-rate volatility when governments were unable to coordinate macroeconomic policies in the 1980s. As in earlier decades, governments attempted to manage payments imbalances and stabilize exchange rates by coordinating intervention in foreign-exchange markets and lending from surplus to deficit states. These attempts had mixed success. Two factors were critical: the enormous volume of private international flows that had to be managed and the Reagan administration's opposition to coordinated foreign-exchange intervention. As we shall see, however, the first factor was the most important. Even when the G7 governments

53. Craig R. Whitney, "Blaming the Bundesbank," *New York Times Magazine*, 17 October 1993, pp. 44, 48; *Economist*, 26 September 1992, pp. 49, 89; 9 January 1993, p. 54; *New York Times*, 14 September 1992, pp. A1, D2.

could agree to coordinate intervention, they were able to achieve their exchange-rate objectives only when those objective were consistent with underlying macroeconomic policies. Coordinated foreign exchange market intervention now has limited value as a symptom-management strategy because the volume of capital that flows internationally in response to macroeconomic policies can easily overwhelm it.

In this section, I examine coordinated foreign exchange market intervention and international lending as symptom-management strategies. While central banks devoted enormous sums to coordinated intervention (far more than in the 1960s, for example), it was often unsuccessful unless backed by coordinated interest-rate adjustments. Balance-of-payments lending was predominantly private, as in the 1970s; but international coordination was crucial for both encouraging private international lending and providing actual funds to finance the U.S. payments deficit after private investors lost confidence in the country's ability to repay the real value of its debts.

Coordinated Intervention in Foreign-exchange Markets

Coordinated intervention among the G7 countries has generally attempted to influence the exchange rate between the U.S. dollar and other currencies, particularly the Japanese yen and the German mark. (Later in the chapter I discuss coordinated intervention to stabilize European currencies around the mark.) This focus on the dollar reflects its centrality in the international economy as well as U.S. bargaining power; other governments have not been as successful in gaining foreign support for their currency objectives. A brief review of prominent instances of coordinated intervention reveals both the extensive nature of intervention (except during the first Reagan administration, 1981–84) and its limited effectiveness as a strategy of international macroeconomic adjustment.

In fall 1978, the American dollar came under severe pressure in foreign-exchange markets because of rapid inflation and declining market confidence in the Carter administration. On 1 November the administration raised interest rates to a then-record high of 9.5 percent; and the United States declared that it would intervene heavily to support the dollar in coordination with foreign central banks, drawing on up to $30 billion in foreign currency to be borrowed for the purpose.

The foreign-exchange markets were impressed with the package, and the dollar rose sharply in November assisted by $3.5 billion of U.S. intervention alone. There were no further adjustments to American macroeconomic policies, however, and in December the dollar fell back to October levels despite continued intervention at the same rate. "The episode illustrates the effectiveness of monetary and exchange rate operations in halting a currency's slide. But it also illustrates the limitations of such action if not followed up by more fundamental changes in monetary policy and macroeconomic policy in general."[54] The dollar did not begin to strengthen decisively until the fall of 1979 when a dramatic tightening of American monetary policy was announced.

In the early 1980s, the dollar climbed sharply relative to most overseas currencies because of the combination of stimulative fiscal policies and restrictive monetary policies pursued in the first four years of the Reagan adminstration. Before 1985 administration officials rejected frequent foreign proposals for coordinated efforts to stabilize exchange rates and correct currency misalignments, in part because they believed that it was important to use monetary policy to stabilize domestic prices rather than exchange rates.[55] British Prime Minister Margaret Thatcher concurred (at least until 1984–85, as discussed earlier). As a consequence, the United States and Britain experienced severely overvalued exchange rates, and currency overvaluation exacted enormous costs on their tradeable goods industries.[56]

American policy changed radically in 1985, to favor coordinated exchange-rate management. Incoming Treasury Secretary James Baker reversed the nonintervention policy in response to growing criticism from private industry and an increasingly protectionist Congress. A focus on coordinated market intervention also shifted attention from American budget problems and shared some of the burden of adjustment with foreign governments, thus serving the Treasury Department's interests in internal government politics.[57] The change in American policy led to coordinated intervention in 1985 to correct currency misalignments, particularly after the September 1985 Plaza Accord. Extensive intervention was effective only because macroeco-

54. Marston, "Exchange Rate Policy Reconsidered," pp. 101–3 (quotation on p. 102).

55. See Destler and Henning, *Dollar Politics*, for a detailed account of the Reagan administration's policy.

56. On these costs, see Marston, "Exchange Rate Policy Reconsidered," pp. 91–96.

57. Destler and Henning, *Dollar Politics*, chap. 3.

nomic policies were adjusted to support it. (See my discussion of this important episode earlier in the chapter.)

Coordinated intervention in foreign-exchange markets was limited between the fall of 1985 and early 1987 because the United States refused to cooperate to stabilize exchange rates unless Japan and Germany agreed to stimulate domestic demand. As I mentioned earlier, Reagan administration officials talked down the dollar to pressure Germany and Japan to reflate; if they did not, their exchange rates would become severely overvalued, thereby hurting their export industries.[58] Eventually, the two countries did agree to relax monetary and fiscal policies, and the United States became increasingly concerned that the dollar was going into a free-fall.

These changes set the stage for a resumption of coordinated foreign exchange market intervention, agreed to in the Louvre Accord of February 1987. This accord introduced the notion of loosely defined target ranges for the mark and yen against the dollar.[59] These ranges were adjusted a number of times in response to American demands and changing market sentiments.[60] Sharp fluctuations in the dollars value in 1987 and 1989 caused the G7 to widen the target ranges until they became "devoid of much meaning."[61]

Without lasting agreements on target ranges, intervention in recent years has been ad hoc, occurring when governments agree that markets are clearly overshooting appropriate currency values. Intervention has sought to dampen wide swings in the dollar's value, propping it up in the face of declining market confidence in American policies or interest rates or after American efforts to talk down the dollar threaten to become too successful (e.g., the spring of 1987, August 1993, and May–June 1994). Intervention to support the dollar alternated with intervention to prevent it from rising above levels that the United States and other governments consider necessary to reduce the American trade deficit.[62] Coordinated intervention has been frequent even when par-

58. Funabashi, *Managing the Dollar*, chap. 7.

59. The Louvre negotiations are recounted in Funabashi, *Managing the Dollar*, chap. 8; Volcker and Gyohten, *Changing Fortunes*, pp. 266–68, 282–84.

60. For accounts of concerted intervention during these years, see Funabashi, *Managing the Dollar*; Destler and Henning, *Dollar Politics*, chap. 4; and Dominguez and Frankel, *Does Foreign Exchange Market Intervention Work?* chap. 5.

61. Dobson, *Economic Policy Coordination*, p. 70.

62. For a list of intervention episodes between 1985 and early 1991, see Dominguez and Frankel, *Does Foreign Exchange Intervention Work?* p. 96. Major episodes of coordinated

ticipating countries disagree over macroeconomic policy preferences; for example, it was intensive in early 1991 despite divergent interest-rate policies. Similarly, deep disagreements between the United States and Germany and Japan over monetary and fiscal policies did not prevent coordinated intervention to support the dollar in August 1992 and dampen the rise of the yen in August 1993. Indeed, countries have often favored exchange-rate policy coordination as a way to deflect foreign pressure for adjustments in fiscal and interest-rate policies.

Coordinated foreign exchange market intervention has also been extensive within the EMS. The rules of the ERM require that participating central banks intervene whenever market rates approach the limits of permissible fluctuation around central ERM parities. Central banks spent the equivalent of tens of billions of dollars in efforts to maintain ERM currency rates during the crises of 1992–93. These efforts were ultimately unsuccessful because of limited coordination of monetary policies and rampant speculation. Nevertheless, the efforts were substantial (the volume of intervention far exceeded that in any previous period) and did help to maintain fixed exchange rates for almost two years after German reunification. Even governments and central banks that bitterly criticized each others' monetary policies coordinated intervention until they were overwhelmed by speculative flows.[63]

The ERM crises of 1992–93 revealed both the extent of coordinated intervention and the degree to which its success depends upon macroeconomic policy coordination. Ultimately, fixed exchange rates could not withstand a policy divergence between Germany and other ERM countries. The French franc survived speculative attacks in September 1992 and January 1993 because heavy coordinated intervention was backed by increases in French interest rates. In contrast, massive co-

---

intervention since 1991 are reported in *New York Times*, 30 August 1992, p. III:11; 20 August 1993, pp. D1, D4; 5 May 1994, pp. A1, D20; *Globe and Mail*, 25 June 1994, pp. B1, B5.

63. For example, the Bundesbank spent about $30 billion on 16 September 1992 ("Black Wednesday") in support of other European currencies, mainly the British pound (*New York Times*, 2 October 1992, p. D1), even though this intervention inflated the German money supply and complicated the bank's efforts to reduce inflation. Ultimately, these efforts failed because of an inability to coordinate what might be called "declaratory policy." Bitter public discord between British and German authorities—especially Bundesbank President Schlesinger's comments in favor of a broader ERM realignment, including the pound—undoubtedly fueled speculation. *Globe and Mail*, 12 October 1992, pp. B1, B2; *Economist*, 19 September 1992, p. 16.

ordinated intervention in September 1992 failed to save the pound because the British government loudly refused to raise interest rates until it was too late; and the franc was forced out of the ERM in the summer of 1993 because the French government was no longer willing to raise domestic interest rates to defend the franc in the face of deepening recession and growing domestic discontent at the high interest rates that necessarily accompanied the "franc fort" policy.[64]

The preceding review reveals that international coordination of foreign exchange market intervention has been extensive since 1978 and the resources devoted to intervention enormous. Nevertheless, it is far less effective in stabilizing exchange rates than it was in the 1960s. The level of coordination is not lower (except for 1981–84), but the nature of the problem has changed dramatically. Coordinated intervention can have an effect, particularly when it signals government intentions that alter foreign exchange traders' expectations. Expectations can be altered even by relatively small volumes of coordinated intervention. But intervention cannot stabilize exchange rates amid differences in macroeconomic policies: "All the foreign exchange reserves in the G7 vaults are not enough to defend an exchange rate that investors, operating in modern capital markets, decide is inconsistent with fundamentals."[65] In the 1960s, however, it was often successful even when states were pursuing inconsistent policies because international capital mobility was relatively low until the end of the decade (see Chapter 4). The repeated failure of coordinated intervention has recently dampened enthusiasm for this strategy. After central banks jointly spent an estimated $3 to $5 billion in support of the dollar on 4 May 1994 and another estimated $3 billion on 24 June 1994, only to see the dollar plunge to new lows, many G7 governments rejected the idea of additional intervention in discussions surrounding the 1994 Naples economic summit.[66]

The episodes of currency-market intervention I have described reveal interesting trends in political power. The United States continues to

64. *Economist*, 26 September 1992, p. 89; 9 January 1993, pp. 52, 54, 66, 68; 6 February 1993, pp. 76, 82; 17 July 1993, pp. 41–42; 7 August 1993, pp. 21–24.

65. Dominguez and Frankel, *Does Foreign Exchange Intervention Work?* p. 137.

66. Only Japan pressed for more intervention. Estimates of the volume of intervention from *New York Times*, 5 May 1994, p. D20; *Globe and Mail*, 25 June 1994, p. B5. Regarding G7 discussions, see *Wall Street Journal*, 11 July 1994, p. A3; *Globe and Mail*, 9 July 1994, pp. B1, B6.

dominate interregional policy coordination, remaining the driving force behind intervention to influence the dollar's value in terms of the yen or the major European currencies. The United States is more tolerant of exchange-rate fluctuations and more willing to use currency movements as a bargaining lever than either Japan or leading European governments are. Consequently, it has often supported coordinated market intervention only after the dollar appreciated or depreciated far more than other governments believe appropriate (e.g., when the dollar rose in the early 1980s or when it fell in 1992, 1993, and 1994), and often only after other governments adjusted monetary and fiscal policies.

It is important to remember, however, that the United States essentially did not participate in efforts to stabilize European currencies in 1992–93, in contrast to American involvement in intra-European exchange-rate politics in the 1960s. The sharp decline in the dollar's value in the summer of 1992 helped to trigger the September ERM crisis by encouraging capital inflows into Germany, thus driving up the mark against the dollar and other European currencies. Washington was late to join because President Bush was preoccupied with reelection and the German government was unwilling to consider policy coordination with the United States until the American government dealt with its own budget deficit and reconsidered the low-interest-rate policy that had contributed to strains in the ERM. The Bush administration also declined discrete European requests to intervene in support of exchange rates within the ERM in September 1992, believing that American action would not be effective except at an excessive cost.[67] Even though the Clinton administration's budget moved toward meeting European concerns, the United States remained uninvolved during the European exchange-rate crisis in July–August 1993. Exchange rates within Europe have become a purely European issue.

International Financing of Payments Imbalances

International borrowing and lending to finance payments imbalances, a symptom-management strategy closely linked to intervention in foreign-exchange markets, reflect the same changed economic conditions that weakened currency-market intervention. Current account imbalances were enormous in the late 1970s and 1980s, and short-term

---

67. *New York Times*, 27 September 1992, pp. I:1, I:14; 1 August 1993, p. I:16.

international capital flows played a major role in financing (and therefore permitting) them. Deficit governments encouraged borrowing to avoid severe currency depreciation and higher interest rates. Surplus governments, on the other hand, encouraged lending to dampen pressures for currency appreciation and to sustain exports.

As in the 1970s, this international financing was conducted mainly through private international capital markets but with notable differences. In the 1970s, when national and international capital markets were partially insulated from each other by moderate levels of private market linkages and by government controls, deficit states could issue bonds in the Euromarkets denominated in foreign currencies to raise foreign currency to maintain reserve holdings amid current account deficits (see table 12). The interest rate paid on these bonds was determined by Euromarket factors and could diverge from the borrowing country's domestic interest rates. Thus, private international financing of payments imbalances could partly insulate monetary policy from international market pressures, although (as I noted in Chapter 5) private international lenders eventually became unwilling to buy Eurobonds issued by governments that did not restrain inflationary policies.

In the 1980s the integration of national and international capital markets significantly changed the role that private international borrowing and lending played in the process of macroeconomic adjustment. The erosion of technological and governmental barriers between national and international markets meant that governments could no longer use transactions on private international capital markets to insulate domestic monetary policy from international market pressures. Governments that wanted to encourage private capital inflows or outflows to finance trade imbalances found they could do so only by altering the relationship between domestic and foreign interest rates. Deficit states such as Canada, Britain, and (after 1985) the United States could attract capital inflows to finance budget and current account deficits only by raising domestic interest rates—or, in the case of the United States, by persuading foreign states to lower their interest rates. Therefore, by the mid-1980s private international borrowing and lending was no longer separate from domestic monetary policy as a strategy of international macroeconomic adjustment; domestic interest rates now had to be adjusted to attract or repel the short-term capital needed to offset current account imbalances.

The United States was the largest borrower of private international capital, and it was partially exempt from this constraint. From 1981 to 1985, the government pursued expansionary fiscal policies combined for the most part with restrictive monetary policies, which raised American interest rates well above levels in other countries. In response to this differential, private investment flowed into the United States and into government securities (treasury bills) and corporate securities. Private capital inflows were sufficiently large to drive up the dollar despite a growing trade deficit.

Foreign investors continued to lend heavily to the United States in 1984–85 despite declining American interest rates and the widespread view that the dollar was overvalued. These factors ought to have deterred rational lenders because foreign loans to the United States were denominated in dollars. The United States is the only country that can borrow from foreigners in its own currency without paying a substantial risk premium. Normally, if governments want to attract buyers of domestic currency assets (such as treasury bills), they must offer substantially higher interest rates to offset the foreign-currency risk faced by foreign investors or domestic investors who have access to international markets. Consequently, any country other than the United States that wants to borrow from abroad must either issue bonds denominated in foreign currencies (in which the issuer accepts the exchange risk) or raise domestic interest rates. Because the U.S. dollar is the world's leading reserve and transactions currency, foreign lenders have been willing to invest directly in American dollar assets, including government treasury bills, without receiving an interest-rate premium commensurate with the risks they were taking.

In the early 1980s private foreign lending to the United States permitted the country temporarily to avoid market constraints on expansionary fiscal policies. Capital inflows directly or indirectly financed at least half the federal budget deficit.[68] Foreign financing also allowed the United States to avoid the inflation that usually accompanies radically expansionary fiscal policies: imports rather than an increase in the domestic price level met the excess of consumption and investment over output caused by fiscal expansion. In political terms, foreign financing permitted the government to cut taxes and stimulate private

68. Gilpin, *Political Economy of International Relations*, p. 331.

domestic consumption (an effect that helped the Republicans win two presidential elections) while the country embarked on a major military buildup.

The fact that international loans to the United States were denominated in dollars meant that some foreign lenders lost badly when the dollar fell in 1985–87. The real value of these foreign loans declined sharply, as did the real U.S. debt burden. If the debt had been denominated in lenders' currencies, the dollar cost of servicing the foreign debt would have increased. As one observer noted in October 1985, "for the first time a debtor nation stands to benefit both on its capital account and on its trading account from devaluing its currency."[69] By devaluing the dollar, "the United States would in effect expropriate and wipe out a substantial fraction of its debt; the drop of the dollar between March 1985 and March 1986, in fact, may have reduced the debt by as much as one third."[70]

The willingness of private foreign investors to finance American budget and trade deficits has been a subject of some concern since 1986. This issue has crucial implications for American power: since the 1980s its strong international bargaining position on macroeconomic adjustment policy issues has rested in part on the willingness of private foreign investors to lend money to the United States in U.S. currency, thereby insulating the country from some international market pressures. Weak foreign confidence in American policies has occasionally nudged up U.S. interest rates,[71] but policy coordination and favorable economic conditions have continued to insulate American monetary policy from the potential constraints of its dependence on foreign borrowing. For example, foreign private lending contracted sharply in 1987 in response to investor fears that the dollar would continue to tumble. Rather than see the dollar collapse, the central banks of surplus countries stepped in to finance the American current account deficit. Japan, Germany, Taiwan, and other surplus states made official purchases of treasury bills and dollar securities. The dollar foreign exchange reserves of these central banks increased dramatically in 1987

69. Peter Drucker, cited in ibid., p. 334.

70. Gilpin, *Political Economy of International Relations*, p. 334. Others estimate that Japanese investors lost the yen equivalent of $320 billion because of the dollar's decline since 1985; *Economist*, 7 May 1994, p. 90.

71. *Newsweek*, 18 May 1987, p. 58; *New York Times*, 14 October 1990, p. F2.

in contrast to slow growth in the years 1981–86 when American current account deficits were financed mainly by private lending.[72] In addition, the Japanese Ministry of Finance exercised its powers of "administrative guidance to encourage Japanese institutional investors to hold more US assets than they might choose on profit-maximizing grounds in order to keep the dollar from depreciating further than it already had by then."[73]

The limited effectiveness of this large-scale intergovernmental lending contrasts sharply with the effectiveness of much smaller loans in the 1960s, again demonstrating the declining usefulness of symptom-management strategies when capital is internationally mobile. For example, a rescue operation in 1964 lent $3 billion to Britain and permitted it to support the fixed parity for sterling during an apparently severe balance-of-payments crisis. In 1987 foreign central banks lent $120 billion to the United States but did not prevent the dollar from depreciating by 14 percent (in terms of SDRs) over the course of the year.[74] The success of symptom-management policies in preserving national policy-making autonomy in the 1960s was critically dependent upon relatively small imbalances.

After 1987, private foreign lending to the United States resumed. A major factor was American success in persuading the Japanese and German governments to keep interest rates low to increase the attractiveness of dollar investments. Private Japanese purchases of U.S. treasury securities were especially important and actively encouraged by the Japanese government. This encouragement, backed by low Japanese interest rates, reflected a clear political understanding between the two governments. Japan was willing to finance American deficits in exchange for continued access to the American market (temporarily assured by the Reagan and Bush administrations' resistance

72. Stephen Marris, *Deficits and the Dollar: The World Economy at Risk*, updated ed. (Washington, D.C.: Institute for International Economics, 1987), pp. xxvii–xxxi. Similarly, the Bank of Japan bought dollars in 1993–94 ($34.5 billion from March 1993 to April 1994) when long-term capital outflows from Japan to the United States shrank, although the dollar continued to fall. *Financial Times*, 9 July 1994, p.8; *Economist*, 7 May 1994, p.90

73. Dominguez and Frankel, *Does Foreign Exchange Intervention Work?* p. 19.

74. But it probably prevented the dollar from falling even further. The estimate of 1987 increase in foreign central bank holdings of U.S. dollars is from Destler and Henning, *Dollar Politics*, p. 61. The decline in the dollar is calculated from IMF, *International Financial Statistics Yearbook, 1988* (Washington, D.C.: IMF, 1988), p. 717.

to congressional trade protectionism) and continued American defense.[75]

By 1990, fears had returned about the continued willingness of Japanese and other foreign investors to finance American budget and trade deficits. Interest rates were rising in Japan and Europe, and concern about a credit crunch intensified as Japanese financial problems became more apparent. To date, however, the United States has not been seriously affected by a shortage of foreign capital. Its overall payments position was strengthened in 1991 by more than $40 billion in foreign payments to finance Gulf War expenditures. Long-term capital flows between the United States and Japan (foreign direct investment, purchases of securities and real estate) swung sharply from large net inflows into the United States in the late 1980s and 1990, to a net outflow to Japan in 1991, to a small inflow into the United States in 1992. Large short-term capital outflows from Japanese banks, repaying substantial short-term borrowing in the late 1980s, helped to fill the gap created by the decline in Japan's long-term U.S. investment. Within the United States, the decline in foreign purchases of treasury bills did not create problems for financing the budget deficit because recession weakened private sector demand for loans, encouraging Americans to invest in treasury bills.[76] The situation appeared to change in 1994. Japanese investors repatriated funds to strengthen their domestic balance sheets, strong economic growth in the United States generated greater competition between the public and private sectors for borrowed funds, and outflows of portfolio and direct investment from the United States to Latin America and East Asia accelerated. Even though the Federal Reserve increased short-term interest rates to forestall future inflation, the sharp decline in the dollar in spring 1994 pushed up long-term interest rates. Rising long-term interest rates demonstrated that American policy was vulnerable to international market pressures, and encouraged the administration to do more to support the dollar.[77]

Thus, in the early 1990s international policy coordination and fortuitous economic conditions insulated the United States from the interna-

75. Gilpin, *Political Economy of International Relations*, pp. 328–40.

76. *New York Times*, 22 March 1992, pp. I:1, I:12; 22 February 1993, pp. A1, D3; *Economist*, 16 May 1992, p. 104; 19 June 1993, p. 74; *Globe and Mail*, 1 April 1991, p. B13.

77. *Economist*, 7 May 1994, p. 90; 16 July 1994, p. 74; *New York Times*, 30 April 1994, pp. I:1, I:49.

tional market pressures that normally result from heavy foreign indebtedness, although there were signs in 1994 that this might be changing. But for the 1980s and early 1990s, the symptom-management strategy of borrowing to finance payments deficits has continued to be useful. For other governments, however, private international financing of current account imbalances can be achieved only by adjusting domestic interest rates—an internal strategy of adjustment.

INTERNATIONAL COORDINATION OF INTERNAL POLICIES OF ADJUSTMENT

Divergent macroeconomic policies generated enormous international payments imbalances and currency volatility in the late 1970s, the 1980s, and the early 1990s. Capital controls and symptom-management policies, traditionally used to maintain international economic stability amid crossnational differences in fiscal and monetary policies, no longer worked because international capital markets were so highly developed. States faced strong political incentives to coordinate macroeconomic policies to help them achieve their domestic objectives.

Consistent with the economic-structural argument I have developed, monetary and fiscal policies were the central issues in G7 economic diplomacy. Governments suffering from current account imbalances and adverse international capital flows frequently called on foreign governments to alter macroeconomic policies to help reduce those imbalances. One example is foreign demand in the early 1980s for a relaxed U.S. monetary policy. In the European Community, France and other countries frequently asked Germany to pursue more expansive policies to permit other governments to stimulate their economies without generating capital outflows, trade deficits, and exchange-rate depreciation. Conversely, after 1985 Germany and Japan repeatedly called on the United States and other deficit countries to reduce fiscal deficits and tighten credit in order to reduce the payments surpluses that were pushing up the mark and the yen. On other occasions, one country might ask foreign governments to adopt policies that would make it easier for it to alter its own policies. For example, the Carter and Reagan administrations pressured foreign governments to cut taxes and increase spending because they hoped that stronger foreign demand for American goods would help sustain the economy and make it easier to restrain monetary and fiscal policies without causing a U.S. recession.

Despite widespread interest in macroeconomic policy coordination, mutual agreements to adjust monetary and fiscal policies proved difficult to negotiate and implement. We can best understand the reasons by examining the record of negotiations and policy coordination from 1978 to 1994. In this section I provide a chronological account of efforts to coordinate policies and demonstrate that international bargaining power and the institutional structures of individual G7 countries were the key factors behind actual patterns of coordination.

Ad Hoc Coordination of Monetary and Fiscal Policies

The first clear instance of negotiated mutual policy adjustment began late in 1977 and peaked at the Bonn summit in 1978. The contrast between U.S. expansionary policies and more restrictive policies abroad was generating large payments imbalances. The Carter administration called on Japan and Germany to pursue more expansive fiscal policies to sustain their domestic growth and stimulate imports from the United States, thereby stimulating the American economy and offsetting the deflationary impact of the tighter monetary policy that Washington wanted to introduce. The administration had joined with the British Labour government and the OECD secretariat in urging Germany and Japan to reflate in 1977, and those countries had been pressured to commit themselves to stimulate their economies if growth fell below previously announced targets (see Chapter 5). Growth did not match government predictions in 1977–78, which made it difficult for Germany and Japan to resist foreign pressure for more stimulative policies.

For a deeply divided Japanese government, intense American pressure combined with growing domestic concern about economic slowdown to produce macroeconomic policy adjustments. Late in 1977, the government agreed to a growth target of 7 percent in 1978, to be achieved in part by a substantial increase in bond-financed domestic spending, especially on public-works projects.[78] After this success, American efforts shifted to Germany, culminating in the package announced at the Bonn summit. The German government commited itself to introducing fiscal stimulus equivalent to 1 percent of GNP—approxi-

78. Destler and Mitsuyu, "Locomotives on Different Tracks," pp. 250–56.

mately twelve billion marks. In exchange, President Carter committed his administration to restraining monetary growth and decontrolling oil prices. (The German government and other critics believed that U.S. oil prices below world-market levels inflated world demand and therefore world oil prices.) The Japanese government, under continuing American pressure, reiterated its commitment to the 7-percent growth target and agreed to introduce additional budget measures if actual growth fell below that rate.[79]

Agreement at the summit was possible because international pressures for policy changes coincided with domestic pressures:

> Each of the three governments called upon to make the most specific contributions to the bargain—the United States, Germany, and Japan—was internally divided. Within each, one faction supported the policies being demanded of their country internationally, but it was initially in the minority. In each case, the domestic advocates of the internationally desired policy were able to use the summit process to shift the internal balance of power in their favour.[80]

Internationally, the Bonn summit agreement and concurrent changes in Japanese fiscal policy reflected American power. Other states in Europe and organizations such as the OECD, IMF, and EC had advocated Japanese and German fiscal reflation, but only the United States could impose sufficient diplomatic pressure and offer large enough concessions (to Germany on energy issues) to secure a change in foreign policies. American pressure on Japan and Germany continued through the summer and fall of 1978, but by late 1978 the issue was eclipsed by the dramatic deterioration in the dollar. In the spring of 1979, Japan's trade surplus with the United States declined sharply, in part because of Japanese reflation; and American interest in Japanese macroeconomic policy adjustments dissipated. More broadly, the second oil price shock and the resulting inflation (which

79. Robert D. Putnam and Nicholas Bayne, *Hanging Together: The Seven-power Summits* (London: Heinemann Educational Books for the Royal Institute of International Affairs, 1984), pp. 78–102; Robert D. Putnam and C. Randall Henning, "The Bonn Summit of 1978: A Case Study in Coordination," in Richard N. Cooper et al., *Can Nations Agree? Issues in International Economic Cooperation* (Washington, D.C.: Brookings Institution, 1989); and Destler and Mitsuyu, "Locomotives on Different Tracks," pp. 256–58.

80. Putnam and Bayne, *Hanging Together* (1984), pp. 97–98 (quotation); Destler and Mitsuyu, "Locomotives on Different Tracks," pp. 254–55.

some blamed on negotiated policy adjustments in 1977–78) pushed the issue of coordinated reflation off the international agenda for almost a decade.[81]

After the second oil shock, widespread concern about renewed inflation meant that the 1979 and 1980 G7 summits focused on mutual support for the restrictive policies proposed by most leading governments.[82] From 1981 to 1984, demands for international macroeconomic policy coordination came from the governments of countries hurt by the first Reagan administration's tight monetary and stimulative fiscal policies.[83] Foreign capital flowed into the United States to take advantage of high interest rates and finance the growing American budget deficit, pushing up the dollar sharply. The willingness of foreign investors to buy American government securities, even after the dollar became overvalued and American interest rates began to fall in 1983–84, made it easier for Washington to ignore the external consequences of its macroeconomic policy choices and reject foreign criticism.

Foreign governments were unable to persuade Washington to coordinate its monetary, fiscal, or exchange-rate policies internationally. The sensitivity of international capital markets to interest-rate differentials pressured other governments to follow American anti-inflationary policies regardless of domestic preferences.[84] Governments that objected to Reagan administration policies had limited bargaining power because most also had sizable trade surpluses with the United States due to stimulative American fiscal policies, and feared that demands for American budgetary restraint would trigger American demands for foreign fiscal expansion.[85] Governments were also divided among themselves. Expansionist governments in France and Canada wanted the United States to relax its monetary policy, and were willing to tolerate expansive

81. Destler and Mitsuyu, "Locomotives on Different Tracks," pp. 258–68; Putnam and Bayne, *Hanging Together* (1984), pp. 98–104.

82. Putnam and Bayne, *Hanging Together* (1984), p. 104. International consultations influenced American policy; strong German support encouraged the new chairman of the Federal Reserve, Paul Volcker, to take a very hard line on inflation; Volcker and Gyohten, *Changing Fortunes*, p. 168.

83. International debates in these years are chronicled in Putnam and Bayne, *Hanging Together* (1987). For the perspective of an American insider, see Nau, *Myth of America's Decline*, chaps. 7 and 8.

84. Nau, *Myth of America's Decline*, chap. 7 and p. 346.

85. Volcker and Gyohten, *Changing Fortunes*, pp. 185–86.

fiscal policy. But more conservative governments in Britain, Germany, and Japan supported tight U.S. monetary policy and deplored lax fiscal policy. At the 1982 Versailles summit countries agreed on more extensive multilateral surveillance of national policies, but key governments continued to be unwilling to alter policies in response to foreign criticism.

By 1985, Reagan administration leaders were beginning to understand that the United States was being harmed by their unilateral policies and became more interested in international coordination to correct growing external problems. The dollar was sharply overvalued, and American manufacturing industries (excluding defense) had suffered badly. In Congress, powerful protectionist pressures threatened to undermine the liberal international trading system. The United States was also rapidly becoming the world's largest debtor country because of heavy foreign borrowing to finance budget and trade deficits. The Reagan administration hoped to correct these problems in part by persuading foreign countries to stimulate domestic demand, thereby increasing imports from the United States and reducing the trade deficit. The trade deficit could have been addressed by tightening American fiscal policy; but the administration failed to achieve a deficit-cutting agreement with Congress in the spring of 1985, making fiscal restraint unlikely and increasing the appeal of a change in foreign government policies.[86]

Japan and Germany initially resisted American demands to reflate, which they feared would lead to renewed inflation, and continued to demand that the United States adjust its own macroeconomic policies to reduce international imbalances—in particular, lower its budget deficit. During 1985–86, the Reagan administration backed its demands for foreign reflation by pointing to the danger of congressional protectionism if the American trade balance did not improve and threatening to let dollar volatility continue unchecked (although by late 1986 Washington was becoming concerned that dollar volatility was scaring foreign lenders and impeding efforts to finance the American budget

---

86. C. Randall Henning and I. M. Destler, "From Neglect to Activism: American Politics and the 1985 Plaza Accord," *Journal of Public Policy*, 8 (1988), esp. p. 326. Nau, *Myth of America's Decline*, pp. 267–85, emphasizes how American diplomatic efforts in 1985–89 were driven by the need to cope with the international consequences of the inability to solve fiscal problems domestically.

and trade deficits).[87] "A key obstacle to macroeconomic coordination in 1985–87 was the Germans' fear that the Reagan administration would be politically unable to carry out any commitment it might make to cut the U.S. budget deficit, no matter how well-intentioned the president."[88]

Despite these conflicts over fiscal policy, governments agreed to coordinate exchange rates and, on occasion, interest-rate adjustments. As I discussed earlier, the G5 countries coordinated intervention to lower the dollar in January–March and September–November 1985. Japan and the European G5 countries were willing to coordinate exchange-rate policies with the United States because the U.S. had recently relaxed its monetary policy and taken steps to reduce its budget deficit, as other countries had long demanded. Discord over fiscal policy did not prevent leading central banks from agreeing to coordinate interest-rate reductions in March 1986, and the U.S. Federal Reserve and the Bank of Japan agreed on a further cut in April 1986.[89]

By early 1987, foreign governments were willing to reflate in return for American agreement to join coordinated foreign exchange market intervention to stabilize currencies and commit to reducing its budget deficit. The bargain was struck among G7 finance ministers in the Louvre Accord in February 1987.[90] The ministers established a system for coordinated intervention in foreign-exchange markets, and there were explicit negotiated mutual adjustments to macroeconomic policies. The German government promised to increase a planned 1990 tax-reduction package and move it ahead to 1988. Japan agreed to pass a supplementary budget in the spring of 1987 which would stimulate domestic demand, and to cut interest rates. The United States committed itself to reducing its budget deficit by restraining spending. The October 1987 stock-market crash (triggered in part by U.S.-German differences over interest rates) was met by immediate coordinated action among central banks to provide liquidity and prevent the crisis

87. International debates during 1985–86 are chronicled in Funabashi, *Managing the Dollar*, and Putnam and Bayne, *Hanging Together* (1987).

88. Putnam and Henning, "Bonn Summit of 1978," p. 103.

89. Funabashi, *Managing the Dollar*, pp. 46–50; Dobson, *Economic Policy Coordination*, p. 86; Nau, *Myth of America's Decline*, pp. 270–72; Volcker and Gyohten, *Changing Fortunes*, p. 274.

90. Discussed in detail in Funabashi, *Managing the Dollar*, chap. 8; and Volcker and Gyohten, *Changing Fortunes*, pp. 266–68, 282–84. This agreement was preceded by a less substantial agreement between the United States and Japan in October 1986.

from spreading. The shock also encouraged the German and American governments to implement the fiscal-policy commitments made in the Louvre Accord.[91]

From 1987 to 1989 monetary and fiscal policies in the three leading countries reflected the impact of the Louvre bargain. Japan kept interest rates low and monetary growth rapid in order to stimulate domestic demand and encourage Japanese investors to buy American treasury securities, thereby financing American budget and trade deficits and preventing the dollar's collapse.[92] For example, the Bank of Japan and the U.S. Federal Reserve coordinated interest-rate adjustments in April and May 1987 to encourage Japanese investors to buy American treasury bills. The Japanese government also increased domestic spending, even though this action conflicted with the Ministry of Finance's desire to begin paying off the enormous government debt that had accumulated since the 1970s.[93] Japanese monetary and fiscal policy adjustments had the intended impact: domestic demand was strong, the economy became less export dependent, and the current account surplus shrank.[94] The budget deficit shrank in 1988–89, although not because Japan had failed to implement stimulative policies. Instead, strong economic growth produced stronger-than-expected growth in government revenues, thereby shrinking the deficit.[95]

German macroeconomic policy in 1987–89 also revealed the impact of international policy coordination. The Bundesbank's 1987 efforts to support the dollar resulted in rapid money-supply growth, which fed higher inflation in 1988 and 1989.[96] Although the Bundesbank briefly raised interest rates (contrary to American preferences) in September and October 1987, it lowered them in coordination with other G7 central banks in the wake of the October 1987 stock-market crash. On a number of occasions in 1988 and 1989, the bank resisted raising interest rates to contain inflation because of anticipated protests from

91. Dobson, *Economic Policy Coordination*, pp. 118–19, 128, 130.

92. *New York Times*, 14 January 1988, pp. A:1, A:33; *Economist*, 19 November 1988, p. 93; 14 January 1989, p. 71; 1 April 1989, pp. 65–66.

93. Volcker and Gyohten, *Changing Fortunes*, p. 271; *Economist*, 29 October 1988, p. 35; 22 July 1989, p. 67; *New York Times*, 15 January 1988, pp. 25–26.

94. *Economist*, 2 July 1988, pp. 56, 58; 29 October 1988, p. 35; *Globe and Mail*, 20 June 1990, p. B6.

95. Dobson, *Economic Policy Coordination*, p. 94.

96. German money supply targets were overshot in 1986, 1987, and 1988. *Economist*, 5 August 1989, pp. 15–16.

other EC countries and the United States.[97] The German government resisted foreign demands for accelerated tax cuts and spending increases, but tax cuts (including those announced as part of the Louvre Accord) produced a fiscal policy more stimulative than other G7 countries in 1986–88, according to the OECD's calculations of cyclically adjusted budget balances.[98] Table 15 shows that the government's budget deficit increased in 1987 and 1988 despite strong economic growth. Like Japan, Germany continued to run fiscal deficits in the late 1980s despite its desire to reduce the national debt.[99]

American macroeconomic policies after 1987 also revealed the impact of international policy coordination, although in a somewhat perverse fashion. Coordinated reflation in Japan and Germany relieved international market pressure on the United States to adjust its own policies, especially the budget deficit at the heart of international imbalances. The Federal Reserve did occasionally coordinate interest-rate adjustments with foreign central banks, as I noted earlier. There are indications that diplomatic considerations sometimes influenced U.S. budget politics, although the impact was undoubtedly minor. For example, in September 1987 President Reagan agreed to sign deficit-cutting legislation worked out with Congress. Press reports indicate that this legislation was strongly opposed by Defense Secretary Casper Weinberger and Secretary of State George Shultz because it involved cuts in military spending but was strongly supported by Treasury Secretary James Baker as a sign of U.S willingness to uphold fiscal policy commitments.[100] Foreign diplomatic pressure may also have encouraged the Reagan administration and Congress to reach agreement in their December 1987 budget summit,[101] although the shock of the October 1987 stock-market crash had a more immediate impact, and the long-term results of the budget agreement were less than expected.

But on the whole, the impact of these specific measures was minimal in relation to the total deficit, and international pressure certainly did not cause a dramatic shift in American fiscal policy. The deficit re-

97. *Economist,* 13 February 1988, p. 79; 7 May 1988, pp. 71–72; *Globe and Mail,* 3 March 1989, pp. B1, B8.

98. OECD data reported in *Economist,* 11 March 1989, p. 67; see also Dobson, *Economic Policy Coordination,* p. 96.

99. "Survey of the World Economy," *Economist,* 24 September 1988, pp. 47–48.

100. *New York Times,* 4 October 1987, p. E2.

101. As suggested by Dobson, *Economic Policy Coordination,* pp. 119, 126–27.

mained very large despite rapid economic growth.[102] Budget battles between the Reagan and Bush administrations and Congress were not directly influenced by diplomatic pressures. Relaxed monetary and fiscal policies abroad, combined with exchange-rate coordination and balance-of-payments lending, permitted the United States to continue to run enormous fiscal deficits and finance them with foreign borrowing without triggering a collapse in the dollar's value.[103]

In addition to ad hoc policy adjustments, the late 1980s also saw the creation of a more systematic process of international consultation and coordination based on multilateral surveillance of economic policies and conditions. The 1985 American move toward macroeconomic policy coordination also created an interest in developing a mechanism for reviewing the economic policies and performance of other countries with an eye to pressing them to adopt policies that would reduce the American trade deficit.[104] Like the U.S.-proposed reserve indicator schemes in the early 1970s, this idea met foreign opposition. American officials wanted to establish a set of economic indicators to be reviewed in regular meetings of G7 finance ministers as well as target ranges for key exchange rates. Reviews would signal when specific countries needed to make policy adjustments. The United States hoped to use the system to pressure Japan and Germany to ease monetary policy, stimulate domestic demand, and reduce export surpluses. Not surprisingly, Japanese and German officials resisted American proposals to go beyond mere consultations, fearing that the United States would use any signaling mechanism to demand inflationary fiscal policies—as they believed the Carter administration had done in 1977–78.

Countries reached agreement at the 1986 Tokyo summit to establish a system of indicators to be reviewed at regular meetings of G5 and G7 finance ministers and central bank governors, although the notion of automatic policy adjustments was dropped. Instead, the summit communiqué asked the finance ministers to review individual economic forecasts, "taking into account indicators such as GNP growth rates, inflation rates, interest rates, unemployment rates, fiscal deficit ratios,

102. Nau, *Myth of America's Decline,* pp. 268–69, 283–84.
103. *Economist,* 30 September 1989, p. 12.
104. Destler and Henning, *Dollar Politics,* p. 55n11.

current account and trade balances, monetary growth rates, reserves, and exchange rates." Most important, the communiqué invited

the Finance Ministers and Central Bankers . . . to make their best efforts to reach an understanding on appropriate remedial measures whenever there are significant deviations from an intended course; and recommend that remedial efforts focus first and foremost on underlying policy fundamentals.[105]

The new multilateral surveillance system got underway in 1988. G5 and G7 finance ministers, deputy finance ministers, and central bank governors began to meet regularly to review trends in economic conditions and national policies.[106] In 1988 and 1989, government policies were moving in directions necessary to restore international equilibrium (e.g., domestic demand was increasing in Japan, and the U.S. budget deficit was shrinking), so no drastic remedial measures were proposed.[107] Communiqués from finance ministers' meetings and economic summits stressed the need to adjust domestic policies, especially fiscal ones, to eliminate external payments imbalances. The governments with the largest budget deficits—the United States, Canada, and Italy—needed to cut their deficits, while Japan and Germany needed to strengthen domestic demand and adopt microeconomic reforms to stimulate domestic demand and imports. These recommendations were broadly consistent with policies that governments claimed to be pursuing already and probably had little independent impact.

The use of concrete indicators had mixed results, however, and discouraged any attempt to establish further quantitative guidelines for policy adjustment. Projections prepared early in 1988 contained substantial forecasting errors: economic growth and trade adjustment in the United States and Japan was much faster than projected, and inflationary pressures were greater than anticipated. "As a result, the projections on which the surveillance exercise was based were called into question, mak-

105. The communiqué is reprinted in Funabashi, *Managing the Dollar*, p. 268.

106. Multilateral surveillance procedures are described in detail in Dobson, *Economic Policy Coordination.*

107. Andrew Crockett, "The Role of International Institutions in Surveillance and Policy Coordination," in Ralph C. Bryant et al., eds., *Macroeconomic Policies in an Interdependent World* (Washington, D.C.: Brookings Institution, IMF, and Centre for Economic Policy Research, 1989), p. 360.

ing it difficult to agree on the implications for further policy change."[108] Even when statistical indicators were accurate, governments disagreed over their significance and policy implications.[109] Multilateral surveillance was limited to being an ongoing forum for ad hoc bargaining.

Interest in new measures of macroeconomic policy coordination declined after 1988, although policy in the three leading countries continued to incorporate adjustments made in 1987. Current account imbalances shrank in 1988 due to coordinated policy adjustments begun in 1985–87,[110] thereby reducing international market pressure for new negotiated policy adjustments and relieving the sense of crisis. The urgency underlying negotiations also decreased because of the emerging consensus that international capital markets were able to finance larger payments imbalances than observers had thought.[111]

Leading governments lost interest in new measures for more overtly political reasons. Reflation in Japan and Germany had reduced the American trade deficit, and domestic concern about the American budget deficit had risen. Consequently, the United States relaxed pressure on foreign governments to alter their macroeconomic policies. For their part, foreign governments were increasingly unwilling to continue adjusting their policies while the main source of international imbalance—the U.S. budget deficit—remained immune to international pressures.[112] The budget deficit did decline in relation to GDP in 1987–89 (see table 15) due mainly to rapid economic growth; the paralysis in fiscal policy-making had been undisturbed even by the October 1987 stock-market crash. The election of President Bush, who was fervently opposed to tax increases, and his failure to attack the deficit seriously in the first budget of his administration, strengthened the perception that American fiscal policy-making was irresponsible. It was criticized in unusually sharp language at an OECD ministerial meeting in May 1989,[113] and the BIS called it "deplorable."[114] The American govern-

108. Dobson, *Economic Policy Coordination*, pp. 58–59.

109. Volcker and Gyohten, *Changing Fortunes*, pp. 270, 278–79.

110. Dobson, *Economic Policy Coordination*, pp. 121–23.

111. This view was endorsed by the OECD and the IMF. *Economist*, 20 January 1990, p. 73; 30 June 1990, p. 63.

112. Dobson, *Economic Policy Coordination*, p. 133.

113. *Globe and Mail*, 1 June 1989, p. B4.

114. *Globe and Mail*, 13 June 1989, p. B23.

ment's inability to control the budget deficit, despite years of promises, undoubtedly soured the environment for international policy coordination.[115]

Interest in new measures of international coordination also declined in 1988–89 as the clear problems of 1985–87 were replaced by greater uncertainty about the threats to international economic stability. Signs of renewed inflation emerged in 1988, and evidence of recession appeared in some countries in 1989. These conflicting signs led to internal government conflicts about whether interest rates needed to be raised to fight inflation or lowered to avoid recession.[116]

International consultations did have an impact on these internal debates. According to a participant in the G7 deputy finance ministers' meetings in 1987–89, policy coordination among central banks contributed to

> the generalized tightening of monetary policy in the 1988–89 period, when growth was stronger than expected and inflationary pressures began to emerge in some countries. Treasuries in those countries experiencing particularly strong inflationary pressures supported this generalized tightening and cautioned their less-troubled colleagues to do so as well—which they did.[117]

According to another analyst, these meetings encouraged finance ministries to adopt lower, more convergent targets for inflation rates because "finance ministers are naturally reluctant to state a commitment to a higher inflation rate than their counterparts in other countries." Such "coordination of objectives" did have an impact on macroeconomic policies,[118] and it continued into 1990, shown by the G7 response to the jump in oil prices after Iraq's invasion of Kuwait. At a G7 finance ministers' meeting in September 1990, participants agreed not to shield consumers from higher oil prices and emphasized the

115. See, for example, the comments of senior Japanese official Toyoo Gyohten in Volcker and Gyohten, *Changing Fortunes*, pp. 271–72, 309.

116. *Economist*, 12 May 1990, p. 67.

117. Dobson, *Economic Policy Coordination*, p. 126.

118. David Currie, "International Cooperation in Monetary Policy: Has It a Future?" *The Economic Journal* 103 (January 1993), p. 184.

need for restrictive, anti-inflationary monetary policies despite evidence of slowed economic growth.[119]

As international payments imbalances and political concern about them declined after 1988, the G7's attention shifted from international macroeconomic policy coordination toward other issues: Third World debt, financing the Gulf War, and the breakup of the Soviet Union. Declining interest in coordination was signaled by the fact that G7 finance ministers did not meet between October 1989 and March 1990. They met in April 1990, primarily to discuss the weakness of the Japanese yen and to consider a request from the Japanese finance minister for cuts in foreign interest rates. The finance ministry hoped that lower foreign interest rates would relieve pressure on the yen and discourage the Bank of Japan from raising Japanese interest rates. This international initiative reflected an internal dispute between the Bank of Japan, whose new governor wanted to suppress inflationary pressures, and the finance ministry, which was concerned about preventing an economic slowdown and collapsing prices on the recently overheated Tokyo stock exchange and in Japanese real estate markets. The United States and Germany rejected the Japanese request, ostensibly because they preferred to maintain high interest rates to fight domestic inflation. Canada's finance minister shared this view and dismissed the possibility of international policy coordination, arguing that "in the end, everything really starts with our domestic policy. . . .We can't change our policy as a base for doing something for another country."[120]

It is difficult to discern the logic behind the American and Canadian rejections of the Japanese request because both governments wanted to lower interest rates but had avoided doing so because they feared their currencies would decline.[121] Meeting the Japanese request might have served their own domestic policy interests as well as Japan's; indeed, the Bank of Canada subsequently began to reduce its interest rates. The episode demonstrates a remarkably parochial approach to monetary policy-making. Equally interesting, it shows the asymmetry in

119. *New York Times*, 24 September 1990, pp. D1, D13.

120. *Globe and Mail*, 9 April 1990, pp. B1, B4 (quotation); *New York Times*, 8 April 1990, p. 10.

121. For the views of United States officials, see *New York Times*, 26 March 1990, pp. C1, C8. For the views of Canadian policymakers, see "Minutes of Bank of Canada Board of Directors' Meeting," 11 May 1990, *Bank of Canada Review*, July 1990, p. 22.

international policy coordination: similar American requests for foreign assistance have rarely been so rudely rejected. Japan reciprocated by not sending its finance minister to the G7 finance ministers' meeting in May 1990, leading to press speculation about the G7's growing irrelevance.[122]

Since 1990, two distinct macroeconomic policy issues have received sustained diplomatic attention. First, the United States (occasionally joined by other G7 states and international organizations) has pressed for more stimulative Japanese fiscal and monetary policies to reduce Japan's trade surplus. Second, the United States and many EC governments have called on Germany to relax restrictive monetary policies that the Bundesbank has adopted to contain the inflationary consequences of deficit-financed reunification spending. The American budget deficit continues to attract foreign criticism but is rarely a central issue on international meeting agendas because foreign critics have largely abandoned hope of influencing American policy.

The bilateral Structural Impediments Initiative (SII) talks in the spring of 1990 demonstrated continuing American influence on Japanese policy. Held under the threat of congressional protectionism, these talks were supposed to address the fundamental causes of the American trade deficit with Japan. In June 1990 Japan agreed to a large-scale expansion of bond-financed public-works spending, which the United States viewed as a way to increase Japanese domestic demand and stimulate imports from the United States.[123] For its part, the U.S. government restated its commitment to reducing the federal budget deficit and increasing the national savings rate. Simultaneously, President Bush announced that he would consider tax increases as part of a deficit-reduction package to be negotiated with Congress. Some senior administration officials suggested that Japanese pressure and other foreign criticism influenced this decision, although domestic considerations were clearly central.[124]

American officials renewed pressure for Japanese fiscal and monetary stimulus late in 1991. Japan had been spared the criticism that American officials had leveled at high German interest rates earlier that year

122. *Globe and Mail*, 8 May 1990, p. B25.

123. *New York Times*, 29 June 1990, pp. A1, D2; *Economist*, 30 June 1990, pp. 34–35; 21 July 1990, pp. 77–78; 5 January 1991, pp. 28–29.

124. *New York Times*, 29 June 1990, pp. A1, A12; 1 July 1990, pp. E1, E2, E4; *Globe and Mail*, 27 June 1990, p. A7; 29 June 1990, p. B1.

largely because the U.S.-Japan trade imbalance was shrinking and Japan had made concessions in the SII talks. By late 1991, however, hopes for U.S. economic recovery after the Gulf War were being replaced by fears of a credit crunch, and the Bush administration was concerned about the effect that economic stagnation might have on President Bush's reelection prospects. Simultaneously, concern was growing in Japan about the Bank of Japan's tight monetary policy. Introduced in mid-1989 to halt the speculative bubble in real estate and equity markets, it was threatening the stability of the Japanese financial system and growth in the real economy. Late in December 1991, the Bank of Japan followed the U.S. Federal Reserve's lead in sharply cutting interest rates, a move that was widely interpreted as a measure to head off American criticism at the forthcoming summit between President Bush and Japanese Prime Minister Miyazawa.[125] At that meeting, Bush and Miyazawa announced a general agreement to stimulate their economies by continuing to lower interest rates and increasing Japanese spending on public-works projects. American officials had been pressing for this increased spending to help the Japanese government meet its target of 3.5-percent growth in GDP in fiscal year 1992.[126]

This agreement, vaguely worded but grandly titled "Strategy for World Growth," set the pattern for U.S.-Japan negotiations over the next two years. Cuts in U.S. interest rates were matched by the Bank of Japan,[127] and the Japanese government announced major fiscal stimulus packages in March and August 1992 and April and September 1993. By the spring of 1992, as European economies began to go into recession, EC governments (later joined by international organizations such as the OECD and the IMF) joined American-led calls for Japanese fiscal stimulus.[128]

125. *Economist*, 4 January 1992, p. 69.

126. *New York Times*, 9 January 1992, pp. A1, A10.

127. See chart comparing U.S. and Japanese interest rates in *Globe and Mail*, 5 February 1993, pp. B1, B4. In April 1992, the U.S. Federal Reserve cut its federal-funds rate from 4 to 3.75 percent in response to the tumbling Tokyo stock exchange and fears that this could depress the New York stock exchange, thus slowing U.S. recovery. American officials denied that Japanese concerns were an issue in the rate cut, but a Japanese official said, "It's likely that was part of their decision, and we appreciate it very much." *Globe and Mail*, 11 April 1992, p. B1 (quotation); 10 April 1992, pp. B1, B9; *Economist*, 18 April 1992, pp. 13–14.

128. *Globe and Mail*, 27 April 1992, pp. A1, A2; 28 April 1992, pp. A1, A2; 27 May 1992, p. B15; *Economist*, 4 July 1992, pp. 33–34; *New York Times*, 2 May 1993, p. 9.

Nevertheless, Japanese monetary and fiscal policy changes were driven as much by domestic economic problems as by international diplomatic pressures. The tight monetary policy introduced in 1989–90 triggered a sharp decline in equity prices on the Tokyo stock exchange, serious problems in the financial sector, and eventually a sharp slowdown in the goods-producing sector. Cuts in official interest rates and various fiscal stimulus packages were intended to prop up the stock market and encourage banks to resume lending as well as to meet international pressures. But these strategies failed to strengthen domestic demand. The various spending measures had little effect on the government's overall fiscal balance. Table 15 shows that the central government deficit was small and shrinking in 1990–92, and the Japanese government sector as a whole was in surplus in after 1988.[129]

Foreign governments began to discuss Japanese fiscal policy in greater detail and to discount Japanese claims in international meetings. Some observers argued that not all announced spending had occurred and that actual increases were partially offset by spending cuts in other areas.[130] The Clinton administration took the lead in questioning the substance of Japanese policy announcements, demanding that the government cut taxes to boost domestic demand directly. This demand met strong opposition from Japan's Ministry of Finance, which was determined to reduce the government debt accumulated in the 1970s and 80s. Tax cuts appealed to a variety of Japanese political leaders, particularly those in the coalition that replaced the Liberal Democratic Party after the July 1993 election. In the summer and fall of that year, the idea also gained support among Japanese businesses, which were suffering from weakening foreign demand due to the rising yen and weak domestic demand. (Recall that American leaders had been talking down the dollar in spring–summer 1993 to pressure the Japanese government to introduce fiscal stimulus.) Nevertheless, divisions within the coalition government precluded the strong action needed to overcome the Ministry of Finance's opposition to this strategy, and the stimulus package announced in September 1993 did not include tax cuts.[131] After further domestic struggles, a temporary in-

129. *Economist,* 11 July 1992, pp. 65–66.
130. For a careful, nongovernmental assessment of Japanese policy that makes these points, see Jan VanDenBerg, "Japanese Stimulus: Truth and Advertising," *International Economic Insights* 4 (July–August 1993).
131. *Economist,* 21 August 1993, pp. 61, 64; 28 August 1993, pp. 31–32; *Globe and Mail,*

come tax cut was introduced in April 1994. In combination with earlier budget packages, this measure did help stimulate domestic demand and growth in mid-1994. Continued American pressure helped to persuade the new goverment of Prime Minister Tomiichi Murayama to extend the tax cut for another year in September 1994.[132]

This review demonstrates the difficulties involved in actually coordinating policies and assessing their impact. Clearly, the policy-making process in Japan has been heavily influenced by the United States, and foreign pressure probably encouraged an earlier, sharper easing of monetary policy and a more stimulative fiscal policy. Despite that fact, Japanese bureaucratic and domestic politics have been the dominant influence. My review also suggests the importance of domestic political-institutional structures in accounting for the outcomes of policy coordination; the strength of the Ministry of Finance and the weakness of the 1993–94 coalition government affected Japan's inability to introduce the tax cuts favored by foreign governments.

The other main issue in international macroeconomic diplomacy in 1990–94 was foreign concern about high German interest rates. These rates, caused by the Bundesbank's efforts to contain the inflationary consequences of heavy deficit spending on reunification, drew strong criticism from the Bush administration but created especially severe problems among Germany's EMS partners. For most of the 1980s, the EMS had functioned to coordinate monetary policies indirectly through fixed exchange rates. Commitments in the ERM to maintain fixed parities meant foregoing exchange-rate fluctuations as a regular mechanism of international macroeconomic adjustment and instead coordinating interest rates to prevent exchange-rate changes. Of course, the ERM was never symmetrical; Germany set its own interest rates in relation to domestic economic conditions, and others followed (although international pressures probably encouraged somewhat lower interest rates in 1987–89 and 1992–94 than Germany would have chosen solely on the basis of domestic conditions). So long as the German inflation rate was low, other ERM governments believed that sacrificing nominal autonomy in monetary policy meant they were actually increasing their ability to achieve national objectives of noninfla-

10 April 1993, p. B12; 30 August 1993, p. B7; 17 September 1993, pp. B1, B12; *New York Times*, 14 April 1993, p. D2.

132. *Economist*, 12 February 1994, pp. 34–35, 80; 9 July 1994, pp. 34, 39; 10 September 1994, pp. 33–34; 24 September 1994, pp. 32–33; *Financial Times*, 9 July 1994, p. 2.

tionary growth. Fixing currencies in terms of the low-inflation mark increased the credibility of national anti-inflationary goals, thereby making it possible for other governments to achieve low inflation and prevent currency depreciation with lower interest rates than would otherwise be necessary.

This arrangement depended on low inflation rates in Germany. But the government's reunification policies were inflationary, which undermined the entire ERM arrangement. The decision in July 1990 to exchange East German marks for West German marks at parity and the reluctance to finance reunification by cutting spending in western Germany or raising taxes meant that reunification would be financed mainly by heavy borrowing. The Bundesbank refused to accommodate the inflationary consequences and instead pushed up interest rates sharply beginning in late 1990.

At G7 meetings in 1991–92, rising German interest rates and the government's unwillingness to raise taxes or cut other spending to finance reunification attracted foreign concern. Criticism was led by American officials who feared that German policy would reduce American exports to Europe and interfere with efforts to lower U.S. interest rates. Some European governments were also critical, although their concerns were tempered by strong import demand in Germany and weak investor confidence in German policies, which tended to depress the mark's value and reduce pressure on other governments to match German interest-rate hikes.[133]

Foreign concerns apparently did cause the Bundesbank to delay raising interest rates in the spring and summer of 1991; it then increased them less than expected in August 1991 (after the London G7 summit).[134] But Chancellor Kohl's 1990 campaign promise not to raise taxes to finance reunification, combined with entrenched support for current spending in western Germany, made it politically difficult for his government to respond to foreign and domestic calls for a more balanced fiscal policy. The government's failure to heed Bundesbank advice on the economic aspects of reunification created turmoil within the bank and led to the resignation of bank president Karl Otto Pohl

133. *Economist*, 26 January 1991, p. 71; 27 April 1991, pp. 79–80; 31 August 1991, p. 53; *Globe and Mail*, 26 April 1991, pp. B1, B4; *New York Times*, 2 May 1991, pp. D1, D4.

134. *Economist*, 3 August 1991, pp. 72–73; 17 August 1991, p. 72; *Globe and Mail*, 28 March 1991, p. B8; 16 August 1991, pp. B1, B2; *New York Times*, 13 July 1991, pp. 33, 41.

in May 1991, thus encouraging the Bundesbank to take a hard line on inflation to restore its credibility.[135]

American demands for German policy changes intensified in late 1991 and early 1992. Tumbling American interest rates had failed to revive the economy; the dollar began to decline in the fall of 1991, and the Bush administration became increasingly preoccupied with the effect that a weak economy could have on the president's reelection prospects.[136] Late in December 1991, the Bundesbank raised German interest rates while the United States and Japan lowered theirs.[137] American officials tried to use Japanese support to persuade Germany and other European governments to join the Bush administration's "Strategy for World Growth."[138] Those efforts failed, despite increasing European concern about high German interest rates.[139]

G7 and OECD ministerial meetings in the first half of 1992 expressed concern about German policies, but heavy American pressure on the German government generated public antagonism rather than policy adjustments. German officials were particularly critical of American demands for fiscal restraint while the United States was unable to reduce its own budget deficit substantially. They also criticized American demands that Germany take international considerations into account in formulating monetary policy at a time when declining U.S. interest rates were causing turmoil in international currency markets and threatening to reignite inflation.[140] European governments were unwilling to join the United States in calling for lower German interest rates, although such views were expressed more often and forcefully in EC meetings. This lack of support reflected in part the Bush administration's loss of international credibility after its failure to tackle the budget deficit and its heavy-handed pressure on the Federal Reserve to cut interest rates. Equally important, governments such as France and Italy had decided to seek influence over German policy by creating

135. *Economist*, 4 May 1991, pp. 75–76; 18 May 1991, p. 84; 23 November 1991, p. 73; *Globe and Mail*, 17 May 1991, p. B5.

136. *Globe and Mail*, 7 November 1991, pp. B1, B8; *Economist*, 9 November 1991, pp. 12–13; 30 November 1991, p. 76.

137. *Economist*, 4 January 1992, p. 69.

138. *New York Times*, 9 January 1992, pp. A1, A10.

139. *Globe and Mail*, 27 January 1992, pp. B1, B2.

140. *Globe and Mail*, 7 July 1992, pp. B1, B4; 27 April 1992, pp. A1, A2; 19 May 1992, p. B10; *New York Times*, 27 September 1992, pp, I1, I14.

supranational institutions (for example, a single European central bank) rather than by directly confronting the Bundesbank.

The Bush administration paid much less attention to the issue of German interest rates after its failure to negotiate a coordinated growth strategy at the Munich G7 summit in July 1992. At the same time, the EMS crisis forced other European governments to become more active. The Bundesbank did respond to foreign concerns, raising interest rates less than expected in July 1992 and cutting rates modestly despite indications of continued inflationary pressures in September 1992, February 1993, July 1993, and October 1993.[141] Nevertheless, these cuts were too small to save the EMS; the pound and the lira were forced out shortly after the September 1992 rate cut, and ERM bands widened for most remaining currencies after the July 1993 cuts.[142] As I noted earlier, the Bundesbank almost certainly would have made a deeper rate cut in September 1992 if Britain, France, and other EC governments had agreed to devalue their currencies as part of a general EMS realignment.[143] Paradoxically, the Bundesbank did cut interest rates in early September 1993, despite virtually no change in economic conditions or indicators. This surprise move led to speculation that the Bundesbank had refused to act earlier to save the EMS in order to preserve its independence rather than to achieve any specific monetary policy goals.[144]

The two tracks of macroeconomic diplomacy (U.S.-Japan and EC-U.S) converged in 1993–94. Easing German monetary policy, combined with moves toward fiscal expansion in Japan and President Clinton's efforts to reduce the U.S. budget deficit, produced some unusually harmonious G7 meetings in the spring of 1993, between the two ERM crises. American officials believed that their diplomatic efforts, backed by the new credibility that the Clinton administration's budget plan gave to American proposals for international policy adjustment, had enhanced fiscal stimulus in Japan and (in tandem with

141. *Economist,* 18 July 1992, p. 80; 6 February 1993, p. 7; 3 July 1993, p. 5; 17 July 1993, pp. 41–42; *Globe and Mail,* 16 July 1992, pp. B1, B8; 17 July 1992, pp. B1, B11; 22 October 1993, pp. B1, B10; *New York Times,* 5 February 1993, p. D1.

142. *Economist,* 7 August 1993, pp. 21–24.

143. *Economist,* 29 August 1992, pp. 51–52; 19 September 1992, pp. 69, 89–90; 26 September 1992, pp. 49, 89; *Globe and Mail,* 12 October 1992, pp. B1, B2.

144. *Globe and Mail,* 10 September 1993, pp. B1, B2.

EC efforts) monetary easing in Germany.[145] Growing European concern about high unemployment[146] also seemed to converge with American interest in a coordinated growth strategy, as did European and American interests in Japanese reflation to reduce its trade surplus.

Nevertheless, while there was increasing convergence on broad objectives, differences over means continued to block negotiated policy adjustments. Conservative governments and finance ministries called for microeconomic policy changes to make labor markets more flexible (thereby encouraging new hiring) and rejected the neo-Keynesian approach of expanded capital spending accommodated by relaxed monetary policies, which was advocated by the European Commission and some governments. Those governments included the Clinton administration and the French government. The Clinton administration's call for the establishment of numerical national growth targets was rejected at the July 1993 Tokyo summit and, while the communique emphasized growth, it did not commit any government to specific policy changes.[147]

At G7 meetings later in 1993 and in the first half of 1994, Washington continued to urge Germany and Japan to reflate more strongly. The Clinton administration's efforts to formulate a G7 growth strategy at finance ministers' meetings and the Naples economic summit were not successful, encouraging some speculation about declining American influence and U.S.-European interdependence.[148] Similarly, while concern about instability in foreign exchange, equity, and bond markets was widespread in the spring and summer of 1994, there was confusion and disagreement about how to address these problems. Ambitious proposals to strengthen the role of the IMF (celebrating the fiftieth anniversary of the Bretton Woods negotiations) put forward by its managing director and others foundered on the refusal of leading states to contemplate stronger multilateral surveillance of national policies and perennial political discord over the dangers of inflation versus unemployment.[149]

145. *New York Times,* 1 March 1993, pp. D1, D5; 2 May 1993, p. 9.

146. *Economist,* 26 June 1993, pp. 53–54.

147. *Globe and Mail,* 7 July 1993, p. B10; 8 July 1993, pp. A1, A2; 10 July 1993, p. B3; *Economist,* 5 June 1993, p. 77.

148. *New York Times,* 15 March 1994, pp. D1, D5; 20 April 1994, pp. D1, D2; *Wall Street Journal,* 11 July 1994, p. A3; *Globe and Mail,* 9 July 1994, pp. B1, B6.

149. *Economist,* 23 July 1994, pp. 73–74; 8 October 1994, pp. 85–86.

But modest coordinated policy adjustments continued to occur in less ambitious settings. The United States did have some success in bilateral negotiations with Japan, as discussed earlier. With respect to Germany, the Bundesbank continued to reduce interest rates even though its money supply growth targets were repeatedly exceeded and inflation did not fall quickly. Rate cuts apparently were timed to precede international meetings including the October 1993 European Union summit in Brussels and the February 1994 G7 finance ministers' meeting in Frankfurt.[150] Another rate cut in May appeared to be timed to support coordinated intervention to stabilize the dollar, an interpretation privately confirmed by a Bundesbank official.[151]

Overall, it appears that the concerns of other European governments and the United States (though not during the last years of the Bush administration) did influence German monetary policy. Foreign government concerns likely caused the Bundesbank to delay and moderate interest-rate increases and accelerate the downward trend after July 1992. But foreign influence was limited, in large part by the same kind of fiscal policy problems that have plagued the United States since the first Reagan administration. Domestic political obstacles to financing reunification without heavy government borrowing encouraged the institutionally independent Bundesbank to pursue policies opposed by foreign governments and many Germans.

Conclusions

Since the late 1970s, attempts to coordinate international macroeconomic adjustment policies have focused on monetary and fiscal policies because when capital is internationally mobile alternative strategies do not work. Macroeconomic policy-making is becoming internationalized (in the sense that international consultations are continuous and detailed), although final decisions remain the unquestioned prerogative of national governments, and domestic consideration remain central. Negotiated mutual adjustment of monetary and fiscal policies has been more extensive than in any other period I

---

150. *Economist,* 12 February 1994, p. 78; 28 May 1994, p. 80; *Globe and Mail,* 18 February 1994, p. B6.
151. *New York Times,* 12 May 1994, pp. A1, D17.

have discussed, and macroeconomic policies have generally been no more divergent since 1984 than in the 1956–70 period.

But policy coordination has been too infrequent and its influence too modest (especially in the United States) to stabilize an international economy characterized by mobile capital and moderate levels of trade-market integration. Governments continue to try to manage the symptoms of policy divergence through coordinated foreign exchange market intervention backed by international borrowing and lending. Even though the financial resources devoted to symptom-management strategies far exceed those of the 1950s and 60s, private capital flows have frequently overwhelmed these approaches to coordination. States' unwillingness to coordinate macroeconomic policies more closely, the reduced effectiveness of symptom-management strategies, and the inability to devise controls on speculative international capital flows without interfering with trade and investment have left governments unable to avoid sharp exchange-rate fluctuations (an external strategy of adjustment) in response to payments imbalances. Currency volatility and misalignment undoubtedly impose high costs on national economies, but leading governments have often been unwilling or unable to make the negotiated policy adjustments needed to avoid them.

In this section I identify domestic political and institutional factors that help to explain why macroeconomic policy coordination has not been more extensive since the late 1970s and why coordination has varied so much. I also examine the impact of international power relationships on patterns of coordination, arguing that the United States has played a role that differs from that expected by theories of declining American hegemony.

The most obvious obstacle to policy coordination is differences in domestic political interests. Some of these differences are rooted in preferences about trade-offs between growth and price stability, but in theory these variances should not create insurmountable obstacles. Technically, it is possible to reach agreements on macroeconomic policy coordination that permit governments to pursue somewhat different policies while helping each other avoid those that are less preferable to all.[152]

This approach, however, has not really been tried. Governments have seen international policy coordination as a minor adjunct to,

152. Artis and Ostry, *International Economic Policy Coordination*, pp. 12–17.

rather than does an integral part of, macroeconomic policy-making. Thus, differences of domestic political interest pose less serious obstacles to coordination than does the parochial approach to macroeconomic policy making adopted by most governments. Internal policy-making pathologies are even more important, as I consider later in the section. Monetary and fiscal policies were traditionally oriented toward domestic political and economic conditions and long considered to be internal. As I argued in Chapter 2, this was a legacy of low-level international economic integration in the 1930s and 40s, when macroeconomic management became an explicit government objective, and of the even longer association between sovereignty and control over taxing and spending. Monetary and fiscal policy-making institutions were designed to gather information about domestic conditions and achieve domestic targets.

As the international spillover effects of monetary and fiscal policies increased with international market integration, mechanisms were created for considering international factors but were not fully integrated into national decision-making institutions. Meetings among central bankers in the BIS and senior officials from G5 and G7 finance ministries and central banks have become increasingly institutionalized, especially since the 1986 Tokyo summit. Nevertheless, individual roles vary considerably.[153] Central bank governors are the key officials in international discussions and national decisions regarding monetary policy, and many central banks have considerable domestic policy-making autonomy. While domestic concerns are central to monetary policy-making in the United States, Japan, and Germany (with smaller European countries following Germany and Canada following the United States), international consultations have had an impact since 1985. But central bank officials often fail to recognize links between foreign government policies and their ability to achieve domestic objectives, as when the United States and Canada rejected Japan's proposal for coordinated interest-rate adjustments in April 1990. Furthermore, central banks with some independence from national political leaders sometimes manifest an institutional interest in maintaining their independence from foreign as well as domestic intervenors. This institutional jealousy—shown, for example, by the Bundesbank's approach to

153. Dobson, *Economic Policy Coordination*, pp. 26–30, provides a good brief description of the relevant players and their domestic responsibilities.

Economic and Monetary Union in the EC—often poses an obstacle to ad hoc negotiated policy adjustments and detailed, ongoing consultations to stabilize international markets.

In the case of fiscal policy, institutional links between international consultations and national policy-making are weak in most countries— except in times of crisis, when top political leaders become involved in international consultations, such as the economic summits of 1977–78 and the mid-1980s. According to one participant, few officials who attend G7 deputy finance ministers' meetings "have direct responsibility for domestic economic or fiscal affairs. . . . [The consequence] can be an artificial separation of domestic and international goals that is counterproductive to managing interdependence."[154]

Attempts to coordinate fiscal policy face an even more debilitating obstacle. Arguments in favour of international coordination assume that policy is consciously made to serve macroeconomic objectives, which is clearly not the case in certain leading countries. This situation is most apparent in the United States, where the power to make budgets is shared by the legislative and executive branches. In the 1980s, the two branches had very different political priorities. The conflict produced fiscal policies that reflected the preferences of neither branch and failed to respond to the coordination desires of other governments. This policy-making paralysis was a serious obstacle to international coordination. Foreign governments became less responsive to American calls for policy adjustments because of the government's inability to implement earlier commitments regarding fiscal restraint. According to Paul Volcker (who, as former chairman of the Federal Reserve, presumably has a central banker's bias), American policy in the 1980s showed that "the flexible use of fiscal policy is politically difficult. This difficulty is what limits so sharply the potential for the international coordination of economic policies."[155]

Germany experienced similar fiscal policy problems after reunification, although on a smaller scale. Chancellor Kohl's government was unwilling to raise taxes or sharply cut spending in western Germany to finance reunification spending (a problem compounded by the federal structure of the German political system). This led the Bundesbank to raise interest rates to contain inflationary pressures generated by

154. Ibid., p. 31; see pp. 26–36 for more details of these institutional problems.
155. Volcker and Gyohten, *Changing Fortunes,* p. 292.

Bonn's deficit spending. Higher German interest rates pushed up European and international levels and conflicted with the desire of many foreign governments to relax monetary policy during recession.

The American and German situations were not unique. Virtually all advanced capitalist countries experienced large, persistent fiscal deficits even in the boom years of the late 1980s. In 1985–89, central government fiscal deficits as a proportion of GDP averaged 3.5 percent in the United States, 2.3 percent in Japan, 1.5 percent in Germany, 2.4 percent in France, and 0.6 percent in Britain. (Britain was the only G7 country to experience fiscal surpluses in any of these years.)[156] Large deficits and growing national debts severely constrained government ability to manipulate fiscal policy to achieve growth or external balance objectives.

The political and institutional problems of coordinating macroeconomic policies discouraged monetary and fiscal policy coordination and encouraged governments to coordinate symptom-management policies instead—even though they were rarely effective without monetary and fiscal adjustments. G7 meetings often focused on coordinating foreign exchange market intervention and encouraging international financing of payments imbalances; the political obstacles were lower (except during the first four years of the Reagan presidency), and the officials involved actually had responsibility for this kind of national policy-making.[157]

The experience of recent years reinforces my argument in Chapter 2: monetary and fiscal policy coordination is inherently more difficult than other types of adjustment policy coordination. It involves governments' most important economic policy levers, the domestic political consequences are immense (although this is also a rationale for coordination), and fiscal and monetary policies have traditionally been the domain of national governments. Therefore, states turn to macroeconomic policy coordination only as a last resort, when economic problems cannot be resolved with other policy instruments. In practice, governments have been able to agree to mutual adjustments only in

156. Calculated from table 15. As I have argued, the fiscal deficits of Japan and Germany in 1987–89 resulted in part from American pressure, not simply from internal problems.

157. Dobson, *Economic Policy Coordination*, p. 33. This is a common critique of G7 policy coordination: see, for example, Nau, *Myth of America's Decline*, pp. 257, 285; and Currie, "International Cooperation in Monetary Policy," pp. 182–83.

response to shared perceptions of impending crisis; ongoing attempts to coordinate policies failed in the late 1980s, as did less serious attempts in the 1960s and 70s.

Finally, the record of international macroeconomic diplomacy reveals the continuing importance of international power relationships—in particular, U.S. dominance. Although many governments demanded changes in foreign government policies, the United States was most successful in actually winning changes. The size and relative insulation of the American economy gave Washington a strong bargaining position. International policy coordination contributed only marginally to reducing American fiscal deficits, even though they have been the most important source of international economic imbalance since the early 1980s.[158] The United States felt less pressure to restrain fiscal policy because until 1987 private foreign investors were willing to lend to the country in U.S. currency without demanding an interest-rate premium to cover the exchange-rate risk. They were willing to do so because of the dollar's status as the leading world currency. Thus, it was less costly for the United States to pursue unilateral macroeconomic policies at odds with its trading partners than for any other country. This asymmetry replicates the 1960s, when France and other countries criticized the freedom that the dollar's role gave the United States to spend abroad.

Foreign private investors became more wary of lending to the United States after the dollar fell sharply in 1985–87. Since then, the United States has been less insulated from the costs of its budget deficits, although still more so than any other deficit country. Some observers feared that the Federal Reserve's freedom to lower interest rates in response to recessionary pressures would be constrained by the need to keep interest rates high to attract foreign investment in government debt. In the early 1990s, however, the Treasury Department continued to find buyers for American government securities despite sharp cuts in interest rates and periodic weakness in the dollar. Investors continued to buy American government debt even though interest rates were rising in Europe at the same time they were falling in the United States (1991–92). Financing of the American government def-

---

158. American deficits have been especially destabilizing because they are combined with a low domestic savings rate, which means that they are financed by foreign capital to a greater extent than are the deficits of other advanced capitalist states.

icit was undoubtedly eased by Japan's cooperation in reducing its own interest rates (roughly in parallel with trends in the United States), but the early 1990s also showed that the United States economy was large enough and insulated enough from the international economy to adjust to a sharp decline in capital inflows from Japan.

Thus, the United States is still in a powerful bargaining position with foreign governments, especially Japan. Its size and relative insulation mean that many countries depend more on exports to the United States than the United States depends on exports to them. The threat of American protectionism is a powerful bargaining lever and one that the Reagan and Bush administrations used repeatedly and successfully, pressing for changes in foreign macroeconomic policies that permitted lax U.S. fiscal policies in the late 1980s and early 1990s, even after foreign private investors lost confidence in American economic policy. The threat of congressional protectionism has been most effective with Japan, which depends more heavily on the United States than do other G5 countries.

Because international transactions have been less important to the American economy than to smaller economies, the United States has also been less concerned with exchange-rate volatility. Even Western European countries, which are less dependent upon trade with the United States than is Japan, have been concerned about dollar volatility. That volatility has made it hard to stabilize exchange rates within the European Monetary System. This asymmetric pattern of concern has enhanced American bargaining power; for example, Washington threatened not to cooperate to stabilize exchange rates in order to pressure Japan and Germany to alter monetary and fiscal policies.

The U.S. government was less successful in its demands for foreign macroeconomic policy adjustments in 1991–93 than it was in the late 1980s. In particular, Germany rejected American demands to lower interest rates, although it responded to similar concerns from its EC partners. Perhaps American influence in Europe is declining as EC countries focus on macroeconomic cooperation among themselves (e.g., plans for economic and monetary union) and as intra-EC trade grows relative to trade between the EC and the United States.[159] Nevertheless, the tenor of German-American discussions suggests that the

159. On the latter trend, see "U.S. Uncommonly Inactive in World Economic Arena," *New York Times*, 27 September 1992, pp. I:1, I:14.

lack of credibility in American economic policies was the critical factor. German officials (and other non-Americans in the G7) could hardly take the Bush administration's demands seriously because those demands were so much at odds with the administration's own policies and were obviously driven by the president's narrow reelection interests. Foreign governments were also skeptical of American demands because of earlier experiences during the late 1980s. In those years, Japan and Germany acceded to American demands for reflation while the United States failed to fulfill its own commitment to reduce the budget deficit. It may take some time to restore credibility to American policy and reestablish the trust necessary for policy coordination, as President Clinton and Treasury Secretary Bentsen have publicly acknowledged.[160]

American officials have recently become frustrated with their limited ability to persuade the Japanese government to adopt specific fiscal policy measures, especially tax cuts. But this failure does not reflect a decline in American power. Indeed, the United States has had considerable influence over Japanese macroeconomic policy, encouraging cuts in interest rates and the adoption of a series of fiscal stimulus plans. American officials have demanded increasingly specific fiscal policy adjustments; and Japanese inaction reflects the intrusiveness of those demands into areas that were previously purely domestic as well as the domestic political weakness of recent Japanese governments.

Thus, recent limits on U.S. ability to persuade Japan and Germany to adjust monetary and fiscal policies do not alter the fact that the United States continues to dominate international policy coordination. The country sets the agenda for coordination and has been much more successful than other governments in persuading foreign states to alter macroeconomic adjustment policies, just as in earlier decades.

160. *New York Times*, 22 February 1993, p. D5; 1 March 1993, pp. D1, D5; 2 May 1993, p. 9; *Globe and Mail*, 26 June 1993, p. A8. Toyoo Gyohten, a senior Japanese official, makes a similar point in Volcker and Gyohten, *Changing Fortunes*, pp. 271–72, 309.

CHAPTER SEVEN

Conclusions: International Structures, Domestic Politics, and Policy Coordination

To understand patterns of international economic policy coordination, we need to understand how the structure of the international economy both shapes the problems of economic policy-making and affects the viability and attractiveness of alternative strategies. As international trade markets have become more closely integrated and capital mobility has increased, governments have abandoned adjustment strategies and patterns of coordination that no longer work or have become too costly and have moved toward more effective strategies. Many explanations for international cooperation implicitly assume that the problems addressed by international cooperation are unchanging; therefore, they focus on other variables. This attitude is true of many versions of hegemonic stability theory, which argue that international cooperation has eroded in recent years as American power has declined.[1]

I believe the overall level of international policy cooperation has not declined. Coordination has increased among national monetary and fiscal policies, exchange-rate adjustments, and capital controls. Coordination of trade controls for purposes of international macroeconomic adjustment has been limited in recent years (with the exception of Japanese agreements to liberalize import controls), but this reflects

---

1. Robert Gilpin, *The Political Economy of International Relations* (Princeton: Princeton University Press, 1987), recognizes that economic problems have changed but argues that a posited erosion of American hegemony explains what he views as a breakdown of international cooperation and leadership.

harmony rather than eroding cooperation (see Chapter 1). Because earlier trade policy coordination was so successful in creating an open international trading system and transnational production structures, the costs of comprehensive trade controls for the state that imposed them would now be very high.[2] Coordination of foreign exchange market intervention to stabilize currencies (a symptom-management strategy) was less consistent in the 1970s and the early 1980s than in the 1960s but has been extensive since 1985. Coordination of payments financing through the IMF has declined, but private payments financing continues to exhibit clear political understandings, especially Japanese financing of American budget and trade deficits.

This evidence is inconsistent with the argument that international economic cooperation was highest when the United States was most powerful. International coordination (defined as negotiated mutual adjustment of economic policies) was more extensive in the late 1970s, the 1980s, and the early 1990s than in the 1950s, and coordination of central macroeconomic policies has been higher since the late 1970s than in any earlier period.

Hegemonic stability theories also tend to exaggerate the extent of international policy coordination in the 1950s and 60s. Despite its unquestioned preeminence, the United States was rarely able to persuade foreign states to alter monetary and fiscal policies or exchange rates in the late 1940s, the 1950s, and the 1960s. It was successful in achieving its goals during these years only when they were shared by foreign governments which could not achieve those goals without American financial assistance. American foreign aid and military spending overseas strengthened countries' balance-of-payments positions and allowed them to rebuild their international reserves, both prerequisites for the trade liberalization sought by the United States and supported (to varying degrees) by most allied governments. In contrast, the United States was able to persuade foreign governments to revalue their currencies and reflate their economies on a number of occasions in the 1970s, the 1980s, and the early 1990s. Even if overall trends in the level of policy coordination were consistent with trends in American power, existing power-based arguments do not explain why coordination of certain policies has increased while coordination of others has declined. To explain these shifts, one must understand how the changing

---

2. Of course, serious controversies continue over protection of specific sectors.

structure of the international economy affects the advantages and disadvantages of alternative strategies.

In accounting for the discrepancy between my findings and those elsewhere in the literature, we need to examine how international policy coordination is measured. I argue that we must distinguish between (1) the extent of international coordination, defined as the extent of negotiated mutual adjustment of economic policies; and (2) the degree of stability in the international economy. Stability reflects political factors (the nature of government policies and the extent of international coordination) as well as the structure of the international economy and the nature of international economic problems. Analysts who argue that international coordination has fallen may be mistaking stability for policy coordination, failing to see how changes in the structure of the international economy have made the problem of managing economic relations more difficult. Increased economic integration in the 1970s, 80s, and 90s meant that negotiated mutual policy adjustment had to become more extensive simply to achieve the level of stability achieved in the late 1950s and 1960s. Policy coordination did increase, although not enough to provide the same level of stability. (I discuss the obstacles to more extensive policy coordination later in the chapter).

These criticisms do not mean that American power is irrelevant to patterns of international policy coordination. The United States has been the dominant actor throughout the postwar period, and its attitude has always been central to interregional coordination. As Chapters 3 and 4 reveal, the United States was never able to "simply impose its will on others,"[3] as was asserted by one leading proponent of hegemonic stability theory. In all periods, it has been the most important state, and initiatives it does not support have had no chance of acceptance.

American preferences and negotiating demands have been remarkably consistent over the past three decades, defining the parameters of international debate. In general, American governments have wanted to pursue expansionary macroeconomic policies and to persuade foreign governments to adopt relaxed monetary policies and stimulative

3. Stephen D. Krasner, "United States Commercial and Monetary Policy: Unravelling the Paradox of External Strength and Internal Weakness," in Peter J. Katzenstein, ed., *Between Power and Plenty: Foreign Economic Policies of Advanced Industrial States* (Madison: University of Wisconsin Press, 1978), p. 57.

fiscal policies to minimize resulting American trade deficits and, on occasion, capital outflows.

The United States has also differed consistently from other states on the issue of coordinated intervention to stabilize exchange rates. American officials have often been willing to tolerate greater exchange-rate instability because the large U.S. economy is much less dependent on international commerce than smaller states are. Foreign governments have been severely critical of American unwillingness to join coordinated foreign exchange market intervention, as in the late 1960s, the mid-1970s, and periods during the 1980s. This American stance, however, has usually been mirrored by foreign refusals to revalue currencies and create mechanisms for ongoing exchange-rate adjustments to promote international equilibrium and accommodate shifts in competitiveness. Thus, surplus states' objections to currency revaluation and U.S. objections to coordinated intervention often have been equally important obstacles to exchange-rate coordination.

These differences have set the parameters for international debates on macroeconomic adjustment policies during most of the postwar period. The United States has played the central role at all times and has recently been able to persuade foreign governments to alter their most sensitive policies. Negotiated adjustments to American policies have been much less substantial. Indeed, the United States appears to have maintained a near-hegemonic position in international debates throughout the 1980s.

As I discussed in Chapter 6, American governments in the early 1990s appear less successful in their demands for adjustments in foreign government policies. The Bush and Clinton administrations were able to persuade Japan to lower interest rates (consistent with changing conditions in Japan), but their detailed demands for fiscal expansion, especially through cuts in personal income taxes, achieved limited success only after considerable delay. This situation, however, reflects the intrusiveness of American demands into domestic Japanese policy-making and the domestic political weakness of Japan's governments, not any decline in American power. In the case of the German government's rejection of the Bush administration's demands for fiscal-deficit reduction and lower interest rates (1991–92), the crucial factors were the Bush administration's failure to uphold earlier international commitments regarding the U.S. budget deficit and indifference to foreign concerns about American interest rates and currency policy. In other words, reduced American influence reflected problems in American economic policy, not an erosion of the U.S. structural power position.[4] Nevertheless, if current moves toward greater EC macroeconomic policy coordination prove successful, U.S. ability to influence European policies will decline.

American preeminence has been exercised within a broader context of bipolarity, at least until very recently; and this broader international security structure is crucial for explaining patterns of coordination among the advanced capitalist countries. The Soviet security threat was extremely important in encouraging specific measures of policy coordination and generating U.S. dollar outflows that stimulated Western European and Japanese economic recovery and trade liberalization in the 1950s and 60s. The importance of the Soviet threat has always been recognized in security-oriented literature on international politics and American foreign policy but has only recently become part of mainstream debates on international economic policy cooperation.[5] Many statements of hegemonic stability theory ignore this influence on economic relations among the United States and its allies.[6] Even when analysts acknowledge the existence of the Soviet bloc, they do not use it to explain cooperation within the capitalist bloc.[7]

Nevertheless, the Soviet threat and the alliance were crucial for overcoming the obstacles to international cooperation that neorealist scholars have identified. According to those scholars, the security imperatives in an anarchic international political system force major states to minimize their interdependence and avoid cooperative endeavors that risk relative gains for other states.[8] Without the shared

4. See Henry R. Nau, *The Myth of America's Decline: Leading the World Economy into the 1990s* (New York: Oxford University Press, 1990), especially chaps. 1 and 9, for a general argument about how American economic policy choices affect the country's international influence.

5. An important recent book that takes security relations and alliances into account is Joanne Gowa, *Allies, Adversaries, and International Trade* (Princeton: Princeton University Press, 1994).

6. Ibid, pp. 3–5.

7. For example, Robert O. Keohane states that "a hegemonic state must possess enough military power to be able to protect the international political economy that it dominates from incursions by hostile adversaries." *After Hegemony: Cooperation and Discord in the World Political Economy* (Princeton: Princeton University Press, 1984), p. 39. He goes on to explain cooperation among the capitalist states solely in terms of the dynamics of relations within that group.

8. Kenneth N. Waltz, *Theory of International Politics* (Reading, Mass: Addison-Wesley,

perception of a Soviet security threat, concern about vulnerability and relative gains ought to have discouraged states from coordinating all types of adjustment policy and pursuing expansionary macroeconomic policies that created payments deficits and provided export opportunities for other major countries.[9] NATO membership as well as close U.S.-Japan security ties mitigated these fears. Members of a military alliance against a common adversary need not be so concerned about relative gains from international economic integration and policy coordination with their alliance partners. Joanne Gowa's conclusions about free trade among allies are also relevant to international policy coordination; "cross-national distributional concerns should pose fewer obstacles to the conclusion of an intra-alliance than to a cross-alliance accord."[10] The group as a whole focuses on absolute gains, thus enabling the group to gain in relation to its adversary. Of course, the distribution of relative gains will impede coordination if there is serious uncertainty about whether countries will remain allied,[11] but since 1945 there have been no serious threats that any of the major NATO countries or Japan would face each other as military adversaries.

Interest in joint defense against Soviet threats clearly stimulated economic integration and policy coordination in the late 1940s and 50s— and beyond. For example, Japan's willingness to adjust its policies in the late 1980s in response to American demands reflected in part the importance the Japanese attached to defense cooperation. Although the distribution of coordination's costs and benefits has been a constant issue in economic relations, it is much less important than it would have been without bipolarity and the Soviet threat.

The end of the cold war and the breakup of the Soviet Union have clearly altered the political-security context of international economic policy coordination. Neorealists who focus on the formal structure of anarchy and the distribution of power among states as the key determinants of international politics suggest that cooperation that devel-

---

1979), pp. 105–6; Joseph M. Grieco, "Anarchy and the Limits of Cooperation: A Realist Critique of the Newest Liberal Institutionalism," *International Organization* 42 (Summer 1988).

9. For an argument that mercantilist states should avoid expansion and deficits for security reasons, see Paolo Guerrieri and Pier Carlo Padoan, "Neomercantilism and International Economic Stability," *International Organization* 40 (Winter 1986), pp. 30–32.

10. Gowa, *Allies, Adversaries, and International Trade*, p.113.

11. Grieco, "Anarchy and the Limits of Cooperation," p. 500.

oped during the cold war will break down as the system becomes multipolar and major states are forced by the logic of self-help to reduce their economic integration.[12] But I believe that other elements of the international structure also shape political patterns. The economic structure has been fundamentally altered by policies that favor the development of international integration among the Western allies and Japan, and these changes have affected the calculus of state interests. International trade has grown substantially, to the point that conditions in export markets now have a major effect on economic conditions within even the largest countries. Even more important, international financial markets have become highly integrated, and production has become internationalized through the growth of foreign direct investment and transnational corporations.

Furthermore, these structural changes are durable. Despite severe payments imbalances, exchange-rate volatility and misalignment, and persistent high unemployment since the 1970s, international economic integration has continued to deepen and has changed the interests of the most powerful economic sectors in all the advanced capitalist countries. Transnational corporations and banks now dominate economies and would vehemently oppose any serious return to economic autarky and independence. Chapters 1 and 2 show how difficult it would be for states to reverse their financial integration; the short-term costs of capital flight and economic instability would be so severe that governments could hardly find them worthwhile. For example, in 1992–93 traditionally protectionist states in the EC maintained support for financial market integration despite the problems posed for European exchange-rate cooperation. The alternative example—the Soviet Union—is a poor advertisement for national independence as the ideal path to international security and domestic social and political stability. If states are interested primarily in international security and domestic stability, as realist and statist theorists argue, then governments now face powerful national pressures to maintain economic interdependence, because reversal would trigger domestic instability and possible international decline. In addition, as long as capital markets are integrated internationally, governments have incentives to coordinate their policies (see Chapter 2).

12. John J. Mearsheimer, "Back to the Future: Instability in Europe after the Cold War," *International Security* 15 (Summer 1990).

The world has changed in ways not recognized by narrow neorealist analyses. As Robert Jervis and others have argued, recent history has fundamentally altered the calculus of state interests among the industrialized countries.[13] The costs of violence and autarky have increased dramatically due to advanced war technology and new beliefs about conflict as well as to the changes in the structure of the international economy. The end of bipolarity and the cold war will not trigger the collapse of economic policy coordination among the advanced capitalist countries.

The future stability of the international economy depends heavily on the possibilities for macroeconomic policy coordination. The experience of the past fifteen years suggests that negotiated mutual policy adjustments will continue to be possible when governments share a sense of impending economic crisis—as in 1978, 1985, and 1987. This kind of ad hoc coordination does little to stabilize the international economy on an ongoing basis or prevent large payments imbalances. But states have rejected the creation of international guidelines for monetary and fiscal policies, as shown by ill-fated proposals for multilateral surveillance and automatic policy adjustments. States' unwillingness to coordinate policies to prevent international instability points to some important limitations of the kind of analysis undertaken in this book. I have focused on how changes in the structure of the international economy generate incentives for states to adopt particular forms of policy coordination. But governments often do not respond to incentives generated by the international economy in a rational, optimizing fashion—at least not as those terms are understood in liberal economics and game theory. Monetary and fiscal policies are more important for domestic politics than any other type of economic policy, and governments often believe that they need to be free from international constraints to choose policies that best serve their domestic interests. As I argued in Chapter 2, the domestic importance of these policies generates interest in international coordination (to convince other states to adjust their macroeconomic policies to reduce international imbalances) while making monetary and fiscal policies difficult to coordinate.

13. Robert Jervis, "The Future of World Politics: Will It Resemble the Past?" *International Security* 16 (Winter 1991/92).

It may be misleading to identify differences of domestic political interest as the key obstacles to coordination, however, because one cannot assume that these interests are clear and unproblematic. In practice, governments are often internally divided and do not know (or various factions cannot agree) what policies would best serve their interests. As the historical record suggests, the possibilities for coordination are greater when government leaders disagree among themselves about what policies to pursue. Negotiated adjustments in foreign government policies can alter the attractiveness of various options, thereby influencing a government's perception of national interest.

On the other hand, differences of interest can obstruct coordination when each government has a unified view of its national interest. In that case, they are unlikely to pursue other policies except when coerced. The key dispute has always concerned the priority of price stability or low unemployment.[14] International debates between the United States and surplus states in Western Europe and Japan have often pitted American interests in rapid expansion against foreign concerns about inflation, and these differences pose serious obstacles to coordination. This absence of normative consensus, not the weakness of intellectual consensus (which many economists emphasize)[15] has posed the most serious immediate obstacle to specific proposals for negotiated mutual macroeconomic policy adjustments.

Another obstacle that stems from the domestic political importance of monetary and fiscal policies is governments' desire to avoid constraining their freedom to repond to unpredictable developments. This concern has blocked attempts since the 1960s to establish guidelines for policy adjustments in response to concrete measures of international imbalance. But such a preference is paradoxical. Coordination could reduce uncertainty about the future and prevent international market imbalances that impose powerful constraints on policy-making. In effect, governments have preferred to take their chances with unpredictable burdens imposed by private markets responding to national

14. These are competing goals in the politically relevant short-to-medium term, if not in the long term.

15. Jeffrey A. Frankel, *Obstacles to International Macroeconomic Policy Coordination*, Princeton Studies in International Finance No. 64 (Princeton: Department of Economics, Princeton University, December 1988); Richard N. Cooper, "International Economic Cooperation: Is It Desirable? Is It Likely?" *Bulletin of the American Academy of Arts and Sciences* 39 (November 1985).

policy differences, rather than coordinate in order to reduce the likelihood and magnitude of future international market pressures.

These obstacles reflect the parochial nature of macroeconomic decision making and its institutions (see Chapters 2 and 6). The traditional domestic orientation of monetary and fiscal policy-making encourages governments to see international coordination as a constraint on their autonomy and neglect the possibility that coordination could help them achieve their objectives. As Robert Keohane emphasizes, international cooperation can empower as well as constrain: "International regimes are valuable to governments not because they enforce binding rules on others (they do not), but because they render it possible for governments to enter into mutually beneficial agreements with one another. They *empower* governments rather than shackling them."[16] The failure to recognize this truth has been institutionalized in policy-making agencies that virtually exclude international considerations. Thus, it is often difficult for financial officials to imagine international tradeoffs that would help them balance competing domestic interests.

A crucial exception to these generalizations lies in the move toward Economic and Monetary Union (EMU) in the EC. In the December 1991 Maastricht Treaty on European Union, most EC governments committed themselves to a timetable for harmonizing fiscal and monetary policies and subsequently establishing a single currency and a European central bank. I have not reviewed EMU in detail because of its prospective nature and regional focus. Nevertheless, it is interesting to examine the motives underlying the EMU agreement[17] to see how they relate to my arguments. Strictly economic reasoning was not decisive. While many economists saw EMU as a natural accompaniment to 1992 market integration, they remain deeply divided over the merits of a single currency. Instead, the crucial factors were political. France, one of EMU's strongest proponents, was motivated by a desire to gain greater influence over European monetary policy than it had under the European Monetary System (EMS). In the EMS, Germany set its monetary policies primarily in response to domestic concerns (although international pressures occasionally contributed to policy relax-

16. Keohane, *After Hegemony*, p. 13.
17. For a good overview, see Wayne Sandholtz, "Choosing Union: Monetary Politics and Maastricht," *International Organization* 47 (Winter 1993).

ation, as I describe in Chapter 6). In turn, other governments followed German interest-rate movements to maintain currency stability.

As the French government saw EMU, a European central bank would set European monetary policies in response to broader, pan-European conditions. The Italian and Belgian governments generally supported the French view. None of these governments wanted to replace the anti-inflationary policies of the 1980s with inflationary ones, but all preferred a balance of monetary objectives weighted more toward promoting growth. Monetary union and a single currency would enhance the credibility of national anti-inflationary policies by eliminating the possibility that future governments could pursue inflationary policies for political purposes. This credibility would permit governments to achieve price stability with lower interest rates than would be possible with unilateral policy-making. These governments were responding to the pressures that the single market and international capital flows put on national macroeconomic policy-making autonomy by supporting the creation of supranational institutions that would implement policies closer to their own preferences than those they could achieve independently.

The German government's motives were further removed from economic calculations. Bonn favored EMU as a sign of Germany's commitment to European unity after reunification and in light of increasing links with Eastern Europe. The Bundesbank and its German supporters were skeptical, but their concerns were partly addressed when planners modeled the proposed European central bank on the Bundesbank, ensuring that it would be politically independent and have price stability as its primary objective. Nevertheless, there remains some uncertainty about Germany's ultimate willingness to abandon the mark in favor of a single European currency. EMU would clearly constrain national policy-making autonomy in Germany, while other European governments are already constrained by the EMS. In addition, it might well produce monetary policies that are more tolerant of inflation (and therefore further from the German government's preferences). If Germany accepts EMU, it will make that decision for political reasons that go beyond the implications of changing economic structure.

While plans for EMU suggest that European governments may be modifying the parochial approach that has impeded macroeconomic policy coordination in the past, most EC governments share the fiscal policy-making paralysis that poses a final critical obstacle to international coordination. Persistent fiscal deficits and intense domestic political pressures not to cut spending or raise taxes (or, in Japan's case, not to cut current taxes that finance past deficits) mean that many leading governments are unable to formulate coherent or internally consistent policies or to fulfill commitments made in international negotiations.[18] Not surprisingly, this situation reinforces policy-making's domestic orientation in states that are hesitant to risk negotiated mutual adjustments with foreign governments who may be unwilling or unable to carry out their part of the bargain.[19]

Institutionalized coordination faces serious obstacles rooted in the traditions and institutions of monetary and fiscal policy-making, not in unavoidable conflicts of national interest. These domestic traditions and institutions, which emerged from the experience of the 1930s, resist change. Governments have recently tolerated serious domestic and international economic instability because of a parochial approach to monetary and fiscal policy-making but have shown little willingness to develop alternatives. International consultations among central bankers and senior finance ministry officials are frequent and intensive, yet the deeply rooted obstacles indicate that ongoing coordination of monetary and fiscal policies is unlikely. Negotiated mutual policy adjustments will occur on an ad hoc basis, especially in times of crisis. If so, international capital flows will continue to destabilize national and international economies, and governments will coordinate symptom-management policies (especially foreign exchange market intervention) to try to manage instability. But these policies will not be very effective because international capital flows are too large.

Does the erosion of national policy-making autonomy in the face of

18. This dilemma is a specific example of Helen Milner's suggestion that domestic political situations often leave states unable to implement internationally cooperative policies. "International Theories of Cooperation Among Nations: Strengths and Weaknesses," *World Politics* 44 (April 1992), p. 493.

19. Robert D. Putnam and C. Randall Henning suggest that this problem of involuntary cheating (when states fail to meet international commitments because of domestic politics rather than deliberate cheating) is more important than is commonly recognized. "The Bonn Summit of 1978: A Case Study in Coordination," in Richard N. Cooper et al., *Can Nations Agree? Issues in International Economic Cooperation* (Washington, D.C.: Brookings Institution, 1989), pp. 102–4. My findings are consistent with Putnam and Henning's suggestion.

increasing capital mobility mean that the idea of embedded liberalism is no longer viable?[20] It certainly is true that capital markets can impose severe constraints on the ability of smaller countries to adopt macroeconomic policies tailored to domestic political conditions and that states have abandoned efforts to control capital flows that were a central part of the embedded liberal strategies pursued during the Bretton Woods years. As neo-Marxist scholars emphasize, states that pursue nonorthodox policies and redistributive strategies while other countries pursue orthodox ones face capital flight, precipitating exchange crises and undermining domestic order.[21]

But the record of policy coordination suggests that the idea of embedded liberalism is still viable for some states and under some conditions. While small states in Europe and elsewhere have been severely constrained by capital mobility, the United States clearly has not. Furthermore, American policies and policy coordination have given other governments some scope for pursuing expansionary policies. The Reagan, Bush, and Clinton administrations have all been able to sustain stimulative fiscal policies and low interest rates because of the willingness of private investors to purchase dollar-denominated government securities (see Chapter 6). These stimulative policies often generate strong demand for exports of other countries, thereby strengthening trade balances, and have allowed foreign governments to lower interest rates without seeing their currencies tumble. Similarly, the United States was able to persuade Germany (in the late 1980s) and Japan (in the late 1980s and early 1990s) to lower interest rates and pursue more stimulative fiscal policies. American demands for policy changes represented a Keynesian approach in a new guise, despite talk of the death of Keynesian macroeconomics and the triumph of monetarism. In contrast to earlier Keynesian strategies (such as the locomotive strategies of the 1970s and domestic demand management in the 1960s), the Reagan and Bush administrations focused on stimulating the economy

---

20. On embedded liberalism, see Chapter 1 and John Gerard Ruggie, "International Regimes, Transactions, and Change: Embedded Liberalism in the Postwar Economic Order," in Stephen D. Krasner, ed., *International Regimes* (Ithaca: Cornell University Press, 1983).

21. Robert W. Cox, *Production, Power, and World Order: Social Forces in the Making of History* (New York: Columbia University Press, 1987), p. 305; and Stephen Gill and David Law, "Global Hegemony and the Structural Power of Capital," *International Studies Quarterly* 33 (December 1989).

through tax cuts rather than spending increases and demonstrated even less concern with the problem of fiscal deficits. The United States urged foreign governments to pursue more expansionary fiscal policies even though most were already experiencing budget deficits that dwarfed those of earlier periods. The persistence of deficit spending and American demands for fiscal expansion abroad suggest that despite the 1980s shift toward monetarist rhetoric in economic policy, governments continue to value—and to pursue—Keynesian demand stimulus. Furthermore, policy coordination helped all governments escape the constraints that capital flows would otherwise have imposed on unilateral attempts to stimulate national economies.

Nevertheless, all but the very largest countries now face severe constraints on their ability to pursue stimulative policies when larger governments pursue anti-inflationary ones. This case arose in the early 1980s when the U. S. Federal Reserve raised interest rates to historic heights, and it arose again for many European governments when the Bundesbank pushed up rates in the early 1990s. The strategy of embedded liberalism continues to be relevant for many leading governments, and policy coordination can help make it viable. But the specific compromise of embedded liberalism has shifted: governments are now less willing and able to restrain international economic forces (especially capital flows) in support of demand management to maintain national economic and political stability.

Index

Anglo-American Loan Agreement (1947),
69–70

Baker, James, 212, 229
balance-of-payments financing
American, for Europe and Japan, 53–
55, 60, 62, 71–74, 100, 103, 119
and macroeconomic adjustment, 4, 25,
30
private, 33–34, 160, 170–73, 217–22
See also International Monetary Fund;
entries for individual countries
Bank for International Settlements (BIS),
39, 61, 122, 127–30, 232, 245
Bank of Canada, 121, 234
Bank of Japan, 227–28, 234, 236
bargaining power, 9–10, 14–15, 21, 45–
47, 253
during 1945–55, 54–55, 62, 75, 90
during 1956–70, 94, 119, 145–46
during 1971–77, 181–82
during 1978–94, 193, 203, 215–16,
219, 223–25, 248–50
sources of, 47–50
See also hegemonic stability theory;
United States: power and
hegemony
Basle Agreement, 112
Belgium, 101, 112, 115, 173–74, 261
Bentsen, Lloyd, 208, 250
Bonn economic summit (1978), 14, 223–
24

Britain, xi, 38, 99, 101, 105, 112, 114–16,
134, 137–38, 140–42, 152, 163,
173, 180, 190–92, 217, 247
capital controls, 107, 158–60, 198
capital mobility, 42, 44, 145
convertibility crisis (1947), 60, 69–70
and Euromarkets, 16, 95, 97
exchange rate, 66–68, 101, 109–10,
163–64, 168, 209–10, 215
and G5/G7, 177–79, 223, 226
and International Monetary Fund, 77–
78, 114–16, 124–25, 127–28, 144,
157, 169, 171, 175–76, 181
and United States, 60–61, 66–68, 77–
78, 80, 84
Bundesbank, 159, 185, 209–10, 228, 235,
238–41, 243, 245–46, 261, 264. See
also Germany
Bush, George, 12, 216, 220–21, 230, 232,
235, 238, 240–41, 254, 263

Canada, 38, 112, 114, 134, 173, 217
capital mobility, 42–44
flexible exchange rate, 64–65, 86, 161,
163, 184
and G7, 225–26, 231, 234, 245
and United States, 121
capital controls, 4
on current account, 57–58
during 1945–55, 63–64
during 1956–70, 105–8

capital controls (*cont.*)
  during 1971–77, 150, 158–60, 166,
    185–86
  during 1978–94, 193–94, 198–99,
    205–6
  viability, 34, 158–59, 257
  See also capital mobility; *entries for*
    individual countries
capital mobility
  historical development, 16–18, 94–96,
    103, 154–55, 193–98
  and macroeconomic adjustment, xi, 2,
    5–6, 30–36
  measuring, 37–43
  See also capital controls; Euromarkets;
    entries for individual countries
Carter, Jimmy, 1, 178, 211–12, 222–23,
  230
Clinton, William J. (Bill), 208, 216, 237,
  242, 250, 254, 263
cold war, and policy coordination, x, 53–
  55, 72–74, 81, 89, 103, 147–48,
  255–58
currency convertibility, xi, 60, 62–63, 69–
  70, 93, 102–7, 143–44, 161–62
currency status, 49, 134, 147, 218

domestic politics
  and international structures, 15, 19–20
  and policy coordination, 22–25, 27, 36,
    204, 238, 244–48, 258–60

economic summits, 174, 177. *See also*
  entries for specific meetings
Economic and Social Commission
  (ECOSOC), 78
Economic Cooperation Administration
  (ECA), 68, 81–84, 90. *See also*
  Marshall Plan
Eisenhower, Dwight D., 99
embedded liberalism, 3, 77, 166, 263–64
Employment Act (1946), 52
Euromarkets, 16–17, 41–42, 93–98, 106–
  7, 120, 147, 154, 160, 173, 195,
  217
European Coal and Steel Community
  (ECSC), 59, 90
European Community (EC), xii, 6, 48,
  104, 110, 116, 118, 160, 166, 195,

  208, 222, 235–36, 242–43, 246,
  249, 255, 257
Economic and Monetary Union, 240–
  41, 246, 249, 260–61
  See also European Monetary System;
    Exchange Rate Mechanism
European Monetary System (EMS), 32,
  196, 198, 208, 214, 238–39, 249,
  260–61. *See also* Exchange Rate
  Mechanism
European Payments Union (EPU), 58–62,
  80, 86–87
Exchange Rate Mechanism (ERM), 198,
  208–10, 214–16, 238–39. *See also*
  European Monetary System
exchange rates
  fixed, 6, 53, 64, 68–69, 91, 108–9
  and macroeconomic policy, 85–86,
    133–36, 139, 143, 147, 208, 214–
    15, 238–39
  flexible, 149–51, 153, 155, 161, 163,
    179–80
  and macroeconomic adjustment, 4, 28–
    29, 166, 180–83, 186–87, 199–200,
    206
  mechanisms for adjusting, 162, 164–65,
    254
  1949 devaluations, 65–68
  See also foreign exchange market
    intervention; *entries for individual*
    countries
external policies of adjustment, defined,
  4, 23–5. *See also* capital controls;
  exchange rates; trade controls

fiscal deficits, 142, 152, 189, 192, 247–48
fiscal policy coordination
  during 1945–55, 79–84, 86–88
  during 1956–70, 124–25, 135–36, 144
  during 1971–77, 175, 177–79, 181–82
  during 1978–94, 188, 222–30, 232–33,
    235–42
fiscal policy making, 4, 22–24, 28, 30–31,
  36, 188, 236–38, 245–47, 260–62
Ford, Gerald R., 178
foreign exchange market intervention,
  25, 32–33, 41, 47–48, 111–12,
  161, 164, 167–69, 210–16, 252
foreign exchange markets, 33, 39, 41, 87,
  196, 198

foreign exchange reserves, 25, 33, 39–40, 47–48

France, xi, 38, 59, 65, 112, 115, 134, 137, 140–42, 152, 173, 180, 190–92, 222, 240–41, 247, 261
   capital controls, 17–18, 31, 158–59, 166, 195, 198
   capital mobility, 42, 44–45, 145
   exchange rate, 65, 101–2, 110, 165, 210, 214–15
   and G5/G7, 178, 225–26, 242
   and International Monetary Fund, 65, 114, 125–27, 144, 176
   and United States, 61, 82–83, 115, 117, 248

full employment policies, 52, 56–57, 78, 88, 101

General Agreement on Tariffs and Trade (GATT), 56–57, 87, 103–4

General Arrangements to Borrow (GAB), 116, 127

Germany, 32, 48, 54, 101, 110, 114–15, 135–36, 138, 140–42, 151–53, 161, 170, 173–74, 190–92, 247, 260–61
   capital controls, 17, 107–8, 158–59, 166, 185, 194, 198
   capital mobility, 42, 44, 145
   exchange rate, 32, 38, 48, 110, 161, 167, 184, 206, 209–10, 213–14, 216
   and G5/G7, 178–79, 188–89, 222–24, 226–31, 234, 239–43, 245
   reunification, 239, 243, 246–47, 261
   and United States, x, xii, 82, 107, 120–21, 202, 213–14, 219–20, 235, 238, 240–41, 249–50, 254, 263
   See also Bundesbank

Gilpin, Robert, 7

Gold Pool, 112–13

Great Depression, 3, 22, 56

Group of Five (G5), 156, 177, 206, 230, 245

Group of Seven (G7), 177, 189, 203, 210–11, 213, 215, 222–30, 233–35, 239–43, 245–47

Group of Ten (G10), 102, 116, 122, 124, 127–28, 156, 163, 176

Gulf War, 221, 233

hegemonic stability theory, 7–11, 54, 71–72, 89, 182, 251–53. *See also* United States: power and hegemony

Henning, C. Randall, 14, 47n, 262n

internal policies of adjustment, defined, 4, 23–25. *See also* fiscal policy coordination; fiscal policy making; monetary policy coordination

international capital markets. *See* capital mobility; Euromarkets

International Monetary Fund (IMF), 156, 176–78, 236, 242
   and balance-of-payments finance, 65, 69, 113–16, 119–20, 169–71, 173–74, 252
   and capital controls, 57–58, 63–64, 87, 103–4, 159–60, 185
   Committee of Twenty, 159, 165, 171, 185
   and exchange rates, 53, 65–66, 68 69, 85, 91, 108–10, 162, 164–65, 169, 174
   policy conditionality, 76–77, 115–16, 122–28, 157, 172, 174–76, 181

International Trade Organization (ITO), 56, 78–79

inflation
   sources of, 151
   rates, 141, 151–52, 189, 191

Interest Equalization Tax (IET), 96, 106

interests, national and government, 12, 27, 202, 259

international liquidity, 114–19, 171–72

Italy, 38, 101, 104, 112, 114, 134, 173, 180, 240–41, 261
   capital controls, 158–59, 166, 185, 195
   capital mobility, 44–45
   exchange rates, 65, 168, 209
   and G7, 178, 231
   and International Monetary Fund, 157, 169, 171, 175–76, 181
   and United States, 83

Japan, 37–38, 52, 54, 56, 69, 112, 114, 135–36, 138, 140–42, 152, 161, 164, 170, 173–74, 190–92, 247
   capital controls, 102, 158, 185, 194
   capital mobility, 42, 45, 145

Japan (*cont.*)
  exchange rates, 161, 164, 167, 206,
    213–14, 227
  and G5/G7, 178–79, 188–89, 222–24,
    226–31, 234–35, 240–43, 245
  and International Monetary Fund, 69,
    126n
  and United States, x, xii, 51, 54–55, 94,
    100–101, 103, 121, 136, 138, 152,
    202, 208, 213–14, 219–21, 235–38,
    241–43, 249–50, 254–56, 263
Japan Ministry of Finance, 220, 228, 234,
  237–38
Jervis, Robert, 258
Johnson, Lyndon B., 99, 137

Kennedy, John F., 99, 137
Keohane, Robert O., 8, 12, 255n, 260
Keynesian policies, 52, 81, 136–37, 139,
  143, 242, 263–64
Kindleberger, Charles P., 7
Kohl, Helmut, 239, 246
Korean War, 72, 81, 90
Krasner, Stephen D., 7

London economic summit (1977), 178–
  79
London economic summit (1991), 239
Louvre Accord (1987), 213, 227–28

macroeconomic adjustment policies,
  defined, 3–4, 22–26
Marshall Plan (Economic Recovery
  Program), 53–54, 58, 61, 65, 71–
  75, 79–81, 85, 89, 136. *See also*
  Economic Cooperation
  Administration
Michaely, Michael, 135
Milner, Helen, 11, 14, 262n
Miyazawa, Kiichi, 236
monetary policy coordination, 4, 23–24,
  28–32, 260, 262
  during 1945–55, 79–84, 86–88
  during 1956–70, 124–25, 128–31, 135–
    36, 144
  during 1971–77, 175, 177–79, 181–82
  during 1978–94, 188, 225–29, 233–34,
    236–43, 245–46
money supply growth rates, 140, 152,
  189–90

multilateral surveillance, 127–30, 176–77,
  230–32, 258
Murayama, Tomiichi, 238
Mutual Security Program (MSP), 73

Naples economic summit (1994), 215,
  242
Netherlands, 101, 115, 161, 173–74
Nixon, Richard M., 99, 157–58, 162, 165
North Atlantic Treaty Organization
  (NATO), 94, 256

oil price increases, 150–51, 153, 172,
  182, 224–25
open-economy macroeconomic theory,
  30, 187
Organization for Economic Cooperation
  and Development (OECD), 122,
  127, 138, 156, 177, 223, 232, 236,
  240
  Working Party Three, 127–28, 131–33,
    176
Organization for European Economic
  Cooperation (OEEC), 56–59, 80
Organization of Petroleum Exporting
  Countries (OPEC), 154, 172
Oudiz, Gilles, 202

petrodollar recycling, 154, 160
Plaza Accord (1985), 207
Pohl, Karl Otto, 239
policy coordination
  definition, 11–13
  incentives for, ix, 4–5, 22–27, 34–35,
    201–4
  measuring, 14–15, 253
  and welfare, 26–27, 46, 193, 201–3
  power. *See* bargaining power
Putnam, Robert D., 14, 20n, 47n, 262n

Rambouillet economic summit (1975),
  168, 178
Reagan, Ronald, 12, 206–7, 210–13, 220–
  23, 226, 229–30, 263
Roosa, Robert, 120
Ruggie, John Gerard, 3, 137
Russell, Robert, 128–29

Sachs, Jeffrey, 202
Schmidt, Helmut, 178

Shultz, George, 164, 229
Smithsonian Agreement (1971), 163
Soviet threat, 51, 53, 58, 72, 74, 81, 90,
    255–57. *See also* cold war
Special Drawing Rights (SDR), 116–18
Structural Impediments Initiative (SII),
    235–36
swap arrangements, 112, 161
Sweden, 135, 173
Switzerland, 42, 107–8, 173–74
symptom-management policies, defined,
    4, 24–25. *See also* balance-of-
    payments financing; foreign
    exchange market intervention

Thatcher, Margaret, 207, 212
Tokyo economic summit (1986), 230,
    245
Tokyo economic summit (1993), 242
trade controls, 4, 34, 251–52
    during 1945–55, 56–57, 86, 91
    during 1956–70, 93, 104–5
    during 1971–77, 157–58
    during 1978–94, 204–5
trade flows
    and macroeconomic adjustment, 5, 28–
        30, 35–36
    measuring, 36–38, 93, 104, 155, 199
Triffin, Robert, 117
Truman, Harry S., 72, 80

United States, 38, 114, 140–42, 151–52,
    173, 190–92
    balance-of-payments deficits, xi, 73–74,
        98–100, 103, 112, 116, 119–21,
        138, 152, 167, 218–21
    budget deficit, 189, 192, 202, 207, 218,
        227–32, 246–48
    capital controls, 96–97, 106–7, 160,
        198
    capital mobility, 16, 42–44, 95–96, 120,
        145
    dollar-gold relation, 106–7, 112–13,
        117, 161–62
    exchange rates, 31, 134–35, 164–65,
        168–69, 184, 206–8, 211–13, 249,
        254

financial assistance, for Western
        Europe and Japan, 53–55, 60, 62–
        63, 71–74, 84, 88–89, 91, 103
    in G5/G7, xii, 178–79, 188–89, 223–
        30, 239–43, 245
    inconvertibility and tariff surcharge
        (1971), 157, 161–62
    and international liquidity, 115–18
    and International Monetary Fund, 58,
        66, 76–77, 85, 114–16, 119–20,
        123, 127, 160, 162, 164–65, 169–
        70
    military spending, and balance of
        payments, 63, 65, 73–74, 86, 94,
        99–100, 103, 148, 167
    postwar objectives, 51–52, 54, 58–59
    power and hegemony, ix–x, 7–11, 49–
        51, 54, 75, 79, 90, 94, 119, 137–
        39, 146, 161, 182, 203, 211, 215–
        16, 219, 224–25, 248–54
    reserve-indicator proposal, 165, 230
    security interests, and economic policy
        coordination, x, 53–55, 71–72,
        74–75, 81, 84–85, 88–89, 94, 103,
        147–48, 255–56
    *See also entries for specific issues and events;
        entries for other countries*
United States Congress, 13, 36, 72, 79–
        80, 202, 205–7, 212, 221, 226,
        229–30, 235
United States Federal Reserve, 22, 106,
        112, 129, 168, 207, 221, 227–29,
        236, 240, 246, 248, 264
United States Treasury Department, 72,
        80, 90, 120, 212, 248

Vietnam War, 99
Volcker, Paul, 246

Wallich, Henry C., 11
Waltz, Kenneth N., 15
Weinberger, Casper, 229
White, Harry Dexter, 123
World War II, impact on economies, 51–
        52

Cornell Studies in Political Economy

EDITED BY PETER J. KATZENSTEIN

Collapse of an Industry: Nuclear Power and the Contradictions of U.S. Policy, by John L. Campbell

Power, Purpose, and Collective Choice: Economic Strategy in Socialist States, edited by Ellen Comisso and Laura D'Andrea Tyson

The Political Economy of the New Asian Industrialism, edited by Frederic C. Deyo

Dislodging Multinationals: India's Strategy in Comparative Perspective, by Dennis J. Encarnation

Rivals beyond Trade: America versus Japan in Global Competition, by Dennis J. Encarnation

Enterprise and the State in Korea and Taiwan, by Karl J. Fields

Democracy and Markets: The Politics of Mixed Economies, by John R. Freeman

The Misunderstood Miracle: Industrial Development and Political Change in Japan, by David Friedman

Patchwork Protectionism: Textile Trade Policy in the United States, Japan, and West Germany, by H. Richard Friman

Ideas, Interests, and American Trade Policy, by Judith Goldstein

Ideas and Foreign Policy: Beliefs, Institutions, and Political Change, edited by Judith Goldstein and Robert O. Keohane

Monetary Sovereignty: The Politics of Central Banking in Western Europe, by John B. Goodman

Politics in Hard Times: Comparative Responses to International Economic Crises, by Peter Gourevitch

Closing the Gold Window: Domestic Politics and the End of Bretton Woods, by Joanne Gowa

Cooperation among Nations: Europe, America, and Non-tariff Barriers to Trade, by Joseph M. Grieco

Pathways from the Periphery: The Politics of Growth in the Newly Industrializing Countries, by Stephan Haggard

The Politics of Finance in Developing Countries, edited by Stephan Haggard, Chung H. Lee, and Sylvia Maxfield

Rival Capitalists: International Competitiveness in the United States, Japan, and Western Europe, by Jeffrey A. Hart

The Philippine State and the Marcos Regime: The Politics of Export, by Gary Hawes

Reasons of State: Oil Politics and the Capacities of American Government, by G. John Ikenberry

The State and American Foreign Economic Policy, edited by G. John Ikenberry, David A. Lake, and Michael Mastanduno

The Paradox of Continental Production: National Investment Policies in North America, by Barbara Jenkins

Pipeline Politics: The Complex Political Economy of East-West Energy Trade, by Bruce W. Jentleson

The Politics of International Debt, edited by Miles Kahler

Corporatism and Change: Austria, Switzerland, and the Politics of Industry, by Peter J. Katzenstein

Industry and Politics in West Germany: Toward the Third Republic, edited by Peter J. Katzenstein

Small States in World Markets: Industrial Policy in Europe, by Peter J. Katzenstein
The Sovereign Entrepreneur: Oil Policies in Advanced and Less Developed Capitalist Countries, by Merrie Gilbert Klapp
International Regimes, edited by Stephen D. Krasner
Business and Banking: Political Change and Economic Integration in Western Europe, by Paulette Kurzer
Power, Protection, and Free Trade: International Sources of U.S. Commercial Strategy, 1887–1939, by David A. Lake
State Capitalism: Public Enterprise in Canada, by Jeanne Kirk Laux and Maureen Appel Molot
Remaking the Italian Economy, by Richard M. Locke
France after Hegemony: International Change and Financial Reform, by Michael Loriaux
Economic Containment: CoCom and the Politics of East-West Trade, by Michael Mastanduno
Mercantile States and the World Oil Cartel, 1900-1939, by Gregory P. Nowell
Opening Financial Markets: Banking Politics on the Pacific Rim, by Louis W. Pauly
The Limits of Social Democracy: Investment Politics in Sweden, by Jonas Pontusson
The Fruits of Fascism: Postwar Prosperity in Historical Perspective, by Simon Reich
The Business of the Japanese State: Energy Markets in Comparative and Historical Perspective, by Richard J. Samuels
"Rich Nation, Strong Army": National Security and the Technological Transformation of Japan, by Richard J. Samuels
Crisis and Choice in European Social Democracy, by Fritz W. Scharpf, translated by Ruth Crowley
In the Dominions of Debt: Historical Perspectives on Dependent Development, by Herman M. Schwartz
Winners and Losers: How Sectors Shape the Developmental Prospects of States, by D. Michael Shafer
Europe and the New Technologies, edited by Margaret Sharp
Europe's Industries: Public and Private Strategies for Change, edited by Geoffrey Shepherd, François Duchêne, and Christopher Saunders
Ideas and Institutions: Developmentalism in Brazil and Argentina, by Kathryn Sikkink
The Cooperative Edge: The Internal Politics of International Cartels, by Debora L. Spar
Fair Shares: Unions, Pay, and Politics in Sweden and West Germany, by Peter Swenson
Union of Parts: Labor Politics in Postwar Germany, by Kathleen A. Thelen
Democracy at Work: Changing World Markets and the Future of Labor Unions, by Lowell Turner
National Styles of Regulation: Environmental Policy in Great Britain and the United States, by David Vogel
The Political Economy of Policy Coordination: International Adjustment since 1945, by Michael C. Webb
International Cooperation: Building Regimes for Natural Resources and the Environment, by Oran R. Young
International Governance: Protecting the Environment in a Stateless Society, by Oran R. Young
Polar Politics: Creating International Environmental Regimes, edited by Oran R. Young and Gail Osherenko
Governments, Markets, and Growth: Financial Systems and the Politics of Industrial Change, by John Zysman
American Industry in International Competition: Government Policies and Corporate Strategies, edited by John Zysman and Laura Tyson